REAL ESTATE
BROKER EXAM

REAL ESTATE BROKER EXAM

LEARNINGEXPRESS®

NEW YORK

Library of Congress Cataloging-in-Publication Data:
Real estate broker exam.—1st ed.
   p. cm.
  ISBN: 978-1-57685-584-3 (alk. paper)
 1. Real estate agents—Licenses—United States—Examinations, questions, etc.
2. Real estate business—Licenses—United States—Examinations, questions, etc.
3. Real property—United States—Examinations, questions, etc.
I. LearningExpress (Organization)
HD278.R389 2007
333.33076—dc22

                          2006100516

Printed in the United States of America

9 8 7 6 5 4 3 2

First Edition

ISBN: 978-1-57685-584-3

Regarding the Information in This Book

We attempt to verify the information presented in our books prior to publication. It is always a good idea, however, to double-check such important information as deadlines and application and testing procedures, as such information can change from time to time.

For more information or to place an order, contact LearningExpress at:
  2 Rector Street
  26th Floor
  New York, NY 10006

Or visit us at:
  www.learnatest.com

About the Contributors ▶

Lloyd Hampton has been a consultant, broker, expert witness, and renowned speaker in the field of real estate for more than 25 years. He was also a coauthor of *Texas Real Estate Sales Exam*.

Carolyn Rogers, CRB, CREI, GRI, LTG, began her real estate career in 1978. She received her broker's license in 1980, sold real estate in the Austin, Texas, area, and has been active in brokerage management in Houston since 1985. Rogers is currently a full-time real estate instructor and has coauthored five textbooks, including *Texas Real Estate Exam*.

Wendy Tilton is the director of training and customer support at TREND, a real estate multiple-listing company in King of Prussia, Pennsylvania. She also serves as an adjunct associate professor of real estate at the New York University Real Estate Institute. Wendy has a Master of Science degree in real estate investment and development and a doctorate in education.

Contents

1 ▶ The Real Estate Broker Exam

CHAPTER SUMMARY

Congratulations! You are about to take the next step in your real estate career—obtaining your broker's license. This chapter provides an overview of the four major national exams, as well as tips on how this book can help you succeed on whatever exam you take.

I f you are planning to take a real estate broker licensing exam, this book can help you to get a top score on your exam. It will show you how to put all the pieces of test preparation together. This book includes four complete practice exams covering the topics from most real estate broker exams. It also has a real estate math review, a real estate glossary, and a CD-ROM to practice your exam on the computer.

▶ Your Upcoming Real Estate Broker Exam

In most states, you will be required to pass an exam to become licensed as a real estate broker. However, the specific exam you will be required to take depends on the state in which you want to become licensed. If you aren't sure which real estate exam you need to take, contact the real estate commission in the state in which you wish to be licensed for detailed information on their specific licensing requirements.

Some states, such as California and New York, administer their own examinations for prospective real estate licensees. Other states use the services of an independent testing company. These are the most commonly used independent testing companies, along with their contact information:

Applied Measurement Professionals (AMP), Inc.
8310 Neiman Road
Lenexa, KS 66214
800-345-6559 or 913-541-0400
www.goamp.com

Promissor
3 Bala Plaza West, Suite 300
Bala Cynwyd, PA 19004
610-617-9300
www.promissor.com

Thomson Prometric
1260 Energy Lane
St. Paul, MN 55108
800-894-9965
www.prometric.com/Experior/default.htm

Psychological Services, Inc. (PSI)
3210 East Tropicana
Las Vegas, NV 89121
800-733-9267
www.psiexams.com

The exams used by these independent testing companies to examine prospective real estate professionals are in a multiple-choice question format and are often administered on the computer. Here's a sample list of the typical topics, and the approximate number of multiple-choice questions in each topic, for the real estate written exams administered by these four testing companies. Keep in mind that some states vary the total number of questions asked in each topic, and many states will also add state-specific questions to the standard exam. For example, in Texas, an additional 30 questions that relate specifically to Texas laws and rules are included on the real estate licensing exam administered by PSI.

AMP
Time limit: 2 hours

Topics	Number of Questions
Listing Property	31
Selling Property	21
Property Management	14
Settlement/Transfer of Ownership	14
Financing	10
Professional Responsibilities/Fair Practice/Administration	10
Total Questions	**100**

Note: At least 10% of the questions on this exam will require the use of mathematics.

Thomson Prometric

Time limit: 2 hours

Topics	Number of Questions
Business Practices and Ethics	16
Agency and Listing	12
Property Characteristics, Descriptions, Ownership, Interests, and Restrictions	12
Property Valuation and the Appraisal Process	6
Real Estate Sales Contracts	12
Financing Sources	10
Property Management	4
Closing/Settlement and Transferring Title	8
Total Questions	**80**

Promissor

Time limit: 4 hours

Topics	Number of Questions
Real Property Characteristics, Definitions, Ownership, Restrictions, and Transfer	16
Assessing and Explaining Property Valuation and the Appraisal Process	12
Contracts, Agency Relationships with Buyers and Sellers, and Federal Requirements	20
Financing the Transaction and Settlement	20
Leases, Rents, and Property Management	12
Total Questions	**80**

Note: Approximately 10% of the questions on this exam will require the use of mathematics.

PSI

Time limit: 2 hours

Topics	Number of Questions
Property Ownership	7
Land Use Controls and Regulations	7
Valuation and Market Analysis	6
Financing	7
Laws of Agency	10
Mandated Disclosures	7
Contracts	10
Transfer of Property	6
Practice of Real Estate	10
Mathematics	6
Specialty Areas	4
Total Questions	**80**

Regardless of whether you take a state-administered real estate exam or one administered by AMP, Thomson, Promissor, or PSI, you will need to know the same basic real estate information. That is why this book can help you no matter in which state you want to become licensed. The topics on the practice exams in this book reflect most of the same topics on different national exams. The study skills, glossary, and math review also contain invaluable information regardless of which exam you take.

About Licensing Requirements and Exams

By now you have realized that different states use different exams. However, even if two states use the same testing company, the exams may cover different topics, cost different amounts, or have different passing scores. Usually, the most accurate and up-to-date information is available through your state's licensing agency. That is why it is essential to contact your state's real estate organization before your exam. For your convenience, here's a list of the contact information for each state's real estate licensing agency.

At the time of publication, the following information was correct, but be aware that websites or other contact information may change at any time.

State Licensing Agencies

ALABAMA
Real Estate Commission
1201 Carmichael Way
Montgomery, AL 36106
334-242-5544
www.arec.state.al.us

ALASKA
Division of Occupational Licensing
Real Estate Commission
550 West 7th Avenue, Suite 1500
Anchorage, AK 99501
907-269-8160
www.dced.state.ak.us/occ/prec.htm

ARIZONA
Department of Real Estate
2910 North 44th Street
Phoenix, AZ 85018
602-468-1414
www.re.state.az.us

ARKANSAS
Real Estate Commission
612 South Summit Street
Little Rock, AR 72201
501-683-8010
www.state.ar.us/arec

CALIFORNIA
Department of Real Estate
P.O. Box 187000
Sacramento, CA 95818-7000
916-227-0931
www.dre.ca.gov

COLORADO
Department of Regulatory Agencies
Division of Real Estate
1560 Broadway, Suite 925
Denver, CO 80202
303-894-2166
www.dora.state.co.us/Real-Estate

CONNECTICUT
Department of Consumer Protection
Occupational and Professional Licensing Division
165 Capitol Avenue
Hartford, CT 06106
860-713-6050
www.ct.gov/dcp

DELAWARE
Real Estate Commission
861 Silver Lake Boulevard, Suite 203
Dover, DE 19904
302-744-4519
www.dpr.delaware.gov/boards/realestate

DISTRICT OF COLUMBIA
Board of Real Estate
941 North Capitol Street NE, Room 7200
Washington, D.C. 20002
202-442-4320
www.dcra.dc.gov

FLORIDA
Division of Real Estate
1940 North Monroe Street
Tallahassee, FL 32399
850-487-1395
www.state.fl.us/dbpr/re

GEORGIA
Real Estate Commission
229 Peachtree Street NE, Suite 1000
Atlanta, GA 30303
404-656-3916
www.grec.state.ga.us

HAWAII
Real Estate Commission
335 Merchant Street, Room 333
Honolulu, HI 96813
808-586-2643
www.hawaii.gov/hirec

IDAHO
Real Estate Commission
633 North Fourth Street
P.O. Box 83720
Boise, ID 83720-0077
208-334-3285
www.idahorealestatecommission.com

ILLINOIS
Department of Financial and Professional Regulation
Attn.: Bureau of Real Estate Professions
320 West Washington Street
Springfield, IL 62786
217-785-0800
www.idfpr.com/dpr/re/realmain.asp

INDIANA
Professional Licensing Agency
Attn.: Real Estate Commission
402 West Washington Street, Room W072
Indianapolis, IN 46204
317-234-3009
www.in.gov/pla/bandc/estate

IOWA
Real Estate Commission
1920 SE Hulsizer Road
Ankeny, IA 50021
515-281-5910
www.state.ia.us/government/com/prof/sales

KANSAS
Real Estate Commission
Three Townsite Plaza, Suite 200
120 SE 6th Avenue
Topeka, KS 66603
785-296-3411
www.accesskansas.org/krec

KENTUCKY
Real Estate Commission
10200 Linn Station Road, Suite 201
Louisville, KY 40223
888-373-3300
www.krec.ky.gov

LOUISIANA
Real Estate Commission
P.O. Box 14785
Baton Rouge, LA 70898-4785
225-765-0191
www.lrec.state.la.us

MAINE
Real Estate Commission
35 State House Station
Augusta, ME 04333
207-624-8603
www.state.me.us/pfr/olr

MARYLAND
Real Estate Commission
500 North Calvert Street
Baltimore, MD 21202
410-230-6200
www.dllr.state.md.us/license/real_est

MASSACHUSETTS
Board of Registration of Real Estate Brokers and
 Salespersons
239 Causeway Street, Suite 500
Boston, MA 02114
617-727-2373
www.mass.gov/dpl/boards/re

MICHIGAN
Department of Consumer and Industry Services
Bureau of Commercial Services
P.O. Box 30018
Lansing, MI 48909
517-241-9288
www.michigan.gov/cis

MINNESOTA
Minnesota Commerce Department
85 Seventh Place East, Suite 500
St. Paul, MN 55101
651-296-6319
www.commerce.state.mn.us

MISSISSIPPI
Real Estate Commission
P.O. Box 12685
Jackson, MS 39236
601-932-9191
www.mrec.state.ms.us

MISSOURI
Real Estate Commission
3605 Missouri Boulevard
P.O. Box 1339
Jefferson City, MO 65102-1339
573-751-2628
pr.mo.gov/realestate.asp

MONTANA
Board of Realty Regulation
301 South Park, Room 430
P.O. Box 200513
Helena, MT 59620-0513
406-444-2961
www.mt.gov/dli/bsd/license/bsd_boards/rre_board/
    board_page.asp

NEBRASKA
Real Estate Commission
1200 "N" Street, Suite 402
P.O. Box 94667
Lincoln, NE 68509-4667
402-471-2004
www.nrec.state.ne.us

NEVADA
Nevada Department of Business and Industry
Real Estate Division
788 Fairview Drive, Suite 200
Carson City, NV 89701
775-687-4280
www.red.state.nv.us

NEW HAMPSHIRE
Real Estate Commission
State House Annex, Room 434
25 Capitol Street
Concord, NH 03301
603-271-2701
www.state.nh.us/nhrec

NEW JERSEY
Department of Banking and Insurance
Attn.: Real Estate Commission
P.O. Box 474
Trenton, NJ 08625-0474
609-292-7053
www.state.nj.us/dobi/remnu.shtml

NEW MEXICO
Real Estate Commission
5200 Oakland Avenue NE, Suite B
Albuquerque, NM 87113
505-222-9820
www.rld.state.nm.us/b&c/recom

NEW YORK
Department of State
Division of Licensing Services
P.O. Box 22001
Albany, NY 12201-2001
518-473-2728
www.dos.state.ny.us/lcns/realest.html

NORTH CAROLINA
Real Estate Commission
P.O. Box 17100
Raleigh, NC 27619-7100
919-875-3700
www.ncrec.state.nc.us

NORTH DAKOTA
Real Estate Commission
200 East Main Avenue, Suite 204
Bismarck, ND 58502
701-328-9749
www.governor.state.nd.us/boards

OHIO
Division of Real Estate and Professional Licensing
77 South High Street, 20th Floor
Columbus, OH 43215
614-466-4100
www.com.state.oh.us/real

OKLAHOMA
Real Estate Commission
Shepherd Mall
2401 NW 23rd Street, Suite 18
Oklahoma City, OK 73107
405-521-3387
www.orec.ok.gov

OREGON
Real Estate Agency
1177 Center Street NE
Salem, OR 97301
Fax: 503-378-4170
www.oregon.gov/REA/index.shtml

PENNSYLVANIA
Real Estate Commission
P.O. Box 2649
Harrisburg, PA 17105-2649
717-787-8503
www.dos.state.pa.us/bpoa

RHODE ISLAND
Department of Business Regulation
Division of Commercial Licensing and Regulation
   Real Estate
233 Richmond Street, Suite 230
Providence, RI 02903
401-222-2246
www.dbr.state.ri.us/divisions/commlicensing/
   realestate.php

SOUTH CAROLINA
Department of Labor Licensing and Regulation
Real Estate Commission
P.O. Box 11847
Columbia, SC 29211-1847
803-896-4400
www.llr.state.sc.us/pol/realestatecommission

SOUTH DAKOTA
Real Estate Commission
221 West Capitol, Suite 101
Pierre, SD 57501
605-773-3600
www.state.sd.us/ddr2/reg/realestate

TENNESSEE
Real Estate Commission
500 James Robertson Parkway
Nashville, TN 37243
615-741-2273
www.state.tn.us/commerce/boards/trec

TEXAS
Real Estate Commission
P.O. Box 12188
Austin, TX 78711-2188
512-459-6544
www.trec.state.tx.us

UTAH
Department of Commerce
Division of Real Estate
P.O. Box 146711
Salt Lake City, Utah 84114-6711
801-530-6747
www.realestate.utah.gov

VERMONT
Office of Professional Regulation
Real Estate Commission
81 River Street
Montpelier, VT 05609
802-828-2363
www.vtprofessionals.org/opr1/real_estate

VIRGINIA

Department of Professional and Occupational
  Regulation
3600 West Broad Street
Richmond, VA 23230
804-367-8526
www.dpor.virginia.gov/dporweb/reb_main.cfm

WASHINGTON

Department of Licensing
Real Estate Section
P.O. Box 9015
Olympia, WA 98507-9015
360-664-6488
www.dol.wa.gov/business/realestate

WEST VIRGINIA

Real Estate Commission
300 Capitol Street, Suite 400
Charleston, WV 25301
304-558-3555
www.wvrec.org

WISCONSIN

Bureau of Direct Licensing and Real Estate
Department of Regulation and Licensing
1400 East Washington Avenue, Room 173
Box 8935
Madison, WI 53708-8935
608-266-2112
www.drl.wi.gov/boards/reb

WYOMING

Real Estate Commission
2020 Carey Avenue, Suite 702
Cheyenne, WY 82002
307-777-7141
http://realestate.state.wy.us

The Right Questions

Once you've found your state's agency, it's important to know the right questions to ask. To find out everything you need to know about your exam, use the following list of questions.

- Which exam is given in my state?
- What are the topics covered on this exam?
- How many questions are there?
- What are the state-specific real estate topics covered on this exam?
- Is the exam multiple choice?
- Is the exam handwritten, or is it given on the computer?
- How do I register?
- How much does the exam cost?
- How long will the exam take to complete?
- Can I use a calculator on the exam?
- If I can use a calculator, what kinds of calculators are permitted?
- Where is the exam given?
- What day is the exam given?

- Can I reschedule my exam?
- What time is the exam?
- What do I have to bring to the exam?
- What is not allowed at the test centers?
- If the exam is given on the computer, will I be allowed to practice on a computer before the exam begins?
- How is the exam scored?
- What is the passing score?
- Are there separate passing scores for different parts of the exam?
- When will I receive my score report?
- What happens if I do not pass the exam?
- Can I retake my exam?
- If I have special needs, how do I arrange for them?

If you are already working for a real estate company, your colleagues can be a good source of information about the tests. If your state requires attending classes at a real estate school as part of the requirements for the broker license, your instructor and the school administration may also be able to provide guidance.

The Association of Real Estate License Law Officials (ARELLO) provides information regarding licensing at their website, www.arello.com.

▶ How This Book Can Help You

The process of preparing for a real estate exam may seem like an overwhelming task, but this book will help you break it into several manageable steps. The first step is to finish this chapter. Then, move on to Chapter 2, which explains how to set up an individualized study plan and presents specific study strategies you can use during your study sessions. You will find out the steps to take in order to maximize your chances for scoring high on your exam. You will also find out when to take sample exams so you can check your scores and still have enough time to focus on the areas in which you need more work. In addition, you will increase your understanding and retention of the real estate material you are studying by using many different study strategies, not just one or two.

While you are reading Chapter 2, take the time to create an individualized study plan that will fit your needs and schedule. This is a crucial step in the test-preparation process. After you finish reading Chapter 2, spend some time using each different study strategy explained in that chapter.

Chapter 3 contains the first of four practice exams. You should take a practice exam before you begin studying. That way, you will be able to find your strengths and weaknesses, and you will be able to focus your studying on exactly the topics that are giving you the most trouble.

After you finish your practice exam, you will find a Real Estate Refresher Course. This review covers several real estate topics that will be on a real estate broker exam. Because you already know which topics on the first exam gave you trouble, you can focus on those topics.

Chapter 14 presents information on brokerage office operations. It provides information related to running a real estate office or company. Topics include federal, state, and local regulations, contracts, policies, procedures, and record keeping.

After the real estate refresher course comes the Real Estate Math Review. This section contains a basic review of arithmetic, algebra, geometry, and word problems. It also covers the types of math questions you will face on a real estate broker exam.

Need help with real estate terms? Chapter 6 provides a Real Estate Glossary with the most commonly tested and used real estate terms. This glossary will help you prepare not only for your exam, but also for your career.

Once you have reviewed the course, the math, and the glossary, it's time for more practice exams. There are three more practice exams in this book. After every exam, you should review which topics still give you the most trouble and study accordingly. For more study tips, start reading Chapter 2.

2 ▶ The LearningExpress Test Preparation System

CHAPTER SUMMARY

Taking the real estate broker exam can be tough. It demands a lot of preparation if you want to achieve a top score. Your career as a broker depends on your passing the exam. The LearningExpress Test Preparation System, developed exclusively for LearningExpress by leading test experts, gives you the discipline and attitude you need to be a winner.

FACT: TAKING A real estate licensing exam is not easy, and neither is getting ready for it. Your future career as a real estate broker depends on your getting a passing score, but there are all sorts of pitfalls that can keep you from doing your best on this exam. Here are some of the obstacles that can stand in the way of your success:

- being unfamiliar with the format of the exam
- being paralyzed by test anxiety
- leaving your preparation to the last minute
- not preparing at all!
- not knowing vital test-taking skills: how to pace yourself through the exam, how to use the process of elimination, and when to guess
- not being in tip-top mental and physical shape
- arriving late at the test site, having to work on an empty stomach, or being uncomfortable during the exam because the room is too hot or too cold

What's the common denominator in all these test-taking pitfalls? One word: control. Who's in control, you or the exam?

Here's some good news: The LearningExpress Test Preparation System puts you in control. In nine easy-to-follow steps, you will learn everything you need to know to make sure that you are in charge of your preparation and your performance on the exam. Other test takers may let the test get the better of them; other test takers may be unprepared or out of shape, but not you. You will have taken all the steps you need to take to get a high score on the real estate broker exam.

Here's how the LearningExpress Test Preparation System works: Nine easy steps lead you through everything you need to know and do to get ready to master your exam. Each step discussed in this chapter includes both reading about the step and one or more activities. It's important that you do the activities along with the reading, or you won't be getting the full benefit of the system. Each step tells you approximately how much time that step will take you to complete.

Step 1. Get Information	50 minutes
Step 2. Conquer Test Anxiety	20 minutes
Step 3. Make a Plan	30 minutes
Step 4. Learn to Manage Your Time	10 minutes
Step 5. Learn to Use the Process of Elimination	20 minutes
Step 6. Know When to Guess	20 minutes
Step 7. Reach Your Peak Performance Zone	10 minutes
Step 8. Get Your Act Together	10 minutes
Step 9. Do It!	10 minutes
Total	**3 hours**

We estimate that working through the entire system will take you approximately three hours, although it's perfectly okay if you work faster or slower. If you take an afternoon or evening, you can work through the whole LearningExpress Test Preparation System in one sitting. Otherwise, you can break it up and do just one or two steps a day for the next several days. It's up to you—remember, you are in control.

▶ Step 1: Get Information

Time to complete: 50 minutes
Activity: Read Chapter 1, "The Real Estate Broker Exam"

Knowledge is power. The first step in the LearningExpress Test Preparation System is finding out everything you can about the real estate broker exam. Once you have your information, the other steps in the LearningExpress Test Preparation System will show you what to do about it.

Part A: Straight Talk about the Real Estate Broker Exam

Why do you have to take this exam, anyway? You have already been through your pre-license course; why should you have to go through a rigorous exam? It's simply an attempt on the part of your state to be sure you have the knowledge and skills necessary for a licensed real estate broker. Every profession that requires practitioners to exercise financial and fiduciary responsibility to clients also requires practitioners to be licensed—and licensure requires an exam. Real estate is no exception.

It's important for you to remember that your score on the real estate broker exam does not determine how smart you are, or even whether you will make a good real estate broker. There are all kinds of skills an exam like this can't test: whether you have the drive and determination to be a top broker, whether you will faithfully exercise your responsibilities to your clients, or whether you can be trusted with confidential information about people's finances. Those kinds of things are hard to evaluate, while a computer-based test is easy to evaluate.

However, this is not to say that the exam is not important. The knowledge tested on the exam is essential knowledge you will need to do your job. Your ability to enter the profession you've trained for depends on your passing this exam. And that's why you are here—using the LearningExpress Test Preparation System to achieve control over the exam.

Part B: What's on the Test

If you haven't already done so, stop here and read Chapter 1 of this book, which gives you an overview of the real estate broker exam. Then, go to your state's website and read the most up-to-date information about your exam directly from the test developers.

▶ Step 2: Conquer Test Anxiety

Time to complete: 20 minutes
Activity: Take the Test Anxiety Quiz

Having complete information about the exam is the first step in getting control of the exam. Next, you have to overcome one of the biggest obstacles to test success: test anxiety. Test anxiety not only impairs your performance on the exam itself, but also keeps you from preparing. In Step 2, you will learn stress management techniques that will help you succeed on your exam. Learn these strategies now, and practice them as you work through the exams in this book, so they will be second nature to you by exam day.

Combating Test Anxiety

The first thing you need to know is that a little test anxiety is a good thing. Everyone gets nervous before a big exam—and if that nervousness motivates you to prepare thoroughly, so much the better. It's said that Sir Laurence Olivier, one of the foremost British actors of the twentieth century, felt ill before every performance. His stage fright didn't impair his performance; in fact, it probably gave him a little extra edge—just the kind of edge you need to do well, whether on a stage or in an examination room.

Test Anxiety Quiz

You need to worry about test anxiety only if it is extreme enough to impair your performance. The following questionnaire will provide a diagnosis of your level of test anxiety. In the blank before each statement, write the number that most accurately describes your experience.

0 = Never   1 = Once or twice   2 = Sometimes   3 = Often

___ I have gotten so nervous before an exam that I simply put down the books and didn't study for it.

___ I have experienced disabling physical symptoms such as nausea and severe headaches because I was nervous about an exam.

___ I have skipped an exam because I was scared to take it.

___ I have experienced dizziness and disorientation while taking an exam.

___ I have had trouble filling in the little circles because my hands were shaking too hard.

___ I have failed an exam because I was too nervous to complete it.

___ **Total: Add up the numbers in the blanks above.**

Your Test Anxiety Score

Here are the steps you should take, depending on your score.

0–2: Your level of test anxiety is nothing to worry about; it's probably just enough to give you that little extra edge.

3–6: Your test anxiety may be enough to impair your performance, and you should practice the stress management techniques listed in this section to try to bring your test anxiety down to manageable levels.

7 or above: Your level of test anxiety is a serious concern. In addition to practicing the stress management techniques listed in this section, you may want to seek additional help.

Above is the Test Anxiety Quiz. Stop and answer the questions to find out whether your level of test anxiety is something you should worry about.

Stress Management before the Test

If you feel your level of anxiety getting the best of you in the weeks before the test, here is what you need to do to bring the level down again:

- **Get prepared.** There's nothing like knowing what to expect and being prepared for it to put you in control of test anxiety. That's why you are reading this book. Use it faithfully, and remind yourself that you are better prepared than most of the people taking the test.

- **Practice self-confidence.** A positive attitude is a great way to combat test anxiety. This is no time to be humble or shy. Stand in front of the mirror and say to your reflection, "I am prepared. I am full of self-confidence. I am going to ace this test. I know I can do it." Say it into a tape recorder and play it back once a day. If you hear it often enough, you will believe it.

- **Fight negative messages.** Every time someone starts telling you how hard the exam is or how it's almost impossible to get a high score, start saying your self-confidence messages. Don't listen to the negative messages. Turn on your tape recorder and listen to your self-confidence messages.
- **Visualize.** Imagine yourself reporting for duty on your first day as a real estate broker. Think of yourself talking with clients, showing homes, and best of all, making your first sale. Visualizing success can help make it happen—and it reminds you of why you are going to all this work in preparing for the exam.
- **Exercise.** Physical activity helps calm your body down and focus your mind. Besides, being in good physical shape can actually help you do well on the exam. Go for a run, lift weights, go swimming—and do it regularly.

Stress Management on Test Day

There are several ways you can bring down your level of test anxiety on test day. They will work best if you practice them in the weeks before the test, so you know which ones work best for you.

- **Deep breathing.** Take a deep breath while you count to five. Hold it for a count of one, and then let it out for a count of five. Repeat several times.
- **Move your body.** Try rolling your head in a circle. Rotate your shoulders. Shake your hands from the wrist. Many people find these movements very relaxing.
- **Visualize again.** Think of the place where you are most relaxed: lying on the beach in the sun, walking through the park, or whatever. Now close your eyes and imagine you are actually there. If you practice in advance, you will find that you need only a few seconds of this exercise to experience a significant increase in your sense of well-being.

When anxiety threatens to overwhelm you right there during the exam, there are still things you can do to manage the stress level:

- **Repeat your self-confidence messages.** You should have them memorized by now. Say them silently to yourself, and believe them!
- **Visualize one more time.** This time, visualize yourself moving smoothly and quickly through the test, answering every question right and finishing just before time is up. Like most visualization techniques, this one works best if you have practiced it ahead of time.
- **Find an easy question.** Find an easy question, and answer it. Getting even one question finished gets you into the test-taking groove.
- **Take a mental break.** Everyone loses concentration once in a while during a long test. It's normal, so you shouldn't worry about it. Instead, accept what has happened. Say to yourself, "Hey, I lost it there for a minute. My brain is taking a break." Put down your pencil, close your eyes, and do some deep breathing for a few seconds. Then you will be ready to go back to work.

Try these techniques ahead of time, and which ones work best for you!

▶ Step 3: Make a Plan

Time to complete: 30 minutes
Activity: Construct a study plan

One of the most important things you can do to get control of yourself and your exam is to make a study plan. Too many people fail to prepare simply because they fail to plan. Spending hours on the day before the exam poring over sample test questions not only raises your level of test anxiety, but is simply no substitute for careful preparation and practice over time.

Don't fall into the cram trap. Take control of your preparation time by mapping out a study schedule. On the following pages are two sample schedules, based on the amount of time you have before you take the real estate broker exam. If you are the kind of person who needs deadlines and assignments to motivate you for a project, here they are. If you are the kind of person who doesn't like to follow other people's plans, you can use the suggested schedules here to construct your own.

Even more important than making a plan is making a commitment. You can't review everything you learned in your real estate courses in one night. You have to set aside some time every day for study and practice. Try for at least 20 minutes a day. Twenty minutes daily will do you much more good than two hours on Saturday.

Don't put off your study until the day before the exam. Start now. A few minutes a day, with half an hour or more on weekends, can make a big difference in your score.

Schedule A: The 30-Day Plan

If you have at least a month before you take the real estate broker exam, you have plenty of time to prepare—as long as you don't waste it! If you have less than a month, turn to Schedule B.

Time	Preparation
Days 1–4	Skim over the written materials from your training program, particularly noting 1) areas you expect to be emphasized on the exam and 2) areas you don't remember well. On Day 4, concentrate on those areas.
Day 5	Take your first practice exam.
Day 6	Score the first practice exam. Use the "For Review" section at the end of the test to see which topics you need to review most. Identify two areas that you will concentrate on before you take the second practice exam.
Days 7–10	Study the two areas you identified as your weak points. Don't forget, there is the Real Estate Broker Refresher Course in Chapter 7, the Real Estate Broker Math Review in Chapter 8, and the Real Estate Glossary in Chapter 9. Use these chapters to improve your score on the next practice test.
Day 11	Take your second practice exam.
Day 12	Score the second practice exam. Identify one area to concentrate on if you want take a third practice exam different from the one you're studying for.
Days 13–18	Study the one area you identified for review. Again, use the Broker Refresher Course, Broker Math Review, and Glossary for help.
Day 19	Take a third practice exam.
Day 20	Once again, identify one area to review, based on your score on the third practice exam.
Days 20–21	Study the one area you identified for review. Use the Broker Refresher Course, Broker Math Review, and Glossary for help.
Days 22–25	Take an overview of all your training materials, consolidating your strengths and improving on your weaknesses.
Days 26–27	Review all the areas that have given you the most trouble in the three practice exams you have taken so far.
Day 28	Take fourth practice exam. Note how much you have improved!
Day 29	Review one or two weak areas by studying the Broker Refresher Course, Broker Math Review, and Glossary.
Day before the exam	Relax. Do something unrelated to the exam and go to bed at a reasonable hour.

Schedule B: The Ten-Day Plan

If you have two weeks or less before you take the exam, use this ten-day schedule to help you make the most of your time.

Time	Preparation
Day 1	Take your first practice exam and score it using the answer key at the end. Use the "For Review" section at the end to see which topics you need to review most.
Day 2	Review one area that gave you trouble on the first practice exam. Use the Real Estate Broker Refresher Course in Chapter 7, the Real Estate Broker Math Review in Chapter 8, and the Real Estate Glossary in Chapter 9 for extra practice in these areas.
Day 3	Review another area that gave you trouble on the first practice exam. Again, use the Broker Refresher Course, Broker Math Review, and Glossary for extra practice.
Day 4	Take your second practice exam and score it.
Day 5	If your score on the second practice exam doesn't show improvement on the two areas you studied, review them. If you did improve in those areas, choose a new weak area to study today.
Day 6	Take a third practice exam and score it.
Day 7	Choose your weakest area from the third practice exam to review. Use the Broker Refresher Course, Broker Math Review, and Glossary for extra practice.
Day 8	Review any areas that you have not yet reviewed in this schedule.
Day 9	Take a fourth practice exam and score it.
Day 10	Use your last study day to brush up on any areas that are still giving you trouble. Use the Broker Refresher Course, Broker Math Review, and Glossary.
Day before the exam	Relax. Do something unrelated to the exam and go to bed at a reasonable hour.

► Step 4: Learn to Manage Your Time

Time to complete: Ten minutes to read, many hours of practice!
Activity: Practice these strategies as you take the sample tests in this book

Steps 4, 5, and 6 of the LearningExpress Test Preparation System put you in charge of your exam by showing you test-taking strategies that work. Practice these strategies as you take the sample tests in this book, and then you will be ready to use them on test day.

First, you will take control of your time on the exam. It's terrible feeling to find that there are five minutes left when you are only three-quarters of the way through the test. Here are some tips to keep that from happening to you.

- **Follow directions.** Some real estate broker exams are given on the computer. If a tutorial is offered before the exam, you should take your time taking the tutorial before the exam. Read the directions carefully and ask questions before the exam begins if there's anything you don't understand.
- **Pace yourself.** If there is a timer on the screen as you take the exam, keep an eye on it. This will help you pace yourself. For example, when one-quarter of the time has elapsed, you should be one-quarter of the way through the test. If you are falling behind, pick up the pace a bit. If you do not take your exam on a computer, use your watch or the clock in the testing room to keep track of the time you have left.
- **Keep moving.** Don't waste time on one question. If you don't know the answer, skip the question and move on. You can always go back to it later.
- **Don't rush.** Although you should keep moving, rushing won't help. Try to keep calm and work methodically and quickly.

► Step 5: Learn to Use the Process of Elimination

Time to complete: 20 minutes
Activity: Complete the worksheet on Using the Process of Elimination

After time management, your next most important tool for taking control of your exam is using the process of elimination wisely. It's standard test-taking wisdom that you should always read all the answer choices before choosing your answer. This helps you find the right answer by eliminating wrong answer choices. Sure enough, that standard wisdom applies to your exam, too.

Let's say you are facing a question like this one:

Alicia died, leaving her residence in town and a separate parcel of undeveloped rural land to her brother Brian and her sister Carrie, with Brian owning one-quarter interest and Carrie owning three-quarters interest. How do Brian and Carrie hold title?
a. as tenants in survivorship
b. as tenants in common
c. as joint tenants
d. as tenants by the entirety

You should always use the process of elimination on a question like this, even if the correct answer jumps out at you. Sometimes, the answer that jumps out isn't correct after all. Let's assume, for the purpose of this exercise, that you are a little rusty on property ownership terminology, so you need to use a little intuition to make up for what you don't remember. Proceed through the answer choices in order.

So you start with choice **a**. This one is pretty easy to eliminate; this tenancy doesn't have to do with survivorship. Because the real estate broker exam is given on a computer, you won't be able to cross out answer choices; instead, make a mental note that choice **a** is incorrect.

Choice **b** seems reasonable; it's a kind of ownership that two people can share. Even if you don't remember much about tenancy in common, you could tell it's about having something "in common." Make a mental note, "Good answer, I might use this one."

Choice **c** is also a possibility. Joint tenants also share something in common. If you happen to remember that joint tenancy always involves equal ownership rights, you mentally eliminate this choice. If you don't, make a mental note, "Good answer" or "Well, maybe," depending on how attractive this answer looks to you.

Choice **d** strikes you as a little less likely. Tenancy by the entirety doesn't necessarily have to do with two people sharing ownership. This doesn't sound right, and you have already got a better answer picked out in choice **b**. If you are feeling sure of yourself, you can mentally eliminate this choice.

If you're pressed for time, you should choose answer **b**. If you have the time to be extra careful, you could compare your answer choices again. Then, choose one and move on.

If you are taking a test on paper, like the practice exams in this book, it's good to have a system for marking good, bad, and maybe answers. We're recommending this one:

X = bad
✓ = good
? = maybe

If you don't like these marks, devise your own system. Just make sure you do it long before test day—while you're working through the practice exams in this book—so you won't have to worry about it during the exam.

Even when you think you are absolutely clueless about a question, you can often use process of elimination to get rid of one answer choice. If so, you are better prepared to make an educated guess, as you will see in Step 6. More often, the process of elimination allows you to get down to only two possibly right answers. Then you are in a strong position to guess. And sometimes, even though you don't know the right answer, you find it simply by getting rid of the wrong ones, as you did in this example.

Try using your powers of elimination on the questions on the Using the Process of Elimination worksheet. The questions aren't about real estate work; they're just designed to show you how the process of elimination works. The answer explanations for this worksheet show one possible way you might use the process to arrive at the correct answer.

The process of elimination is your tool for the next step, which is knowing when to guess.

Use the process of elimination to answer the following questions.

1. Ilsa is as old as Meghan will be in five years. The difference between Ed's age and Meghan's age is twice the difference between Ilsa's age and Meghan's age. Ed is 29. How old is Ilsa?
  a. 4
  b. 10
  c. 19
  d. 24

2. "All drivers of commercial vehicles must carry a valid commercial driver's license whenever operating a commercial vehicle." According to this sentence, which of the following people need NOT carry a commercial driver's license?
  a. a truck driver idling his engine while waiting to be directed to a loading dock
  b. a bus operator backing her bus out of the way of another bus in the bus lot
  c. a taxi driver driving his personal car to the grocery store
  d. a limousine driver taking the limousine to her home after dropping off her last passenger of the evening

3. Smoking tobacco has been linked to
  a. increased risk of stroke and heart attack.
  b. all forms of respiratory disease.
  c. increasing mortality rates over the past ten years.
  d. juvenile delinquency.

4. Which of the following words is spelled correctly?
  a. incorrigible
  b. outragous
  c. domestickated
  d. understandible

Answers

Here are the answers, as well as some suggestions as to how you might have used the process of elimination to find them.

1. d. You should have eliminated choice **a** right away. Ilsa can't be four years old if Meghan is going to be Ilsa's age in five years. The best way to eliminate other answer choices is to try plugging them in to the information given in the problem. For instance, for choice **b**, if Ilsa is 10, then Meghan must be 5. The difference in their ages is 5. The difference between Ed's age, 29, and Meghan's age, 5, is 24. Does 24 = 2 times 5? No. Then choice **b** is wrong. You could eliminate answer **c** in the same way and be left with choice **d**.

2. c. Note the word *not* in the question, and go through the choice one by one. Is the truck driver in choice **a** "operating a commericial vehicle"? Yes, idling counts as "operating," so he needs to have a commercial driver's license. Likewise, the bus operator in choice **b** is operating a commercial vehicle; the question doesn't say the operator has to be on the street. The limo driver in choice **d** is operating a commercial vehicle, even if it doesn't have a passenger in it. However, the cabbie in choice **c** is *not* operating a commercial vehicle, but his own private car.

3. a. You could eliminate choice **b** simply because of the presence of the word *all*. Such absolutes hardly ever appear in correct answer choices. Choice **c** looks attractive until you think a little about what you know—aren't *fewer* people smoking these days, rather than more? So how could smoking be responsible for a higher mortality rate? (If you didn't know that *mortality rate* means the rate at which people die, you might keep this choice as a possibility, but you would still be able to eliminate two answers and have only two to choose from.) And choice **d** is not logical, so you could eliminate that one, too. And you are left with the correct choice, **a**.

4. a. How you used the process of elimination here depends on which words you recognized as being spelled incorrectly. If you knew that the correct spellings were *outrageous*, *domesticated*, and *understandable*, then you were home free. You probably knew that at least one of those words was wrong!

▶ Step 6: Know When to Guess

Time to complete: 20 minutes
Activity: Complete worksheet on Your Guessing Ability

Armed with the process of elimination, you are ready to take control of one of the big questions in test taking: Should I guess? The short answer is *yes*. Some exams have what's called a guessing penalty, in which a fraction of your wrong answers is subtracted from your right answers—but the real estate broker exam doesn't work like that. The number of questions you answer correctly yields your raw score. So you have nothing to lose and everything to gain by guessing.

The more complicated answer to the question "Should I guess?" depends on you—your personality and your guessing intuition. There are two things you need to know about yourself before you go into the exam:

- Are you a risk taker?
- Are you a good guesser?

You will have to decide about your risk-taking quotient on your own. To find out if you are a good guesser, complete the Your Guessing Ability worksheet, because most real estate broker exams have no guessing penalty. Even if you are a play-it-safe person with lousy intuition, you're still safe in guessing. The best thing would be if you could overcome your anxieties and go ahead and mark an answer. But you may want to have a sense of how good your intuition is before you go into the exam.

Your Guessing Ability

The following are ten really hard questions. You are not supposed to know the answers. Rather, this is an assessment of your ability to guess when you don't have a clue. Read each question carefully, just as if you did expect to answer it. If you have any knowledge at all of the subject of the question, use that knowledge to help you eliminate wrong answer choices.

1. September 7 is Independence Day in
   a. India.
   b. Costa Rica.
   c. Brazil.
   d. Australia.

2. Which of the following is the formula for determining the momentum of an object?
   a. $p = mv$
   b. $F = ma$
   c. $P = IV$
   d. $E = mc^2$

3. Because of the expansion of the universe, the stars and other celestial bodies are all moving away from each other. This phenomenon is known as
   a. Newton's first law.
   b. the big bang.
   c. gravitational collapse.
   d. Hubble flow.

4. American author Gertrude Stein was born in
   a. 1713
   b. 1830
   c. 1874
   d. 1901

5. Which of the following is NOT one of the Five Classics attributed to Confucius?
   a. *I Ching*
   b. *Book of Holiness*
   c. *Spring and Autumn Annals*
   d. *Book of History*

6. The religious and philosophical doctrine that holds that the universe is constantly in a struggle between good and evil is known as
   a. Pelagianism.
   b. Manichaeanism.
   c. neo-Hegelianism.
   d. Epicureanism.

7. The third chief justice of the U.S. Supreme Court was
   a. John Blair.
   b. William Cushing.
   c. James Wilson.
   d. John Jay.

8. Which of the following is the poisonous portion of a daffodil?
   a. the bulb
   b. the leaves
   c. the stem
   d. the flowers

9. The winner of the Masters golf tournament in 1953 was
   a. Sam Snead.
   b. Cary Middlecoff.
   c. Arnold Palmer.
   d. Ben Hogan.

10. The state with the highest per capita personal income in 1980 was
   a. Alaska.
   b. Connecticut.
   c. New York.
   d. Texas.

Answers

Check your answers against the correct answers below.

1. c.
2. a.
3. d.
4. c.
5. b.
6. b.
7. b.
8. a.
9. d.
10. a.

▶ How Did You Do?

You may have simply gotten lucky and actually known the answers to one or two questions. In addition, your guessing was more successful if you were able to use the process of elimination on any of the questions. Maybe you didn't know who the third chief justice was (question 7), but you knew that John Jay was the first. In that case, you would have eliminated choice **d** and therefore improved your odds of guessing correctly from one in four to one in three.

According to probability, you should get $2\frac{1}{2}$ answers correct, so getting either two or three right would be average. If you got four or more right, you may be a really terrific guesser. If you got one or none right, you may not be a great guesser.

Keep in mind, though, that this is only a small sample. You should continue to keep track of your guessing ability as you work through the sample questions in this book. Circle the numbers of questions you guess on as you make your guesses; or, if you don't have time while you take the practice exams, go back afterward and try to remember which questions you guessed on. Remember, on an exam with four answer choices, your chances of getting a correct answer is one in four. So keep a separate guessing score for each exam. How many questions did you guess on? How many did you get right? If the number you got right is at least one-fourth of the number of questions you guessed on, you are at least an average guesser, maybe better—and you can go ahead and guess on the real exam. If the number you got right is significantly lower than one-fourth of the number you guessed on, you would be safe in guessing anyway, but maybe you would feel more comfortable if you guessed only selectively, when you can eliminate a wrong answer or at least have a good feeling about one of the answer choices.

▶ Step 7: Reach Your Peak Performance Zone

Time to complete: Ten minutes to read; weeks to complete!
Activity: Complete the Physical Preparation Checklist

To get ready for a challenge like a big exam, you have to take control of your physical, as well as your mental, state. Exercise, proper diet, and rest will ensure that your body works with, rather than against, your mind on test day, as well as during your preparation.

Exercise

If you don't already have a regular exercise program going, the time during which you are preparing for an exam is actually an excellent time to start one. And if you are already keeping fit—or trying to get that way—don't let the pressure of preparing for an exam fool you into quitting now. Exercise helps reduce stress by pumping wonderful good-feeling hormones called endorphins into your system. It also increases the oxygen supply throughout your body, including your brain, so you will be at peak performance on test day.

A half hour of vigorous activity—enough to raise a sweat—every day should be your aim. If you are really pressed for time, every other day is okay. Choose an activity you like, and get out there and do it. Jogging with a friend always makes the time go faster, or take a radio.

But don't overdo it; you don't want to exhaust yourself. Moderation is the key.

Diet

First, cut out the junk. Go easy on caffeine and nicotine, and eliminate alcohol and any other drugs from your system at least two weeks before the exam. Promise yourself a binge the night after the exam, if need be.

What your body needs for peak performance is simply a balanced diet. Eat plenty of fruits and vegetables, along with lean protein and complex carbohydrates. Foods high in lecithin (an amino acid), such as fish and beans, are especially good "brain foods."

The night before the exam, you might "carbo-load" the way athletes do before a contest. Eat a big plate of spaghetti, rice and beans, or your favorite carbohydrate.

Rest

You probably know how much sleep you need every night to be at your best, even if you don't always get it. Make sure you do get that much sleep, though, for at least a week before the exam. Moderation is important here, too. Extra sleep will just make you groggy.

If you are not a morning person and your exam will be given in the morning, you should reset your internal clock so that your body doesn't think you are taking an exam at 3:00 A.M. You have to start this process well before the exam. The way it works is to get up half an hour earlier each morning, and then go to bed half an hour earlier that night. Don't try it the other way around; you will just toss and turn if you go to bed early without having gotten up early. The next morning, get up another half an hour earlier, and so on. How long you will have to do this depends on how late you are used to getting up. Use the Physical Preparation Checklist on page 29 to make sure you are in tip-top form.

▶ Step 8: Get Your Act Together

Time to complete: Ten minutes to read; time to complete will vary
Activity: Complete Final Preparations worksheet

You are in control of your mind and body; you are in charge of test anxiety, your preparation, and your test-taking strategies. Now it's time to take charge of external factors, such as the testing site and the materials you need to take the exam.

Find Out Where the Exam Is and Make a Trial Run

Do you know how to get to the testing site? Do you know how long it will take to get there? If not, make a trial run, preferably on the same day of the week at the same time of day. Make note, on the Final Preparations worksheet on page 30, of the amount of time it will take you to get to the exam site. Plan on arriving 30–45 minutes early so you can get the lay of the land, use the bathroom, and calm down. Then, figure out how early you will have to get up that morning, and make sure you get up that early every day for a week before the exam.

Gather Your Materials

The night before the exam, lay out the clothes you will wear and the materials you have to bring with you to the exam. Plan on dressing in layers; you won't have any control over the temperature of the examination room. Have a sweater or jacket you can take off if it's warm. Use the checklist on the Final Preparations worksheet to help you pull together what you will need.

Don't Skip Breakfast

Even if you don't usually eat breakfast, do so the morning of the exam. A cup of coffee doesn't count. Don't eat doughnuts or other sweet foods, either. A sugar high will leave you with a sugar low in the middle of the exam. A mix of protein and carbohydrates is best: Cereal with milk, or eggs with toast, will do your body a world of good.

Physical Preparation Checklist

For the week before the exam, write down 1) what physical exercise you engaged in and for how long and 2) what you ate for each meal. Remember, you are trying for at least 30 minutes of exercise every other day (preferably every day) and a balanced diet that's light on junk food.

Exam minus 7 days

Exercise: _____ for ____ minutes

Breakfast: _____

Lunch: _____

Dinner: _____

Snacks: _____

Exam minus 6 days

Exercise: _____ for ____ minutes

Breakfast: _____

Lunch: _____

Dinner: _____

Snacks: _____

Exam minus 5 days

Exercise: _____ for ____ minutes

Breakfast: _____

Lunch: _____

Dinner: _____

Snacks: _____

Exam minus 4 days

Exercise: _____ for ____ minutes

Breakfast: _____

Lunch: _____

Dinner: _____

Snacks: _____

Exam minus 3 days

Exercise: _____ for ____ minutes

Breakfast: _____

Lunch: _____

Dinner: _____

Snacks: _____

Exam minus 2 days

Exercise: _____ for ____ minutes

Breakfast: _____

Lunch: _____

Dinner: _____

Snacks: _____

Exam minus 1 day

Exercise: _____ for ____ minutes

Breakfast: _____

Lunch: _____

Dinner: _____

Snacks: _____

Final Preparations

Getting to the Exam Site

Location of exam: _____

Date: _____

Departure time: _____

Do I know how to get to the exam site? Yes _____ No _____
If no, make a trial run.

Time it will take to get to exam site: _____

Things to Lay Out the Night Before

Clothes I will wear	_____
Sweater/jacket	_____
Watch	_____
Photo ID	_____
No. 2 pencils	_____
Calculator	_____
_____	_____
_____	_____

▶ Step 9: Do It!

Time to complete: Ten minutes, plus test-taking time
Activity: Ace the Real Estate Broker Exam!

Fast-forward to exam day. You are ready. You made a study plan and followed through. You practiced your test-taking strategies while working through this book. You are in control of your physical, mental, and emotional state. You know when and where to show up and what to bring with you. In other words, you are better prepared than most of the other people taking the real estate broker exam with you. You are psyched.

Just one more thing: When you are done with the exam, you will have earned a reward. Plan a celebration. Call up your friends and plan a party, or have a nice dinner for two—whatever your heart desires. Give yourself something to look forward to.

And then do it. Go into the exam, full of confidence, armed with test-taking strategies you have practiced until they're second nature. You are in control of yourself, your environment, and your performance on the exam. You are ready to succeed. So do it. Go in there and ace the exam. And look forward to your future career as a real estate broker!

3 ▶ AMP Practice Exam 1

CHAPTER SUMMARY

This is the first of the two AMP practice exams in this book. Take this exam to see how you would do if you took the exam today and find out where your strengths and weaknesses lie.

I f you prefer to take a practice exam on a computer, refer to the insert at the end of this book to see how you can take a free AMP practice test online on our website. Taking exams on the computer is good practice for the real exam. However, if you don't have access to the Internet, taking the exams on paper will accomplish the same goal—letting you know in which areas you are strong and in which areas you need more work.

Take this exam in as relaxed a manner as possible, without worrying about timing. You can time yourself on the second AMP practice exam. You should, however, make sure that you have enough time to take the entire exam in one sitting. Find a quiet place where you can work without interruptions.

The answer sheet is on the following page, and then comes the exam. After you have finished, use the answer key and explanations to learn your strengths and weaknesses. Then use the scoring section at the end of this chapter to see how you did overall.

1. (a) (b) (c) (d)
2. (a) (b) (c) (d)
3. (a) (b) (c) (d)
4. (a) (b) (c) (d)
5. (a) (b) (c) (d)
6. (a) (b) (c) (d)
7. (a) (b) (c) (d)
8. (a) (b) (c) (d)
9. (a) (b) (c) (d)
10. (a) (b) (c) (d)
11. (a) (b) (c) (d)
12. (a) (b) (c) (d)
13. (a) (b) (c) (d)
14. (a) (b) (c) (d)
15. (a) (b) (c) (d)
16. (a) (b) (c) (d)
17. (a) (b) (c) (d)
18. (a) (b) (c) (d)
19. (a) (b) (c) (d)
20. (a) (b) (c) (d)
21. (a) (b) (c) (d)
22. (a) (b) (c) (d)
23. (a) (b) (c) (d)
24. (a) (b) (c) (d)
25. (a) (b) (c) (d)
26. (a) (b) (c) (d)
27. (a) (b) (c) (d)
28. (a) (b) (c) (d)
29. (a) (b) (c) (d)
30. (a) (b) (c) (d)
31. (a) (b) (c) (d)
32. (a) (b) (c) (d)
33. (a) (b) (c) (d)
34. (a) (b) (c) (d)
35. (a) (b) (c) (d)
36. (a) (b) (c) (d)
37. (a) (b) (c) (d)
38. (a) (b) (c) (d)
39. (a) (b) (c) (d)
40. (a) (b) (c) (d)
41. (a) (b) (c) (d)
42. (a) (b) (c) (d)
43. (a) (b) (c) (d)
44. (a) (b) (c) (d)
45. (a) (b) (c) (d)
46. (a) (b) (c) (d)
47. (a) (b) (c) (d)
48. (a) (b) (c) (d)
49. (a) (b) (c) (d)
50. (a) (b) (c) (d)
51. (a) (b) (c) (d)
52. (a) (b) (c) (d)
53. (a) (b) (c) (d)
54. (a) (b) (c) (d)
55. (a) (b) (c) (d)
56. (a) (b) (c) (d)
57. (a) (b) (c) (d)
58. (a) (b) (c) (d)
59. (a) (b) (c) (d)
60. (a) (b) (c) (d)
61. (a) (b) (c) (d)
62. (a) (b) (c) (d)
63. (a) (b) (c) (d)
64. (a) (b) (c) (d)
65. (a) (b) (c) (d)
66. (a) (b) (c) (d)
67. (a) (b) (c) (d)
68. (a) (b) (c) (d)
69. (a) (b) (c) (d)
70. (a) (b) (c) (d)
71. (a) (b) (c) (d)
72. (a) (b) (c) (d)
73. (a) (b) (c) (d)
74. (a) (b) (c) (d)
75. (a) (b) (c) (d)
76. (a) (b) (c) (d)
77. (a) (b) (c) (d)
78. (a) (b) (c) (d)
79. (a) (b) (c) (d)
80. (a) (b) (c) (d)
81. (a) (b) (c) (d)
82. (a) (b) (c) (d)
83. (a) (b) (c) (d)
84. (a) (b) (c) (d)
85. (a) (b) (c) (d)
86. (a) (b) (c) (d)
87. (a) (b) (c) (d)
88. (a) (b) (c) (d)
89. (a) (b) (c) (d)
90. (a) (b) (c) (d)
91. (a) (b) (c) (d)
92. (a) (b) (c) (d)
93. (a) (b) (c) (d)
94. (a) (b) (c) (d)
95. (a) (b) (c) (d)
96. (a) (b) (c) (d)
97. (a) (b) (c) (d)
98. (a) (b) (c) (d)
99. (a) (b) (c) (d)
100. (a) (b) (c) (d)

AMP PRACTICE EXAM 1

▶ AMP Practice Exam 1

1. A tenant in a strip mall pays a monthly rental fee that includes all property maintenance charges, utilities, and cleaning services. This is known as a
   a. net lease.
   b. percentage lease.
   c. ground lease.
   d. gross lease.

2. Agent Schultz has a written agreement with Bob Jones to find a two-story house with at least three bedrooms, two baths, and a full basement in the Happy Meadow subdivision by August 30. What type of agreement does Agent Schultz have?
   a. an open buyer's agent agreement
   b. a dual agent agreement
   c. an exclusive buyer's agent agreement
   d. an agency agreement

3. Agent Carlson, while acting as a buyer's agent, is asked by her client, Mr. Jackson, if any of "those" people lived in the areas she was showing him. Agent Carlson has a duty to disclose anything that would affect the transaction. How should she respond?
   a. She should advise Mr. Jackson of the race of all neighbors that she is aware of.
   b. She should advise Mr. Jackson that they should contact the local law enforcement agency to obtain the information.
   c. She should advise Mr. Jackson to contact the local church to obtain the information.
   d. She should advise Mr. Jackson that, under the Fair Housing Laws, she cannot provide him with that information.

4. Molly Stanka and Richard Trawick, who are not married, want to buy a house together. In order to ensure that if one dies, the other automatically becomes the full owner, their deed must state that they are
   a. joint tenants.
   b. tenants in common.
   c. tenants in severalty.
   d. tenants by the entirety.

5. In a condominium, the owners own proportionate interests in
   a. land adjacent to the property.
   b. the structure and amenities.
   c. commercial businesses licensed to operate within the property.
   d. the air space enclosed by the structure.

6. Broker Damon negotiated the sale of an investment property for Max. Broker Damon had no agreement or authority to do so, but Max accepted the assistance and closed the deal with Broker Damon's help. What type of agency is this?
   a. This is not an agency.
   b. agency by estoppel
   c. agency by ratification
   d. agency by appointment

7. After John Rawlings bought his apartment, he started receiving his own property tax bills. This indicates that he has bought into a
   a. condominium.
   b. cooperative.
   c. leasehold.
   d. syndicate.

8. Man-made additions to real estate are known as
   a. chattels.
   b. trade fixtures.
   c. parcels.
   d. improvements.

9. No one seems to own the vacant lot next to Henry's house, so he has used it for a garden for many years now. He may have a good chance of going to court and obtaining ownership by
   a. condemnation.
   b. closing.
   c. adverse possession.
   d. remainder.

10. In order to reach the lake, the Chengs have a permanent right of way across their neighbor's lakefront property. The Chengs own
   a. an easement appurtenant.
   b. a license.
   c. a deed restriction.
   d. a lien.

11. Which of the following is an example of voluntary alienation of real property?
   a. a condemnation sale
   b. a foreclosure auction
   c. a deed of trust
   d. a transfer by escheat

12. In general, the lien with first claim on the real estate is the one first
   a. agreed upon.
   b. signed.
   c. recorded.
   d. foreclosed.

13. Mary and John Applegate asked Agent West for the best way to take title to the property on which they had made an accepted offer. What should Agent West do?
   a. He should advise the Applegates to ask their parents.
   b. He should advise the Applegates to contact a competent attorney.
   c. He should have her broker advise the Applegates of the best way to take title.
   d. He should advise the Applegates to contact the county recorder.

14. An appraiser determines that a commercial property, if fully leased, would produce $250,000 in rent on a monthly basis. A vacancy factor of 9% is applied, and by using a capitalization rate of 12%, the market value of the property is estimated at
   a. $22,750,000
   b. $25,000,000
   c. $189,583
   d. $2,777,777

15. How may a buyer's agent be paid?
   a. only by the buyer directly at closing
   b. a finder's fee may be paid directly by the seller outside of closing
   c. only by the buyer prior to closing
   d. by the listing broker through a commission split

16. Broker Asha Patel listed Joe Slack's house and subsequently showed it to her sister, who made an offer to purchase. What is the broker's responsibility of disclosure in this situation?
   a. No disclosure is required.
   b. The broker must disclose her family relationship to the purchaser.
   c. No disclosure is required if the full terms of the listing are met.
   d. It was a violations of fiduciary duties for the broker to show the property to a relative.

17. An acre contains approximately
   a. 5,270 square yards.
   b. 40,000 square feet.
   c. one-quarter square mile.
   d. 43,560 square feet.

18. Common covenants found in a mortgage could be any of the following EXCEPT a promise to
   a. keep the property in good repair.
   b. pay all real estate taxes as they come due.
   c. provide unlimited access to the mortgagee.
   d. not destroy or remove any improvements securing the loan.

19. The lender's underwriting criteria specify a maximum housing expense to income ratio of 35% of gross monthly income. If the applicant proves annual earnings of $75,000 in the previous year, and that salary rate is continuing, the maximum monthly PITI would be
   a. $2,187.50
   b. $2,625
   c. $6,250
   d. $2,571.42

20. A legal description that includes phrases such as "starting at the intersection of Smith and Baird roads and proceeding westerly 150 feet more or less to a stream" is referred to as
   a. metes and bounds.
   b. rectangular survey.
   c. lot and block.
   d. recorded plat.

21. The listing broker will receive a commission fee of 6% on the first $200,000 of sale price and 4% on any amount above $200,000. If the property sells for $419,000, how much is the total commission?
   a. $25,140
   b. $20,760
   c. $21,140
   d. $16,760

22. An abstract of title contains
   a. the summary of a title search.
   b. an attorney's opinion of title.
   c. a registrar's certificate of title.
   d. a quiet title lawsuit.

23. The Real Estate Settlement Procedures Act (RESPA) applies to
   a. all residential financing.
   b. land contracts.
   c. first mortgages only.
   d. financing of one- to four-family residences.

24. Broker Lu must have an escrow account
   a. before the state licensing agency will issue his broker's license.
   b. when he holds earnest money for any transaction.
   c. before his agents can enter into any listing agreements.
   d. at no time; he can put the money into his personal account.

25. A tract of land is being sold for $1,350,000, and the seller stated that there were 123 acres. The buyer ordered a survey, and the agreement states that if the total acreage varies by more or less than three acres, the sale price will be adjusted by $0.29 per square foot for the difference. What will be the final sales price if the survey reveals 125.2 acres?
   a. $1,581,576.50
   b. $1,377,791.28
   c. $1,322.208.68
   d. $1,377,208.28

26. Which of the following best describes the role of an agent who seeks a particular type of property for a client?
   a. general agent
   b. independent contractor
   c. special agent
   d. limited power of attorney

27. Property managers often make management decisions about tenant selection and budgets for their clients. In these relationships, the property manager is acting as a(n)
   a. special agent.
   b. power of attorney.
   c. independent contractor.
   d. general agent.

28. Which of the following is a requirement for a valid agency relationship?
   a. written agreement
   b. compensation
   c. mutual consent
   d. brokerage license

29. Jessie has shown the Evans family 27 homes, and they have selected one and made an offer. During negotiations, Mrs. Evans found another house she wanted to see. After Jessie showed them the second house, they wanted to make an offer on it. How will Jessie advise these buyers?
   a. They should make an offer on the second house and take whichever seller accepts first.
   b. They have already committed to the first seller and cannot terminate.
   c. They may withdraw the first offer but will forfeit the earnest money.
   d. They must withdraw the offer on the first house before making the second offer.

30. The best and most desired way of ending a special agency relationship is
   a. discharge by either principal.
   b. resignation by the agent.
   c. death or disability of the client.
   d. performance of the objective.

31. What happens if the agent has not located a buyer by the end of the listing period?
   a. The listing is automatically extended for an additional 30 days.
   b. The listing price is reduced by 5%.
   c. The agency relationship terminates.
   d. The broker can sue for reimbursement of marketing expenses.

32. Pete Mayfield has contracted with three brokers to sell his country property. He has agreed to pay a commission to the broker who brings a ready, willing, and able buyer and who meets his terms. What type of arrangement is this?
   a. The brokers are in violations of license laws.
   b. This is a listing by ratification.
   c. This is an open listing.
   d. This is a multiple listing.

33. Which of the following is included in an agent's responsibilities to the party the agent is NOT representing?
- **a.** The agent must disclose any material facts about the property.
- **b.** The agent must provide truthful information about the principal.
- **c.** The agent must give counsel and advice to the other party.
- **d.** The agent has no responsibilities to the other party.

34. The buyer broker contract states that the agent is to locate a specific property in a particular area for the client to purchase. The contract specifies price, location, amenities, and terms. The agent locates an acceptable property and, on behalf of the client, assists him or her in obtaining a ratified offer to purchase. All of the following are true at this point in the transaction EXCEPT that the agent
- **a.** has earned and is entitled to the commission fee.
- **b.** continues to owe fiduciary duties to the client.
- **c.** may expose the client to other properties on the market.
- **d.** may withhold from the client that the seller has a backup contract on the property.

35. When representing a buyer in a real estate transaction, the agent must disclose to the seller all of the following EXCEPT
- **a.** the buyer's motivating circumstances.
- **b.** the agent's relationship with the buyer.
- **c.** any agreement to compensate the agent out of the listing broker's commission.
- **d.** any potential for the agent to benefit from referring the parties to a subsidiary of the agent's firm for transaction-related services.

36. A tenant applicant confined to a wheelchair is interested in renting a townhome. A request is made to the landlord to allow the tenant to have an access ramp constructed. Which of the following is true in this situation?
- **a.** The tenant's application must be rejected.
- **b.** The landlord must allow the tenant to make the modification at the tenant's expense.
- **c.** The landlord is required to fund modifications to the property to accommodate the access problem.
- **d.** The landlord may collect an additional deposit to assure compliance.

37. The Civil Rights Act of 1866 prohibits discrimination based on skin color and provides
- **a.** exceptions for some owner-occupied housing.
- **b.** exceptions for certain apartment buildings.
- **c.** exceptions for private clubs.
- **d.** no exceptions.

38. The federal ban on discrimination based on familial status is intended to provide equal access to rentals for
- **a.** unmarried couples.
- **b.** people with children.
- **c.** single tenants.
- **d.** the elderly.

39. Martha James lives in one side of a two-family house. She wants to advertise the other side as nonsmoking. Can she legally do so?
- **a.** Yes, because the right to smoke is not protected by law.
- **b.** Yes, because she occupies part of the house herself.
- **c.** No, because a property owner cannot advertise discriminatory practices.
- **d.** No, because she can legally discriminate only on the basis of credit and income.

40. No federal fair housing laws are violated if a landlord refuses to rent to
  a. families with children.
  b. tenants of Vietnamese descent.
  c. deaf persons.
  d. students.

41. Land can be owned apart from the buildings on it under the arrangement known as a
  a. net lease.
  b. life estate.
  c. reversion.
  d. ground lease.

42. The penalty for a first violation of federal fair housing laws can be as much as
  a. $1,000
  b. $5,000
  c. $10,000
  d. $100,000

43. If the lease states that the landlord will provide heat, the tenant whose apartment is freezing may break the lease claiming
  a. suit for possession.
  b. actual eviction.
  c. constructive eviction.
  d. condemnation of the premises.

44. Credit lenders may not discriminate on the basis of age unless the prospective borrowers are
  a. parents of more than five children.
  b. out-of-state buyers.
  c. part-time workers.
  d. minors.

45. A property manager must determine appropriate insurance coverage for a property. This type is expense is a
  a. a pro rata expense.
  b. a capital expenditure.
  c. fixed expense.
  d. variable expense.

46. Zoning ordinances typically regulate the
  a. number of occupants allowed for each building.
  b. permitted uses of each parcel of land.
  c. maximum rent that may be charged.
  d. adherence to fair housing laws.

47. The new owner who agrees to pay an existing loan but does not officially take personal responsibility for it is
  a. assuming the loan.
  b. taking the property subject to the loan.
  c. subordinating the debt.
  d. alienating the lender.

48. When a borrower is required to maintain an escrow or trust account with the lending institution, money in that account may be used to pay the homeowner's
  a. points.
  b. utility bills.
  c. property taxes.
  d. life insurance.

49. Miguel tried to sell his house as a for-sale-by-owner but eventually decided to list with Fairview Realty. Because he had several interested parties, he reserved the right to sell the property to anyone he may find and owe the broker no fee. What kind of listing is this?
   a. exclusive right to sell
   b. exclusive agency
   c. nonexclusive
   d. open

50. Archie constructed a built-in bookcase in the living room of his home, added a ceiling fan, a table lamp, and a leather club chair for comfortable reading. He is selling his house, and all of these additions are included in the sale. Which of the following is true?
   a. The bookcases and ceiling fan are included in the real estate contract. The lamp and chair are chattel and are sold separately.
   b. All the items must be included in the real estate contract to be legally conveyed.
   c. Only the ceiling fan is real estate, and the other items must be sold on a bill of sale.
   d. All of the items must be sold separately, because they were not part of the real estate when Archie bought the house.

51. What is the type of legal description that uses imaginary grid lines of meridians and baselines?
   a. metes and bounds
   b. recorded plat
   c. compass bearing
   d. rectangular survey

52. A township is
   a. 36 square miles.
   b. one square mile.
   c. the same as a section.
   d. 640 acres.

53. The function of the Federal Housing Administration (FHA) is to
   a. make loans.
   b. insure loans.
   c. guarantee loans.
   d. buy loans.

54. Which of the following is an advantage of a biweekly payment plan?
   a. The borrower pays less per month in return for a longer term.
   b. It is equivalent to 12 monthly payments each year.
   c. There are lower interest rates.
   d. The loan is paid off sooner than scheduled.

55. Real property is
   a. the land and all improvements.
   b. the land, the improvements, and the bundle of rights.
   c. the land and the right to possess it.
   d. the land and buildings.

56. Simon Hersch, a salesperson associated with broker Ella King, lists a house for sale for $120,000, with 6% commission due at closing. Three weeks later, the owner accepts an offer for $115,000, brought in by Simon. Ella's practice is that 45% of commissions go to the office, and the remainder to the salesperson. How much will Simon make on the sale?

   a. $3,105

   b. $3,240

   c. $3,795

   d. $3,960

57. The seller has agreed to pay three points to the lending institution to help the buyers obtain a mortgage loan. The house was listed for $200,000 and is being sold for $180,000. The buyers will pay 10% in cash and borrow the rest. How much will the seller owe to the lender for points?

   a. $1,620

   b. $4,860

   c. $5,400

   d. $6,000

58. The subject house being appraised has no fireplace but does have a garage. The appraiser estimates that a fireplace contributes $3,000 to the value and that a garage contributes $12,000 to value in that neighborhood. A nearby house that recently sold for $198,000 is similar except that it has a fireplace but no garage. The adjusted value of the comparable house is

   a. $213,000

   b. $183,000

   c. $207,000

   d. $189,000

59. The Bakers have a gross income of $60,000. The lender wants them to spend no more than 28% of their income on their housing expenses. A house they can buy for $240,000 has $2,400 in annual property taxes. Homeowners insurance would cost about $400 a year. At today's interest rates, monthly payments would be $6.65 per $1,000 borrowed on a 30-year mortgage. What is the smallest amount the Bakers can expect to spend for a cash down payment?

   a. $10,334

   b. $48,000

   c. $52,000

   d. $64,510

60. In determining the market value of the subject property, which of the following would be of most importance?

   a. market value less depreciation

   b. selling price of comparable properties

   c. market value of recently sold comparable properties

   d. adjustment between market value and market price

61. In order to appraise property valued over $1,000,000 in a federally related transaction, the person performing the appraisal would need to be

   a. state certified.

   b. federally licensed.

   c. certified by the bank.

   d. approved by the government.

62. Land consisting of a quarter section is sold for
$1,850 per acre. The total sale price is
 a. $296,000
 b. $592,000
 c. $290,000
 d. $1,850,000

63. Rita Mendez has $86,576 left on her 8.5%
mortgage. Her monthly payment is set at
$852.56 for principal and interest (she pays her
own taxes and insurance). How much of her
next payment will go to reduce the principal?
 a. $116.76
 b. $239.31
 c. $613.25
 d. $735.80

64. How many acres are contained in a parcel 121
feet wide and 240 yards deep?
 a. 1
 b. $1\frac{1}{2}$
 c. 2
 d. $2\frac{1}{2}$

65. How much is the FHA annual mortgage insurance premium for the month in which the
remaining principal owed is $92,347?
 a. $0.05
 b. $12
 c. $38.48
 d. $46.17

66. Sue Addison owns an apartment building that
was constructed in 1965. According to federal
law, which of the following must be attached to
the leases Sue prepares for prospective tenants?
 a. a report of the building's radon level
 b. a lead-based paint disclosure statement
 c. an illustration of the building's location relative to electromagnetic fields (EMFs)
 d. any known instances of groundwater contamination in the building's water supply

67. The difference between replacement cost and
reproduction cost results from the different
 a. lots on which the properties are placed.
 b. times when the structures are built.
 c. handbooks used to estimate labor and
 materials.
 d. materials and techniques used for
 construction.

68. An appraiser arrives at a gross rent multiplier
by analyzing the
 a. building's amount of depreciation from all
 causes.
 b. income and recent sale prices of nearby
 properties.
 c. vacancy rates in the overall community.
 d. cost of constructing an equivalent building
 on a similar lot today.

69. The buyer gives the owner a $5,000 payment and a written agreement stating that, on July 1 of the following year, the buyer will purchase the property for $150,000 cash or the owner may keep the money. This transaction is known as

   a. a lease with an option to purchase.

   b. a purchase contract with a delayed settlement.

   c. an option agreement.

   d. a limited partnership.

70. A broker has contacted owners in a certain subdivision and advised them that several members of a particular religious sect have bought homes in the area. The broker has offered to list properties at a reduced rate, and encouraged the owners to sell quickly. What is this?

   a. steering

   b. anti-trust

   c. blockbusting

   d. channeling

71. Khan is buying a house and has 30 days in which to obtain financing as specified in the sales contract. The contract states that he must notify the seller within that period if he cannot obtain financing, or risk default if he does not close. It states that "time is of the essence" applies to financing approval. Which of the following is true?

   a. Khan can take care of matters at his convenience.

   b. The financing approval is more important than the time frame.

   c. The lender must see that the contract has been completely fulfilled prior to closing.

   d. Khan must adhere to the time frame, which will end at 11:59 P.M. on the 30th day.

72. Broker Ames told Sybil that her neighborhood was undergoing a change in racial makeup and that if she did not sell soon, she would lose most of the equity in her home. She listed and entered into a contract to sell out of fear. She soon discovered that the broker was guilty of blockbusting. What can Sybil do?

   a. Nothing; the agreement is firm.

   b. She must sell but may have grounds to sue the broker.

   c. She can cancel but must pay the broker's commission.

   d. The contract is voidable at the option of the seller.

73. Land developers subdivide land and assign lot and block numbers to identify certain parcels or lots in the subdivision. This is a legal description known as

   a. block survey system.

   b. recorded plat description.

   c. developer plat survey.

   d. municipal survey system.

74. A broker enters into an agreement with a tenant to secure a buyer/sublessee for the operation of the tenant's unlicensed beauty salon, which has recently been closed down by the city. The buyer signs a document allowing her to take over the business. Which of the following statements is true in this situation?

   a. The buyer can now open the doors for customers.

   b. The sublease is void because it is for an illegal purpose.

   c. The broker is entitled to his or her fee.

   d. The tenant is released from his or her lease.

75. The buyer has been held to be in default on a contract of sale. If buyer and seller had not agreed on liquidated damage, the seller could do which of the following?
   a. Obtain a court order preventing the buyer from purchasing another property.
   b. Sue the buyer for compensatory damages.
   c. Have the buyer incarcerated.
   d. Require the buyer to find a substitute purchaser.

76. The best way for a broker acting as a dual agent to minimize his or her risk is to
   a. negotiate a win/win transaction from which each party walks away satisfied.
   b. obtain written acknowledgment from both parties that they consent to the agent acting for both sides.
   c. obey each party's instructions even if they are in conflict.
   d. give notice to each party of any information useful in negotiation.

77. A contract in which an owner promises to pay compensation to a broker for providing a buyer, but is free to enter into the same agreement with other brokers, is known as
   a. an exclusive right to sell contract.
   b. a net listing.
   c. an open listing.
   d. personal service agreement.

78. A retail center generates $250,000 annual effective income with expenses of $213,450 including monthly debt service of $6,540. The property appreciates at approximately 5.5% per year. What is the annual cash flow?
   a. $50,300
   b. $36,550
   c. $30,010
   d. $43,760

79. To be valid, a listing contract must contain all of the following EXCEPT
   a. signatures of all interested parties.
   b. legal description of the property.
   c. expiration date.
   d. final contract price.

80. A prospect for the lease of a commercial property feels the need for adversarial representation and hires a broker to negotiate the lease on his behalf. The contract entered into between the prospect and the broker is called
   a. an authorization to negotiate.
   b. a buyer broker agreement.
   c. a property management agreement.
   d. a cooperative brokerage agreement.

81. Andre Benoit listed his condominium with Suzanne Cepeda for $167,900. His monthly association fee is $390, payable in advance on the first of the month. The sale is closing August 8, and Suzanne has informed him that the fee will be prorated at closing. Which of the following is the correct course of action?
   a. Debit buyer $100.64 and credit seller.
   b. Credit buyer $100.64 and debit seller.
   c. Debit buyer $276.76 and credit seller.
   d. Debit buyer $289.34 and credit seller.

82. Which of the following would terminate a listing agreement?
   a. the death of the broker
   b. the retirement of the salesperson
   c. the receipt of an offer to purchase
   d. the expiration of the salesperson's license

83. The typical relationship between broker and salesperson for tax purposes is known as
   a. indentured servant.
   b. independent contractor.
   c. statutory agent.
   d. transaction facilitator.

84. A broker lists properties acquired through foreclosure by a bank. Upon sale of the property, the bank covenants and warrants the property's title only against defects occurring during the bank's ownership and none prior to that time. This conveyance is a
   a. general deed.
   b. general warranty deed.
   c. special warranty deed.
   d. bargain and sale deed.

85. Herbert is closing on the sale of his house on June 30. The sale price is $350,000, and the balance on his mortgage loan is $287,561. He will owe $1,400 in property taxes, and the payoff on a home improvement lien is $32,558. He is paying Tops Realty a fee of 5% of the sale price and will have other closing costs of $2,547. How much will Herbert net?
   a. $25,934
   b. $8,434
   c. $11,559.95
   d. $8,934.05

86. The Hansons' home was listed with a broker, but they located a buyer at Mr. Hanson's place of employment and sold the property themselves. However, they were still obligated to pay a brokerage fee. What kind of listing had they agreed to?
   a. a net listing
   b. an open listing
   c. an exclusive right to sell
   d. an exclusive agency

87. Which of the following estates is NOT conveyed by deed?
   a. fee simple estate
   b. leasehold estate
   c. freehold estate
   d. easement

88. The listing broker's commission is earned when
   a. the property is listed.
   b. an offer has been accepted.
   c. financing has been arranged.
   d. the property is finally closed.

89. A deed is the instrument used to convey ownership of
   a. personal property.
   b. short-term use of real estate.
   c. real property.
   d. crops and other produce.

90. Ed Klein has a large lake on his property. He sells a permit to his friend Melissa, allowing Melissa to fish in Ed's lake at any time for one year. Melissa's right to use Ed's property is known as
   a. a license.
   b. an encroachment.
   c. an easement by necessity.
   d. a prescriptive right.

91. Repair or remodeling of a property generally adds to its worth. In recognition of the role contractors and suppliers play in increasing the value of a property, in many states they are assured payment for their goods and services by being able to file a
  a. declaratory judgment against the owner.
  b. *lis pendens* against the title insurance company.
  c. mechanic's lien against the property.
  d. registration with the new owner.

92. The Smiths offer to buy the Escobars' house for $125,000, with the closing scheduled for June 15. The Escobars sign a written acceptance, with the provision that the closing is to be on June 16. At this point, which of the following can occur?
  a. The Smiths can back out of buying the house with no penalty.
  b. The Escobars can hold the Smiths to a June 15 closing.
  c. The Escobars can hold the Smiths to a June 16 closing.
  d. The Smiths can sue for specific performance on June 15.

93. The party most likely to sue for specific performance in the purchase of real estate is the
  a. buyer.
  b. seller.
  c. broker.
  d. mortgage insurance company.

94. Jill Adams, a property owner, just received a bill from her local taxing authority in the amount of $2,040. Property taxes in this jurisdiction are based on 80% of assessed value, and the rate is $1.50 per hundred. What value has the assessor placed on Jill's property?
  a. $136,000
  b. $170,000
  c. $163,200
  d. $190,000

95. When real estate is purchased through a lease option, the money initially paid in return for the option can be applied to the eventual purchase price
  a. only in those states where the law allows it.
  b. if it is so agreed in the contract.
  c. if the lease is for a one-year period.
  d. under no circumstances.

96. The Millers put their house on the market, the Blicks made a written purchase offer, and the Millers accepted the offer in writing. When is the contract valid?
  a. immediately
  b. as soon as the signatures are notarized
  c. when the Blicks are notified of the acceptance
  d. when it is placed in the public records

97. Jim Fox is 17 when he signs a contract to lease a small house. After the property manager accepts his offer, the lease contract is
  a. void.
  b. voidable.
  c. valid.
  d. unenforceable.

98. Of the following, which lien has the lowest priority?

  a. property taxes
  b. a mortgage or trust deed
  c. unsecured judgment
  d. a special assessment

99. Which of the following statements is true of a land contract?

  a. The buyer is given the right to possess.
  b. The seller has a lien on the title.
  c. The buyer has legal title to the property.
  d. The seller cannot provide any of the financing.

100. A buyer paid $5,000 for an option to purchase a property within 180 days for $200,000. Within a month, the buyer made an offer to buy the property immediately for $180,000. Which of the following is true in this situation?

  a. The option money is forfeited.
  b. The owner may accept the offer for $180,000.
  c. The buyer is in default of the option agreement.
  d. Both parties are in violation of contract law.

▶ Answers

1. a. A net lease is one in which the tenant pays some ownership expenses along with his or her rent, such as maintenance, taxes, etc.

2. c. Agent Schultz has an exclusive buyer's agent agreement and, therefore, would be entitled to a commission, even if Mr. Jones bought his home through another agent or a for-sale-by-owner.

3. d. Under the Federal Fair Housing laws, agents cannot identify a member of a protected class to potential buyer(s). Local law enforcement agencies and churches do not provide similar information.

4. a. Joint tenants are often known as "joint tenants with right of survivorship." If Jane dies, Richard will automatically receive Jane's share, no matter what her will might say.

5. b. Ownership of a condominium unit includes a share of the structure and any common areas, as well as exclusive use of the air space within a designated unit.

6. c. Broker Damon had no authority to act as an agent, but Max accepted the benefits of his acts, thereby ratifying the agency representation.

7. a. A condominium is owned in fee simple, just as a single house would be. By contrast, the owner of a cooperative apartment receives shares in a corporation that owns the whole building and pays property taxes on it.

8. d. Improvements, which become part of the real property, include man-made additions such as sewers, roads, and buildings.

9. c. Adverse possession can sometimes give the use of title after occupancy of a parcel of land without permission or objection for a long period of time, the number of years varying from state to state.

10. a. An easement appurtenant allows the owner a particular use of an adjoining parcel's land. The Chengs do not have a license because they have a permanent right; a license may be withdrawn or canceled.

11. c. Only the trust represents the owner's own decision; the other transfers would be involuntary.

12. c. The general rule is that the lien first recorded takes priority.

13. b. Agents should always advise their buyers and sellers to contact competent professional personnel concerning questions of law, taxes, or accounting.

14. a. ($250,000 × 12 × 0.91) ÷ 0.12 = $22,750,000

15. d. A buyer's agent may be paid a portion of the listing commission by a cooperating broker. This does not create an agency relationship with the seller.

16. b. The seller's agent must disclose any relationship between the agent or broker and any prospective buyer. It may be a family or business relationship.

17. d. Students should memorize the size of an acre, which some estimate at "somewhat more than 200 feet by 200 feet."

18. c. The mortgagee must follow all rules about entering the property. Other covenants might be prompt payment and maintaining adequate hazard and casualty insurance coverage.

19. a. ($75,000 ÷ 12) × 0.35 = $2,187.50

20. a. The intersection and the stream are known as monuments, which mark the corners of a metes and bounds legal description. Because one boundary is a stream and subject to natural change, the phrase *more or less* is used.

21. b. $299,000 × 6% = $12,000
($419,000 − $200,000) × 4% = $8,760
$12,000 + $8,760 = $20,760

22. a. An abstract reports the results of a full title search of the public records.

23. d. RESPA sets requirements for all federally related mortgages and home equity loans on one- to four-family residences.

24. b. A broker is not required to have an escrow account unless he or she accepts monies to be held for the benefit of others.

25. b. 125.2 acres − 123 acres = 2.2 acres more × 43,560 sq. ft. per acre = 95,832 sq. ft. 95,832 sq. ft. × $0.29 per sq. ft. = $27,791.28 additional
$1,350,000 + $27,791.28 = $1,377,791.28 final sales price

26. c. The special agent is employed to provide a specific service, such as finding the buyer a property that meets the buyer's requirements.

27. d. The general agent is empowered to make binding decisions on behalf of the principal. Approving leases and property expenditures are among those activities.

28. c. Of the listed suggestions, only mutual consent is required. Agency is sometimes formed by the behavior of the parties; compensation is generally a result of the completion of the task assigned in the agreement, and licensure is immaterial in agency.

29. d. An offer may be withdrawn at any time prior to written acceptance and notification to by the offeree to the offeror.

30. d. Performing the object of the assignment ends the relationship.

31. c. If the object of the special agency is not performed by its expiration date, the listing expires.

32. c. An open listing is nonexclusive, so the seller may sell the property and owe no commission, or one of the brokers may earn a fee as the procuring cause of a sale.

33. a. The agent is required only to provide the other party with all of the pertinent facts about the condition of the property and to make honest statements about the transaction.

34. d. The buyer's broker must disclose all known information to the client about the property or the seller. The fact that there is a backup contract is pertinent information, and the buyer must be informed.

35. a. The duty of confidentiality extends to buyer clients.

36. b. If the tenant pays, there is no violation of building codes, and the tenant agrees to restore the property to its original condition, the landlord must approve the ramp.

37. d. The fact that no exceptions are provided for discrimination based on color is the most important aspect of this act.

38. b. Familial status refers to a parent or guardian who lives with one or more children under the age of 18.

39. a. No law offers equal protection for smoking.

40. d. Occupation and source of income are not protected classes under federal laws.

41. d. A ground lease, usually for many years, allows the tenant to erect and own buildings on rented land.

42. c. HUD's penalty for a first offense can be $10,000. The Justice Department may fine for a pattern of repeat violations up to $100,000.

43. c. The landlord's deliberate neglect of a duty may break a lease through the process known as constructive eviction.

44. d. The Equal Credit Opportunity Act was amended in 1976 to add age as a protected class, except where the would-be borrower is a minor.

45. c. Although insurance rates may change, they are a fixed expense in an annual budget to operate a property.

46. b. Typical zones permit residential, multifamily, or commercial buildings within a given zone.

47. b. Taking title to property subject to an existing mortgage acknowledges the existence of the debt but does not incur personal liability.

48. c. The escrow account is used to ensure prompt payment of bills, including property taxes, homeowners insurance premiums, and occasionally costs for homeowners associations or flood insurance.

49. b. Miguel appointed one exclusive broker, Fairview Realty, as his agent. He is obligated to pay only if the broker procures a satisfactory buyer.

50. a. The bookcase and the fan were personal property prior to being attached to the house. They are fixtures and must be sold with the real estate. The lamp and chair are personal property or chattel and should be sold on a bill of sale.

51. d. The rectangular or government survey method was established by the U.S. government in 1785 and is used to describe approximately 70% of the land area in the United States.

52. a. A township is a division of land in a rectangular survey system that is six miles square, or 36 square miles.

53. b. The FHA does not lend any money; it administers an insurance program that allows homebuyers to borrow almost the full purchase price with a low down payment.

54. d. Biweekly plans involve 26 half-payments a year, the equivalent of 13 full payments. The extra payment goes entirely to reduce principal, shortening the remaining term.

55. **b.** The land includes the surface, subsurface, and airspace above. Real estate includes the land and all man-made improvements. Real property is the land, the improvements, and the legal rights of ownership, which include possession, control, enjoyment, exclusion, and disposition.

56. **c.** $115,000 sales price × 6% commission = $6,900 total commission to broker
$6,900 × 55% split to Simon = $3,795 fee paid to Simon

57. **b.** Points are paid on the amount borrowed, not on the selling price. The buyers are borrowing 90% of the sale price, or $162,000. Each point is 1% of that figure, so three points are $162,000 × 0.03 = $4,860.

58. **c.** The appraiser subtracts the value of the fireplace from the sales price of the comparable house, and then adds the value of the garage that is found in the subject property.
$198,000 − $3,000 + $12,000 = $207,000

59. **d.** The Bakers' monthly gross income is $5,000 ($60,000 ÷ 12). The lender allows them a monthly mortgage payment no higher than 28% of $5,000 = $1,400. From that $1,400 must be subtracted a month's property taxes ($2,400 ÷ 12 = $200) and a month's homeowner insurance premium ($400 ÷ 12 = $33.33). That leaves $1,167 to pay for the mortgage itself, principal, and interest. At $6.65 per thousand dollars, $1,167 will pay for $175.49, or $175,490 borrowed on a mortgage ($1,167 ÷ $6.65 = $175.49). If they buy for $240,000 and borrow $175,490, the Bakers will need $64,510 as a cash down payment ($240,000 − $175,490).

60. **c.** The market value of the comparable (recently sold) properties is used to determine market value for the subject property

because it reflects what buyers are willing to pay for similar properties, not what they are currently priced at.

61. **a.** Under the Financial Institutions Reform, Recovery, and Enforcement Act (FIRREA), appraisers need to be certified by the state to perform an appraisal as part of a federally related transaction when the property value exceeds $1,000,000.

62. **a.** A section of land is 640 acres. A quarter section contains 160 acres.
160 × $1,850 = $296,000

63. **b.** A year's interest on the present debt would be $7,358.96 ($86,576 × 0.085). A month's interest is $613.25 ($7,358.96 ÷ 12). The principal portion of her payment is $239.31 ($852.56 − 613.25).

64. **c.** 240 yards = 720 feet (240 yards × 3 feet in a yard)
121 feet × 720 feet = 87,120 square feet
87,120 square feet ÷ 43,560 square feet in an acre = 2 acres

65. **c.** The annual FHA mortgage insurance premium rate is 0.5%.
$92,347 loan balance × 0.005 = $461.74 annual premium
$461.74 ÷ 12 months = $38.48 monthly premium

66. **b.** Federal law requires that a lead-based paint disclosure form be given to all tenants and buyers if the building was constructed before 1978.

67. **d.** Reproduction of a building uses the original materials and techniques for an exact duplicate of the original; replacement uses modern methods for an equivalent building that will serve the same purpose as the original.

68. b. A gross rent multiplier estimates how much investors seem willing to pay for property yielding a given amount of income. This is only a rough estimate, as it does not consider some important factors, such as vacancies and expenses.

69. c. In an option contract, the buyer purchases the right to buy a property at fixed terms within a defined period of time. If the option is not executed, the owner gets to keep the deposit.

70. c. Inducing or attempting to induce an owner to sell because of the entry of any member of a protected class under fair housing laws is a violation of federal law. Blockbusting is also called *panic peddling*.

71. d. Any party who fails to take care of his or her responsibilities in a timely manner is subject to being held in default of the contract. Time is of the essence is a legal clause meaning exact time frames must be met.

72. d. Contracts made under duress are voidable at the option of the innocent party.

73. b. Land developers use the recorded plat method to assign lot, block, and section numbers to a tract of land and record it in the county where the land is located.

74. b. A court would refuse to enforce any contract in violation of the law or public policy.

75. b. After disposing of the property, the seller may calculate losses, and seek to recover compensatory damages from the defaulting buyer.

76. b. A dual agent should make sure each party realizes the situation and gives written consent.

77. c. With an open listing, the owner may employ any number of brokers, but only the broker who delivers the buyer is paid a fee.

78. b. $250,000 income − $213,450 total expenses including debt service = $36,550 Appreciation is not included in the cash flow analysis.

79. d. The final contract price will not be determined until after an offer is presented and accepted.

80. b. A contract wherein the broker represents a buyer or tenant is called a buyer broker agreement or an exclusive right to represent agreement.

81. d. The buyer will reimburse Andre for August 9 through August 31.
$390 monthly fee ÷ 31 days in August = $12.58 per day
31 days − 8 days = 23 days the buyer will owe the seller $12.58 × 23 = $289.34

82. a. The death of either party will cancel the listing.

83. b. The relationship most salespersons have with their brokers is that of independent contractor under IRS rules.

84. c. The grantor warrants the title only, because the grantor owned the property. A general warranty deed is a full warranty deed including the covenants of seisin, quiet enjoyment, against encumbrances, and further assurance.

85. b. $350,000 sales price × 5% = $17,500 commission
$350,000 − $287,561 first lien − $32,558 second lien − $1,400 taxes − $2,547 costs − $17,500 commission = $8,434.00 net to Herbert

86. c. An exclusive right to sell obligates the owner to pay a brokerage fee regardless of who located the buyer. In an exclusive agency, the owner is not liable for payment of a fee if they sell the property themselves.

87. b. A rental or leased property is a leasehold estate and possession is conveyed by the lease agreement.

88. **b.** Although most commissions may not be paid until the closing, the listing agent's assignment has actually been completed when a buyer is produced who is willing and able to purchase on the seller's terms.

89. **c.** A deed conveys ownership of real property; personal property is conveyed by lease, bill of sale, or title.

90. **a.** A license is a privilege to use the land of another for a specific purpose. It may not be assigned, and ends upon expiration, revocation, or withdrawal.

91. **c.** Contractors and others are permitted to file a mechanic's lien against the improved property.

92. **a.** When the Escobars made a counteroffer, it constituted a rejection of the original offer. The Smiths are now free and may accept or reject the counteroffer.

93. **a.** Although a seller's problems might be solved with money damages, a buyer might prefer forcing the seller to sell because each parcel of real estate is unique.

94. **b.** $2,040 divided by 1.5 × 100 divided by 0.8 = $170,000

95. **b.** Lease option contracts can be very flexible, and the parties may make any arrangement that suits them.

96. **c.** Acceptance of an offer must be communicated to the offeror.

97. **b.** The lease contract appears to be valid, but if it is not completed when Jim turns 18, he may disavow it, thus making it voidable.

98. **c.** Property taxes, special assessments, and secured liens have priority over all others.

99. **a.** The buyer may take possession of the property, but legal title remains with the owner until the terms of the purchase are met.

100. **b.** Either party is permitted to attempt to renegotiate the terms of the transaction.

▶ Scoring

Remember that this practice exam is not correlated exactly to your state's real estate broker exam; your official test will also include state-specific questions. To evaluate how you fared on this practice exam, find the number of questions you got right, and divide by 100 (the number of questions on this exam). This will give you your score as a percentage. A passing score would be about 70% on this practice exam.

For now, what's much more important than your overall score is how you did on each of the areas tested by the exam. You need to diagnose your strengths and weaknesses so that you can concentrate your efforts as you prepare. The question types are mixed in the practice exam, so in order to tell where your strengths and weaknesses lie, you'll need to compare your answer sheet with the AMP Practice Exam 1 for Review below, which shows which of the categories each question falls into.

Use your score in conjunction with the Learning-Express Test Preparation System in Chapter 2 of this book to help you devise a study plan using the Real Estate Broker Refresher Course in Chapter 7, the Real Estate Broker Math Review in Chapter 8, and the Real Estate Glossary in Chapter 9. You should plan to spend more time on the sections that correspond to the questions you found hardest and less time on the lessons that correspond to areas in which you did well.

Once you have spent some time reviewing, take the second AMP practice exam in Chapter 10 to see how much you've improved.

AMP Practice Exam 1 for Review

Topic	Question Numbers
Financing	18, 19, 44, 47, 48, 53, 54, 59, 63, 65, 88, 93, 96
Listing Property	8, 10, 12, 16, 17, 20, 21, 32, 37, 46, 49, 50, 51, 52, 55, 58, 60, 61, 67, 68, 70, 73, 77, 79, 81, 82, 84, 85, 86, 87, 88
Property Management	1, 14, 27, 36, 38, 39, 40, 41, 42, 45, 66, 74, 78, 80
Professional Responsibilities/ Fair Practice/Administration	3, 13, 24, 26, 28, 30, 31, 33, 76, 83
Selling Property	2, 6, 15, 25, 29, 34, 43, 56, 62, 69, 71, 72, 75, 92, 93, 95, 96, 97, 98, 99, 100
Settlement/Transfer of Ownership	4, 5, 7, 9, 11, 22, 23, 35, 57, 64, 89, 90, 91, 94

4 ▶ Promissor Practice Exam 1

CHAPTER SUMMARY

This is the first of the two Promissor practice exams in this book. Take this exam to see how you would do if you took the exam today and find out what are your strengths and weaknesses.

I f you prefer to take a practice exam on a computer, refer to the insert at the end of this book to see how you can take a free Promissor practice test on our website. Taking exams on the computer is good practice for the real exam. However, if you don't have access to the Internet, taking the exams on paper will accomplish the same goal—letting you know in which areas you are strong and in which areas you need more work.

Take this exam in as relaxed a manner as possible, without worrying about timing. You can time yourself on the second Promissor practice exam. You should, however make sure that you have enough time to take the entire exam in one sitting. Find a quiet place where you can work without interruptions.

The answer sheet is on the following page, and then comes the exam. After you have finished, use the answer key and explanations to learn your strengths and weaknesses. Then use the scoring section at the end of this chapter to see how you did overall.

1.	ⓐ	ⓑ	ⓒ	ⓓ	31.	ⓐ	ⓑ	ⓒ	ⓓ	61.	ⓐ	ⓑ	ⓒ	ⓓ
2.	ⓐ	ⓑ	ⓒ	ⓓ	32.	ⓐ	ⓑ	ⓒ	ⓓ	62.	ⓐ	ⓑ	ⓒ	ⓓ
3.	ⓐ	ⓑ	ⓒ	ⓓ	33.	ⓐ	ⓑ	ⓒ	ⓓ	63.	ⓐ	ⓑ	ⓒ	ⓓ
4.	ⓐ	ⓑ	ⓒ	ⓓ	34.	ⓐ	ⓑ	ⓒ	ⓓ	64.	ⓐ	ⓑ	ⓒ	ⓓ
5.	ⓐ	ⓑ	ⓒ	ⓓ	35.	ⓐ	ⓑ	ⓒ	ⓓ	65.	ⓐ	ⓑ	ⓒ	ⓓ
6.	ⓐ	ⓑ	ⓒ	ⓓ	36.	ⓐ	ⓑ	ⓒ	ⓓ	66.	ⓐ	ⓑ	ⓒ	ⓓ
7.	ⓐ	ⓑ	ⓒ	ⓓ	37.	ⓐ	ⓑ	ⓒ	ⓓ	67.	ⓐ	ⓑ	ⓒ	ⓓ
8.	ⓐ	ⓑ	ⓒ	ⓓ	38.	ⓐ	ⓑ	ⓒ	ⓓ	68.	ⓐ	ⓑ	ⓒ	ⓓ
9.	ⓐ	ⓑ	ⓒ	ⓓ	39.	ⓐ	ⓑ	ⓒ	ⓓ	69.	ⓐ	ⓑ	ⓒ	ⓓ
10.	ⓐ	ⓑ	ⓒ	ⓓ	40.	ⓐ	ⓑ	ⓒ	ⓓ	70.	ⓐ	ⓑ	ⓒ	ⓓ
11.	ⓐ	ⓑ	ⓒ	ⓓ	41.	ⓐ	ⓑ	ⓒ	ⓓ	71.	ⓐ	ⓑ	ⓒ	ⓓ
12.	ⓐ	ⓑ	ⓒ	ⓓ	42.	ⓐ	ⓑ	ⓒ	ⓓ	72.	ⓐ	ⓑ	ⓒ	ⓓ
13.	ⓐ	ⓑ	ⓒ	ⓓ	43.	ⓐ	ⓑ	ⓒ	ⓓ	73.	ⓐ	ⓑ	ⓒ	ⓓ
14.	ⓐ	ⓑ	ⓒ	ⓓ	44.	ⓐ	ⓑ	ⓒ	ⓓ	74.	ⓐ	ⓑ	ⓒ	ⓓ
15.	ⓐ	ⓑ	ⓒ	ⓓ	45.	ⓐ	ⓑ	ⓒ	ⓓ	75.	ⓐ	ⓑ	ⓒ	ⓓ
16.	ⓐ	ⓑ	ⓒ	ⓓ	46.	ⓐ	ⓑ	ⓒ	ⓓ	76.	ⓐ	ⓑ	ⓒ	ⓓ
17.	ⓐ	ⓑ	ⓒ	ⓓ	47.	ⓐ	ⓑ	ⓒ	ⓓ	77.	ⓐ	ⓑ	ⓒ	ⓓ
18.	ⓐ	ⓑ	ⓒ	ⓓ	48.	ⓐ	ⓑ	ⓒ	ⓓ	78.	ⓐ	ⓑ	ⓒ	ⓓ
19.	ⓐ	ⓑ	ⓒ	ⓓ	49.	ⓐ	ⓑ	ⓒ	ⓓ	79.	ⓐ	ⓑ	ⓒ	ⓓ
20.	ⓐ	ⓑ	ⓒ	ⓓ	50.	ⓐ	ⓑ	ⓒ	ⓓ	80.	ⓐ	ⓑ	ⓒ	ⓓ
21.	ⓐ	ⓑ	ⓒ	ⓓ	51.	ⓐ	ⓑ	ⓒ	ⓓ					
22.	ⓐ	ⓑ	ⓒ	ⓓ	52.	ⓐ	ⓑ	ⓒ	ⓓ					
23.	ⓐ	ⓑ	ⓒ	ⓓ	53.	ⓐ	ⓑ	ⓒ	ⓓ					
24.	ⓐ	ⓑ	ⓒ	ⓓ	54.	ⓐ	ⓑ	ⓒ	ⓓ					
25.	ⓐ	ⓑ	ⓒ	ⓓ	55.	ⓐ	ⓑ	ⓒ	ⓓ					
26.	ⓐ	ⓑ	ⓒ	ⓓ	56.	ⓐ	ⓑ	ⓒ	ⓓ					
27.	ⓐ	ⓑ	ⓒ	ⓓ	57.	ⓐ	ⓑ	ⓒ	ⓓ					
28.	ⓐ	ⓑ	ⓒ	ⓓ	58.	ⓐ	ⓑ	ⓒ	ⓓ					
29.	ⓐ	ⓑ	ⓒ	ⓓ	59.	ⓐ	ⓑ	ⓒ	ⓓ					
30.	ⓐ	ⓑ	ⓒ	ⓓ	60.	ⓐ	ⓑ	ⓒ	ⓓ					

► Promissor Practice Exam 1

1. A building is owned jointly by three individuals. If their type of ownership includes the right of survivorship, what happens to an owner's interest upon the death of that owner?
   a. Their interest passes automatically to the other owners.
   b. Their interest passes to heirs or devisees.
   c. Their interest passes to the state if there are no heirs.
   d. Their interest passes as directed in their will.

2. Which of the following forms of ownership includes the right of survivorship?
   a. tenants in common
   b. joint tenancy
   c. severalty
   d. community property

3. Which of the following terms is NOT synonymous with the others?
   a. personal property
   b. fixture
   c. personalty
   d. chattel

4. Rugged Outfits Corporation leases retail space in a shopping center for a clothing store. They install counters, shelves, lighting, and other fixtures. These items are now considered
   a. trade fixtures.
   b. personal property.
   c. removal at the end of the lease.
   d. all of the above

5. Which of the following is NOT a physical characteristic of real estate?
   a. scarcity
   b. immobility
   c. indestructibility
   d. nonhomogeneity

6. An estate in land that gives the owner the greatest bundle of rights, without a limitation on the duration of ownership, and allows the owner to control who inherits the property is known as a
   a. conventional life estate.
   b. defeasible fee estate.
   c. legal life estate.
   d. fee simple estate.

7. The process by which government takes private property for a public use is known as
   a. police power.
   b. eminent domain.
   c. condemnation.
   d. escheat.

8. The legal description that refers to principal meridians and baselines is called
   a. recorded plat.
   b. metes and bounds.
   c. rectangular survey system.
   d. reference bearings.

9. How many acres are there in the $SW\frac{1}{4}$ of the $NW\frac{1}{4}$ of the $SE\frac{1}{4}$ of Section 16?
   a. 2.5 acres
   b. 5 acres
   c. 10 acres
   d. 20 acres

10. Under a typical zoning ordinance, a noncon-forming use is a use of property
  a. that violates the zoning ordinance.
  b. that, although it is in violation of the local zoning code, is desired by the local community and, therefore, allowed to continue.
  c. that no longer conforms to the zoning regulations.
  d. that was present before the zoning ordinance or amendment was put in place and is, therefore, "grandfathered."

11. Should there be the need to foreclose on a parcel of real property, any liens will be paid in order of priority. Which lien will be paid first?
  a. mechanic's lien
  b. mortgage lien
  c. first recorded lien
  d. *ad valorem* tax lien

12. Which type of deed provides the grantee with the greatest protection?
  a. general warranty deed
  b. special warranty deed
  c. bargain and sale deed
  d. quitclaim deed

13. The culmination of a real estate transaction is the transfer of ownership from a seller to a buyer. At what point in time does ownership of real property transfer?
  a. when the deed is signed by the grantor
  b. when the deed is delivered and accepted by the grantee
  c. when the deed is signed by the grantee
  d. when the deed is recorded in public record

14. Passage of property to the state when a person dies without a will and without heirs is known as
  a. involuntary alienation.
  b. adverse possession.
  c. eminent domain.
  d. escheat.

15. An easement that is annexed to the land for the benefit of the adjoining property owner and passes with land is known as an easement
  a. by necessity.
  b. appurtenant.
  c. in gross.
  d. by prescription.

16. Which of the following is NOT an element of market value?
  a. Both seller and buyer are willing and acting in their own best interest.
  b. Both parties are well informed or advised as to the property's uses.
  c. The property is exposed in the open market for a reasonable time.
  d. The price paid is the highest price the property will bring in the marketplace.

17. What is the principle of value that states that the value of any part of a property is equal to the value it adds?
  a. contribution
  b. conformity
  c. severance
  d. increasing and diminishing returns

18. An apartment building generates a gross income of $295,000 and a net operating income of $171,500 per annum. The capitalization rate for this type of property for this market area ranges from 7% to 9%. What is the maximum indicated value for this property?
   a. $1,905,555
   b. $2,450,000
   c. $3,277,777
   d. $4,214,285

19. A seven-story building without an elevator would be said to suffer from which type of depreciation?
   a. external obsolescence
   b. physical deterioration
   c. locational obsolescence
   d. functional obsolescence

20. The sales comparison approach requires an appraiser to make adjustments to value. How are the adjustments made?
   a. If the comparable is better, subtract value; if worse, add value.
   b. If the comparable is better, add value; if worse, subtract value.
   c. If the subject is better, subtract value; if worse, add value.
   d. If the subject is better, add value; if worse, subtract value.

21. Capital gains on the sale of a real estate asset is calculated by
   a. sales price minus the basis.
   b. adjusted sales price minus the basis.
   c. realized selling price minus the adjusted basis.
   d. contract sales price minus the adjusted basis.

22. Which of the following statements is true with regard to express and implied contracts?
   a. An express contract must be in writing, and an implied contract is created by the parties' actions.
   b. An express contract is stated in words, whether written or oral, and an implied contract is created by the parties' actions.
   c. An express contract is oral, and an implied contract is created by the parties' actions.
   d. An express contract is written, and an implied contract is oral.

23. Which of the following statements is false with regard to bilateral and unilateral contracts?
   a. Bilateral contracts involve a promise exchanged for a promise.
   b. Unilateral contracts involve a promise exchanged for an act.
   c. A real estate purchase contract is bilateral.
   d. A real estate lease is unilateral.

24. State Oil Company has signed a purchase contract with Betty's Diner to purchase a parcel of property. Betty's Diner has failed to disclose to State Oil that toxic substances were dumped on the property over a ten-year period. Once this omission is discovered by State Oil, the contract is
   a. valid.
   b. voidable.
   c. void.
   d. unenforceable.

25. Which of the following is NOT an essential element of a contract?
   a. offer and acceptance
   b. consideration
   c. earnest money
   d. competent parties

26. Carlos Santos signs a contract to purchase property from Carl Johnson. Carlos later decides not to purchase and transfers his rights to purchase to property to Charlotte Chow. If Carlos were not released from his obligations under the contract, this would be an example of
   a. assignment.
   b. novation.
   c. substitution.
   d. unilateral transfer.

27. In case of a breach of contract, the other party may often enforce specific performance. What is specific performance?
   a. a lawsuit for actual and treble damages
   b. a lawsuit by the non-defaulting party to specifically collect damages agreed to in the contract
   c. a lawsuit to compel action called for in the agreement
   d. all of the above

28. When a contract is signed by all the parties, the contract is said in law to be
   a. performed.
   b. enforceable.
   c. executed.
   d. executory.

29. Alltown Realty has a listing agreement on a parcel of land. This agreement specifies that Alltown Realty will be paid a commission upon sale and closing of the property. The agreement further specifies that Alltown will be paid the commission no matter which firm procures the buyer. The only exception is if the Petersons find their own buyer without the assistance of any broker. This type of listing agreement is a(n)
   a. exclusive right to sell.
   b. exclusive agency.
   c. open listing.
   d. net listing.

30. The law requiring that contracts for the sale of real estate be in writing to be enforceable in a court of law is the
   a. Statute of Contract Construction.
   b. Statute of Frauds.
   c. Statute of Enforceability.
   d. Law of Contracts.

31. Michael and Michelle Murdock have signed a contract to sell their home to Elizabeth Plowsky. Until closing, Elizabeth is said to have what kind of interest in the property?
   a. no title or interest
   b. bare (legal) title
   c. general title
   d. equitable title

32. Which of the following would be an example of a void contract?
   a. a contract signed to transport illegal substances
   b. a contract signed under duress
   c. a contract signed without the agreed earnest money paid
   d. a contract signed by a minor

33. What is required to create an agency relationship between a principal and an agent?
   a. a written contract
   b. a written contract with compensation paid or promised
   c. a principal delegates authority and an agent accepts the delegation
   d. a promise of compensation

34. Stacy Hampton is a salesperson with Allstar Realty. She is showing property to a buyer her firm has not agreed to represent. In this context, Stacy's firm would be considered a(n)
   a. agent.
   b. subagent.
   c. nonagent.
   d. counteragent.

35. An agent who represents a principal in a broad range of functions within the scope of a business and who has the ability to bind the principal, is said to be a(n)
   a. general agent.
   b. special agent.
   c. limited agent.
   d. universal agent.

36. Bob Kenyon is showing a parcel of land that is not on the market to a buyer he does not represent, without the property owner's knowledge. The buyer makes an offer that Bob presents to the owner. The property owner then accepts the offer. Bob has created an agency by
   a. agreement.
   b. action.
   c. circumstance.
   d. ratification.

37. What is a formal, legal relationship between a principal and an agent that entails trust and confidence?
   a. formal agency
   b. legal agency
   c. compensatory relationship
   d. fiduciary

38. Which of the following is a fiduciary duty owed by an agent to a customer?
   a. disclosure
   b. loyalty
   c. accounting
   d. none of the above

39. If an agent represents a seller, which of the following would NOT have to be disclosed to a prospective buyer?
   a. The foundation of the structure needs repair.
   b. There are past due property taxes owed on the parcel.
   c. The seller is in financial trouble and facing foreclosure.
   d. An upcoming improvement project will require that the city take the west 40 feet of the parcel.

40. Which of the following fiduciary duties continues even after the end of the formal relationship with a client?
   a. loyalty
   b. confidentiality
   c. obedience
   d. reasonable care

41. Teresa Tran is a broker who has been hired by a property owner to list and sell a small shopping center. She has been given authority to place a For Sale sign on the property and to place the listing on several websites. She has also been authorized to show the property to prospective buyers and to present any offers to her client. She has been given no other authority with regard to this property. Teresa is a(n)
a. special agent.
b. general agent.
c. authorized agent.
d. implied agent.

42. An intentional misstatement of a material fact designed to deprive a person of money, property, or rights is
a. misrepresentation.
b. puffing.
c. misstatement.
d. fraud.

43. Federal lead-based paint regulation would require all the following EXCEPT
a. disclosure of known lead-based paint hazards.
b. lead warning statements in sales contracts and leases.
c. removal of any lead-based paint in residential dwellings built before 1978.
d. providing buyers and tenants with the EPA booklet on lead-based paint.

44. Should toxic or hazardous materials be discovered on a property, the Comprehensive Environmental Response, Compensation, and Liability Act (CERCLA) regulations would identify which of the following as potentially responsible parties liable for the costs of cleanup?
a. previous owners
b. current owners
c. anyone who transported or installed the hazardous material
d. all of the above

45. The duty of an agent to disclose material facts includes all of the following EXCEPT
a. property defects.
b. agency relationships.
c. presence of HIV/AIDS in a property.
d. proposed zoning changes that may affect the property.

46. John Kleburg is representing a seller. He is aware that a water heater is improperly installed; however, the buyers never ask about the water heater. In this instance, John is guilty of
a. misrepresentation by omission.
b. misrepresentation by commission.
c. puffing.
d. nothing, because the buyers did not inquire about the water heater.

47. What is an exaggerated statement of opinion concerning the condition or value of a property?
a. puffing
b. fraud
c. leading
d. unsubstantiated input

48. Under the Superfund Amendments and Reauthorization Act, a property owner may claim the "innocent landowner" defense to environmental liability if
   a. the landowner purchased the property without knowledge of the environmental hazard.
   b. the seller withheld from the innocent landowner (buyer) information concerning an environmental hazard.
   c. the innocent landowner did not place, or cause to be placed, the hazardous material on the property.
   d. the landowner used reasonable diligence in discovering any environmental hazards prior to acquiring the property and no hazards were found.

49. The federal law that prohibits discrimination, without exception, because of a person's color is the
   a. Civil Rights Act of 1866.
   b. Civil Rights Act of 1968.
   c. Federal Fair Housing Act.
   d. Equal Opportunity in Housing Act.

50. Which of the following is NOT a protected class under the Fair Housing Act?
   a. race
   b. religion
   c. age
   d. sex

51. Under the Fair Housing Amendments Act of 1988, "handicap" was added to the list of protected classes. Under this law, handicap is defined as
   a. any impairment or disability that negatively impacts a person's financial position.
   b. a physical or mental impairment that substantially limits a major life activity.
   c. a physical impairment that limits more than one major life activity.
   d. confinement to a wheelchair or other substantial mobility problems.

52. All of the following are protected under the familial status of Federal Fair Housing EXCEPT a
   a. single parent with two children.
   b. pregnant woman.
   c. married 17-year-old living in an apartment with his spouse.
   d. married couple with six adopted children.

53. The Americans with Disabilities Act (ADA) requires
   a. architectural changes when "readily achievable."
   b. rent discounts to persons with disabilities.
   c. architectural changes whenever requested by a disabled person.
   d. nondiscrimination based on disability by employers with 25 or more employees.

54. Four competing brokers in a small town get together and agree to take only exclusive right to sell listings. Under anti-trust law, this would be an example of
a. price fixing.
b. boycotting.
c. allocation of markets.
d. tie-in arrangements.

55. Carol Crow, a real estate agent, is having lunch with her best friend, Mark Garcia. Mark is an agent with another firm. While waiting for lunch to be served, the two agents start discussing how upset they both are at a local real estate inspector, what a poor job he does, and how it has killed some of their deals. What are the penalties for this violation of anti-trust law?
a. There is no violation in this instance because there was no specific agreement to boycott the inspector.
b. a fine of up to $10,000 and up to one year in the county jail
c. a civil fine of up to $50,000
d. a fine of up to $100,000 and/or up to three years in federal prison

56. The Fair and Accurate Credit Transactions Act (FACT) requires that records containing the personal information of customers be
a. destroyed on an annual basis.
b. retained for at least ten years.
c. disposed of by using a document disposal company.
d. disposed of using reasonable measures.

57. A property is listed for $319,000. It later sells for $312,000. The buyers are getting a 90% loan-to-value-ratio loan paying one point for loan origination and one-and-a-half points for discount. What is the total amount of points paid by the buyers?
a. $7,020
b. $7.177.50
c. $7,800
d. $7,975

58. A closing is taking place on July 16. The value of the property is $260,000 and the tax rate is $1.80 per $100 of valuation. Prorate the taxes using a calendar year, and prorate through the closing date.
a. $2,525.92 debit buyer and credit seller.
b. $2,525.92 debit seller and credit buyer.
c. $2,548.00 debit buyer and credit seller.
d. $2,548.00 debit seller and credit buyer.

59. A loan of $150,000 is made for 30 years with an interest rate of 10%. Assuming a loan factor of $8.78 per $1,000, what is the total interest paid on this loan?
a. $278,329
b. $311,544
c. $324,120
d. $474,120

60. The escrow account cushion that a lender may hold for taxes and insurance is limited under the Real Estate Settlement Procedures Act (RESPA) to
   a. one-twelfth of the annual amount (one month).
   b. one-sixth of the annual amount (two months).
   c. one-quarter of the annual amount (three months).
   d. one-half of the annual amount (six months).

61. Which item may be stated in an advertisement for financing under Regulation Z (Truth-in-Lending) without full disclosure in the advertisement of all the terms of financing?
   a. the down payment and number of payments
   b. the total finance charge and the Annual Percentage Rate (APR)
   c. the price and the Annual Percentage Rate (APR)
   d. None of the above, because full disclosure of all financing terms must be disclosed in all ads regulated under Truth-in-Lending.

62. Which of the following would NOT be true of a fully amortized loan?
   a. equal, steady, periodic payments
   b. payments of part principal and part interest
   c. no other payments or amounts due at maturity
   d. with a balloon payment due at maturity

63. The basic function of the Federal Housing Administration (FHA) is to
   a. insure mortgage loans.
   b. make loans to low- and moderate-income persons.
   c. assist in the building and sale of housing built using federal funds.
   d. sell mortgage-backed securities, which supply funds to the primary market.

64. A seller is selling an investment property. Rent is $1,350 per month paid in advance the first of each month. Prorate the rent for a closing on March 12 using a calendar year.
   a. Debit seller $870.97 and credit buyer.
   b. Debit seller $479.03 and credit buyer.
   c. Debit seller $388.60 and credit buyer.
   d. Debit buyer $401.33 and credit seller.

65. The Equal Credit Opportunity Act (ECOA) shares a number of protected classes with the Federal Fair Housing Act. Which of the following is NOT a protected class under ECOA?
   a. familial status
   b. age
   c. marital status
   d. receipt of public assistance

66. The purpose of the secondary market is to
   a. provide loans for housing as long as the amount does not exceed an amount set each year by Fannie Mae and Freddie Mac.
   b. ensure that the primary market always has an adequate supply of funds for home loans.
   c. to oversee the operations of the Federal Housing Administration (FHA) and the Department of Veterans Affairs (DVA) housing related programs.
   d. oversee the operations of the primary market.

67. Which of the following statements best describes a package mortgage?
   a. a loan with more than one parcel of real estate as collateral
   b. a loan with both real and personal property as collateral
   c. a loan that is packaged with other loans to sell to the secondary market
   d. a standardized loan package to be used in financing the purchase of a single-family home

68. What is a mortgage?
   a. a promise to repay a loan under specific terms and conditions
   b. a pledge of personal liability in case of default
   c. a description of the loan and the collateral on that loan
   d. a pledge of property as collateral

69. What is the total monthly principal, interest, tax, and insurance payment (PITI) on a property that sold for $380,000 on a loan with a 70% loan-to-value ratio for 30 years at 7% interest, using a payment factor of $6.65 per $1,000, assuming the annual taxes are 1.5% of the value of the property and the property insurance costs $890 per year?
   a. $2,088.61
   b. $2,117.44
   c. $2,318.07
   d. $3,133.90

70. Prorate the interest on an assumed, interest-only loan of $245,000 with an interest rate of 6.5% and with a closing on October 21. Use a calendar year and prorate to the closing date.
   a. Debit seller $916.23 and credit buyer.
   b. Debit buyer $916.23 and credit seller.
   c. Debit seller $872.60 and credit buyer.
   d. Debit buyer $872.60 and credit seller.

71. The purposes of a property manager would include all of the following EXCEPT
   a. generating income.
   b. preserving the value of the property.
   c. investing the income stream generated by the property.
   d. reaching the goals set by the property owner.

72. Under a net lease, a tenant would pay a set amount of rent plus a portion of all the following EXCEPT
   a. taxes.
   b. insurance.
   c. maintenance.
   d. debt service.

73. A leasehold estate that has a definite beginning and ending date and does not automatically renew is known as a(n)
   a. estate for years.
   b. periodic estate.
   c. estate at will.
   d. estate for term.

74. A lease that specifies that the rent may be adjusted at predetermined times and amounts is known as a(n)
   a. index lease.
   b. ground lease.
   c. net lease
   d. graduated lease.

75. Most problems in property management may be avoided by
   a. limiting direct contact with the tenants.
   b. keeping the principal informed at all times.
   c. selecting and keeping quality tenants.
   d. getting large security deposits.

76. A tenant leases space in a retail center for a shoe store. If the rent is a flat amount plus some portion of the tenant's gross sales, this is known as a
   a. retail lease.
   b. percentage lease.
   c. sales lease.
   d. divided lease.

77. Joseph Carlton, a salesperson with Golden City Realty, is given some funds to pay a client's landscaper and an electrician while the client is out of town. How should these funds be handled?
   a. Joseph may put the funds in his checking account as long as he can properly account for the money later.
   b. Joseph should give the funds to his broker, who will place the funds into a trust or escrow account.
   c. A salesperson or broker is not allowed to handle the public's monies except for earnest money or rent.
   d. Joseph should give the money to his broker so that his broker may place the funds into Golden City Realty's operating account.

78. A seller wishes to net $90,000 from the sale of a parcel land. The seller will need to pay off the existing purchase-money mortgage of $70,000, a tax lien of $4,000, closing costs of $2,500, and a real estate broker commission of 9%. What will the property need to sell for in order for the seller to reach her goal?
   a. $174,400
   b. $173,654.76
   c. $181,485
   d. $182,967.03

79. A broker wishes to have all of her sales associates operate as independent contractors for income tax purposes. Which of the following would NOT be required to accomplish this goal under IRS regulations?
   a. Pay must be related to sales and not hours worked.
   b. The broker may not direct the sales associates' daily activities.
   c. The broker must file a Statement of Independent Contractor Status with the IRS.
   d. The broker and sales associate must sign a contract establishing the independent contractor status.

80. Any advertisement a broker may place on behalf of a principal must include which of the following?
   a. a statement identifying the person or firm placing the advertisement as a licensed broker
   b. a statement that the firm does business in compliance with Fair Housing law
   c. a full disclosure of all financing terms of any offered seller financing
   d. none of the above

▶ **Answers**

1. a. The right of survivorship means that the deceased's interest would pass automatically to the other owners. The survivors referred to in the right of survivorship include only surviving owners, not surviving family.

2. b. Although community property may include the right of survivorship in some states, only joint tenancy always includes the right.

3. b. A fixture is something that was once personal property that has been so attached to the land so as to become real property.

4. d. Because these items are used by a tenant in a trade or business, they are considered trade fixtures, which are personal property and may be removed before the end of the lease.

5. a. Scarcity is an economic characteristic of land rather than a physical one.

6. b. The highest form of property ownership that includes an unlimited duration, with control over the property even after death, is known as fee simple.

7. c. Although eminent domain is the right by which government takes private property for a public use, condemnation is the process.

8. c. The rectangular survey system, also know as the government survey system, uses principal meridians and baselines, ranges, tiers, townships, and sections.

9. c. $640 \div 4 \div 4 \div 4 = 10$ acres. There are 640 acres in a section. Divide 640 by each of the denominators to find the number of acres in the parcel.

10. d. A nonconforming use is a property use that was in place before the zoning was put into effect or before an amendment was made and, therefore, allowed to stay (grandfathered).

11. d. The property tax lien automatically takes highest priority and is, therefore, the first to be paid.

12. a. The general warranty deed provides the grantee (buyer) the greatest assurances from the grantor.

13. b. The ownership of real property transfers when the deed is delivered and accepted by the grantee. Grantees do not sign deeds, and although recording the deed is wise, it is not required for transfer.

14. d. Escheat is a type of involuntary alienation, but it is more specially the right of government to take property when a person dies without a will and without heirs.

15. b. An appurtenant easement is for the benefit of an adjoining landowner that is considered part of the land and passes with the land when the property is conveyed.

16. d. Market value is the most probable price, not the highest price, the property will bring in the open market.

17. a. Contribution means that the value of any part of a property is equal to the value it contributes.

18. b. Value is estimated using the income approach by dividing the net operating income (NOI) by the capitalization rate (CAP). The lower the capitalization rate the higher the indicated value.
$171,500 \div 7\% = $2,450,000

19. d. Functional obsolescence is a loss of value because of loss of utility, function, or outmoded design. A seven-story building without an elevator has lost function and, therefore, value, because of an outmoded design.

20. a. Adjustments are made to comparables, not the subject property. The sales comparison approach requires that the comparable be made equivalent to the subject property. To do so, if the comparable is better, then subtract value and vice versa.

21. c. Capital gains are calculated by taking the realized selling price (contract sales price less allowed costs of sale) and subtracting the adjusted basis (typically, the purchase price plus costs of purchase and improvements and minus such items as depreciation, any part sold, and casualty losses) to arrive at the capital gain or loss.

22. b. An expressed contract is best stated in writing but may be oral, and an implied contract is created by actions of the parties.

23. d. A real estate lease is a promise of a landlord to let exchanged for a promise of the tenant to buy, and is, therefore, unilateral in nature. An option to buy is an example of a unilateral contract. In an option to buy, a seller promises to sell at specified price and terms but the buyer has not promised to buy. It is a one-sided agreement.

24. b. A contract entered into under an act of misrepresentation or fraud is voidable at the option of the other party. In this example, State Oil may void the contract. However, the contract is not automatically void. State Oil may decide that the large oil and gas reserves on the property will far outweigh the cost of any environmental cleanup costs and may still hold Betty's Diner to the agreement.

25. c. Although earnest is almost always present, it is not required. Consideration is required and may take the form of an exchange of promises.

26. a. Assignment does not release the first party of its obligations under a contract. Novation would do so but generally requires the agreement of the other party.

27. c. Specific performance is a lawsuit to compel the other party to fulfill the promises made in the contract but is not used to collect damages.

28. d. Although a signed contract is often referred to in layman's terms as *executed*, the contract in law is actually executory, meaning that the promises of the parties are yet to be executed or performed.

29. b. The exclusive agency listing agreement obligates the seller to pay a commission to the listing broker no matter which firm procures the buyer, but it does not include a commission in the event that the seller finds a buyer without any broker's assistance.

30. b. The Statute of Frauds requires contracts for the sale of real estate to be in writing to be enforceable in a court of law, thereby helping to prevent acts of fraud.

31. d. Elizabeth is said to have equitable title, which means title in fairness if not in fact. Although Elizabeth holds no real title until transfer of ownership takes place, it is recognized that she has an interest because of the fact that she has the property under contract to purchase.

32. a. A contract to commit an illegal act is not a contract at all and, therefore, void. The other examples are all voidable contracts.

33. c. Although it is recommended to establish an agency relationship in writing and to set forth clearly any commission agreement, neither is required. An agency relationship is created when a principal delegates authority to an agent to act on his or her behalf and an agent accepts that delegation.

34. b. Stacy's firm would be a subagent. A subagent is a firm that is representing another firm's client. Because Stacy's firm did not agree to represent the buyer, it is assumed they represent the other firm's client—the seller.

35. a. Special (limited) agents may not bind the principal and a universal agent may act for the principal in all things under a power of attorney. An agent who may bind the principal within the scope of a trade or business is a general agent.

36. d. An agency created after the fact by a principal agreeing to and benefiting from an agent's actions is called an agency by ratification.

37. d. A fiduciary relationship is a formal relationship between a principal and an agent. Examples would include doctor-patient and lawyer-client relationships.

38. d. There are no fiduciary duties to a customer. Fiduciary duties are owed only to a client, someone whom a broker represents.

39. c. The seller's motivation for selling is generally not material and does not have to be disclosed, but any property or title defects known must be disclosed.

40. b. Confidentiality will survive the transaction. Information learned from or about a client must continue to be held in confidence even after the end of the relationship.

41. a. Because Teresa has not been granted the authority to sign for her client and her authority extends to a single property, she would be classed as a special agent.

42. d. Misrepresentation may be minor, puffing is often an opinion, and misstatements may be made unintentionally, but fraud is both material and intentional.

43. c. The federal lead-based paint regulations are first and foremost disclosure laws. These regulations do not require the removal of lead-based paint.

44. d. Any of the listed entities may be held liable for the cost of cleanup, even if they were not aware of the presence of the hazardous materials.

45. c. Fair Housing law prohibits the disclosure of HIV/AIDS.

46. a. John has withheld a material fact about the property by keeping silent. This is a misrepresentation by omission.

47. a. This type of statement is known as puffing and may or may not be deemed unlawful depending on the severity of the statement and the consumer's reliance upon it.

48. d. In this context, *innocent landowner* means that the landowner not only did not know of the environmental hazard, but also used reasonable diligence in discovering possible hazards. This would include a Phase I environmental assessment.

49. a. The Civil Rights Act of 1866 prohibits discrimination in the sale, purchase, or lease of property and has no exceptions, whereas the 1968 statute does contain a number of exceptions.

50. c. Although age is a protected class in both employment and credit law, it is not a protected class under Fair Housing law.

51. b. The statute defines a handicap as a physical or mental impairment that substantially limits one or more major life activities.

52. c. Familial status is defined as having someone under the age of 18 living with a parent or legal guardian. A spouse does not fall within that definition.

53. a. The Americans with Disabilities Act (ADA) requires architectural changes to be made to accommodate persons with disabilities when the accommodation is "readily achievable" and "without undue financial hardship" on the property owner.

54. a. Price fixing is agreeing with competitors to fix, set, or limit prices or terms.

55. d. This would be considered a violation of anti-trust law. Agents with competing firms should not discuss who they will or will not do business with. It is assumed that the discussion itself was an implied boycott and would, therefore, be punishable by a fine of up to $100,000 and/or up to three years in federal prison.

56. d. The Fair and Accurate Credit Transactions Act (FACT) does not require the disposal of such information, only that reasonable procedures be used when disposing of such records. Although a document destruction company is not required, compliance with the law is assumed when one is used.

57. a. $312,000 \times 90\% \times 2.5\% = \$7,020$

58. b. $260,000 \div 100 \times 1.80 \div 365 \times 197 =$ $2.525.92 to debit seller and credit buyer

59. d. $150,000 \div 1,000 \times 8.78 \times 360 - 150,000 =$ $324,120

60. b. The Real Estate Settlement Procedures act (RESPA) limits the cushion that a lender may hold in the escrow or impound account to one-sixth of the annual amount, which equates to approximately two months.

61. c. The price of the product and the interest rate expressed as an Annual Percentage Rate (APR) may be stated in an advertisement without requiring full disclosure of all terms of the financing.

62. d. A fully amortized loan will have zero due at maturity.

63. a. The basic function of the Federal Housing Administration (FHA) is to insure loans made to low- and moderate-income persons, but the FHA does not lend money.

64. a. Because the rent has been paid in advance for the entire month, we need to calculate the amount of rent that needs to be transferred to the buyer for the remaining 20 days of the month. Remember that we are prorating to the closing date, so the seller gets the rent for the first 11 days and the buyer gets the rent for the remaining 20 days in March. $1,350 \div 31 \times 20 = 870.97$ to debit seller and credit buyer

65. a. Familial status, which is having persons under the age of 18 living with a parent or legal guardian, is not a protected class under ECOA. ECOA does have race, religion, sex, national origin, and color in common with Fair Housing law.

66. b. The secondary market's purpose is to see to it that the primary market always has a steady supply of funds for home loans.

67. b. A package mortgage has both real estate and personal property as collateral. An example would be a furnished vacation home purchased with a single loan that has both the real property and the furnishings as collateral.

68. d. A mortgage is a pledge of property as collateral. Although it repeats many of the terms of the loan, the actual loan document is the promissory note.

69. c. $380,000 \times 70\% \div 1,000 \times 6.65 = \$1,768.90$ principal and interest
$380,000 \times 1.5\% \div 12 = \$475$ tax
$890 \div 12 = \$74.11$ insurance
$1,768.90 + 475 + 74.11 = \$2,318.07$

70. c. Because the buyer will make the November 1 payment that pays the interest for October, the seller needs to pay the buyer for the first 20 days of October. $245,000 × 6.5% ÷ 365 × 20 = $872.60 to debit seller and credit buyer

71. c. A property manager would seldom invest the income generated by a property. However, generating income, preserving the value of the property, and reaching the goals of the client are all common purposes of a professional property manager.

72. d. A net lease does not require the tenant to pay the debt service on the loan. Debt service is the principal and interest on the loan and is paid by the property owner.

73. a. An estate for years has a definite beginning and ending and does not renew automatically.

74. d. An index lease is tied to an economic indicator, a ground lease is a lease of land alone, and a net lease is when a tenant pays some of the property expenses. A graduated lease has predetermined adjustments.

75. c. Selecting and keeping quality tenants will do the most in eliminating management problems over time.

76. b. A percentage lease is most commonly used in retail and includes some portion of the business's gross sales as rent along with a flat amount.

77. b. Joseph should turn any such funds over to his broker so that his broker will deposit the money into a trust or escrow account and not into the firm's operating account.

78. d. $90,000 + $70,000 + $4,000 + $2,500 = $166,500
$166,500 ÷ 91% = $182,967.03
Remember to subtract the 9% from 100% to get the 91%.

79. c. There is no special paperwork that must be filed with the IRS to create the independent contractor status.

80. a. Any advertisement must state that the person or firm is licensed. The other two disclosures may or may not be required, depending on the content of the advertisement.

▶ Scoring

Remember that this practice exam is not correlated exactly to your state's real estate broker exam; your official test will also include state-specific questions. In general, to evaluate how you fared on this practice exam, find the number of questions you got right, and divide by 80 (the number of questions on this exam). This will give you your score as a percentage. A passing score would be about 70% on this practice exam.

For now, what's much more important than your overall score is how you did on each of the areas tested by the exam. You need to diagnose your strengths and weaknesses so that you can concentrate your efforts as you prepare. The question types are mixed in the practice exam, so in order to tell where your strengths and weaknesses lie, you'll need to compare your answer sheet with the following Promissor Practice Exam 1 for Review, which shows which of the categories each question falls into.

Use your score in conjunction with the Learning-Express Test Preparation System in Chapter 2 of this book to help you devise a study plan using the Real Estate Broker Refresher Course in Chapter 7, the Real Estate Broker Math Review in Chapter 8, and the Real Estate Glossary in Chapter 9. You should plan to spend more time on the sections that correspond to the questions you found hardest and less time on the lessons that correspond to areas in which you did well.

Once you have spent some time reviewing, take the second Promissor practice exam in Chapter 11 to see how much you've improved.

Promissor Practice Exam 1 for Review

Topic	Question Numbers
Real Property Characteristics, Definitions, Ownership, Restrictions, and Transfer	1, 2, 3, 4, 5, 6, 7, 8, 9, 10, 11, 12, 13, 14, 15
Property Valuation and the Appraisal Process	16, 17, 18, 19, 20, 21
Contacts and Agency Relationships with Buyers and Sellers	22, 23, 24, 25, 26, 27, 28, 29, 30, 31, 32, 33, 34, 35, 36, 37, 38, 39, 40, 41, 42
Property Conditions and Disclosures	43, 44, 45, 46, 47, 48
Federal Laws Governing Real Estate Activities	49, 50, 51, 52, 53, 54, 55, 56
Financing the Transaction and Settlement	57, 58, 59, 60, 61, 62, 63, 64, 65, 66, 67, 68, 69, 70
Leases, Rents, and Property Management	71, 72, 73, 74, 75, 76
Brokerage Operations	77, 78, 79, 80

CHAPTER

5 ▶

Thomson Prometric (Experior) Practice Exam 1

CHAPTER SUMMARY

This is the first of the two Thomson Prometric (formerly Experior) practice exams in this book. Take this exam to see how you would do if you took the exam today and find out what are your strengths and weaknesses.

If you prefer to take a practice exam on a computer, refer to the insert at the end of this book to see how you can take a free Thomson Prometric practice test online on our website. Taking exams on the computer is good practice for the real exam. However, if you don't have access to the Internet, taking the exams on paper will accomplish the same goal—letting you know in which areas you are strong and in which areas you need more work.

Take this exam in as relaxed a manner as possible, without worrying about timing. You can time yourself on the second Thomson Prometric practice exam. You should, however make sure that you have enough time to take the entire exam in one sitting. Find a quiet place where you can work without interruptions.

The answer sheet is on the following page, and then comes the exam. After you have finished, use the answer key and explanations to learn your strengths and weaknesses. Then use the scoring section at the end of this chapter to see how you did overall.

1.	(a)	(b)	(c)	(d)		31.	(a)	(b)	(c)	(d)		61.	(a)	(b)	(c)	(d)
2.	(a)	(b)	(c)	(d)		32.	(a)	(b)	(c)	(d)		62.	(a)	(b)	(c)	(d)
3.	(a)	(b)	(c)	(d)		33.	(a)	(b)	(c)	(d)		63.	(a)	(b)	(c)	(d)
4.	(a)	(b)	(c)	(d)		34.	(a)	(b)	(c)	(d)		64.	(a)	(b)	(c)	(d)
5.	(a)	(b)	(c)	(d)		35.	(a)	(b)	(c)	(d)		65.	(a)	(b)	(c)	(d)
6.	(a)	(b)	(c)	(d)		36.	(a)	(b)	(c)	(d)		66.	(a)	(b)	(c)	(d)
7.	(a)	(b)	(c)	(d)		37.	(a)	(b)	(c)	(d)		67.	(a)	(b)	(c)	(d)
8.	(a)	(b)	(c)	(d)		38.	(a)	(b)	(c)	(d)		68.	(a)	(b)	(c)	(d)
9.	(a)	(b)	(c)	(d)		39.	(a)	(b)	(c)	(d)		69.	(a)	(b)	(c)	(d)
10.	(a)	(b)	(c)	(d)		40.	(a)	(b)	(c)	(d)		70.	(a)	(b)	(c)	(d)
11.	(a)	(b)	(c)	(d)		41.	(a)	(b)	(c)	(d)		71.	(a)	(b)	(c)	(d)
12.	(a)	(b)	(c)	(d)		42.	(a)	(b)	(c)	(d)		72.	(a)	(b)	(c)	(d)
13.	(a)	(b)	(c)	(d)		43.	(a)	(b)	(c)	(d)		73.	(a)	(b)	(c)	(d)
14.	(a)	(b)	(c)	(d)		44.	(a)	(b)	(c)	(d)		74.	(a)	(b)	(c)	(d)
15.	(a)	(b)	(c)	(d)		45.	(a)	(b)	(c)	(d)		75.	(a)	(b)	(c)	(d)
16.	(a)	(b)	(c)	(d)		46.	(a)	(b)	(c)	(d)		76.	(a)	(b)	(c)	(d)
17.	(a)	(b)	(c)	(d)		47.	(a)	(b)	(c)	(d)		77.	(a)	(b)	(c)	(d)
18.	(a)	(b)	(c)	(d)		48.	(a)	(b)	(c)	(d)		78.	(a)	(b)	(c)	(d)
19.	(a)	(b)	(c)	(d)		49.	(a)	(b)	(c)	(d)		79.	(a)	(b)	(c)	(d)
20.	(a)	(b)	(c)	(d)		50.	(a)	(b)	(c)	(d)		80.	(a)	(b)	(c)	(d)
21.	(a)	(b)	(c)	(d)		51.	(a)	(b)	(c)	(d)						
22.	(a)	(b)	(c)	(d)		52.	(a)	(b)	(c)	(d)						
23.	(a)	(b)	(c)	(d)		53.	(a)	(b)	(c)	(d)						
24.	(a)	(b)	(c)	(d)		54.	(a)	(b)	(c)	(d)						
25.	(a)	(b)	(c)	(d)		55.	(a)	(b)	(c)	(d)						
26.	(a)	(b)	(c)	(d)		56.	(a)	(b)	(c)	(d)						
27.	(a)	(b)	(c)	(d)		57.	(a)	(b)	(c)	(d)						
28.	(a)	(b)	(c)	(d)		58.	(a)	(b)	(c)	(d)						
29.	(a)	(b)	(c)	(d)		59.	(a)	(b)	(c)	(d)						
30.	(a)	(b)	(c)	(d)		60.	(a)	(b)	(c)	(d)						

▶ Thomson Prometric (Experior) Practice Exam 1

1. An example of breach of contract is best described as
   a. the substitution of a new contract.
   b. failure to make payment when it is due.
   c. the transfer of rights under a contract.
   d. a bilateral termination of an agreement.

2. Mary White and Elizabeth Brown, widowed sisters, are buying a home together. To ensure that each sister's share will go to her children if she dies, they should purchase the property as
   a. tenants in severalty.
   b. tenants by the entirety.
   c. tenants in common.
   d. joint tenants with right of survivorship.

3. When tenant Heather Grayson opened her ice cream shop in the mall, she installed counters and special freezers. When Heather closes the shop, can she remove them?
   a. It depends on whether her lease specifically states that she can.
   b. No, because as a tenant she gives up the right of possession.
   c. Yes, if she repairs any damage caused by their removal prior to the expiration of the lease.
   d. No, because, as fixtures, they have become part of the real estate.

4. The Law of Agency
   a. protects sellers.
   b. defines the rights and duties of principal and the agent.
   c. protects buyers.
   d. protects the real estate professional.

5. The Simons have defaulted on their loan payments and are behind in paying the rest of their bills, so their home is being sold in a foreclosure auction. Of the many liens against it, which will have first claim on the proceeds of the sale?
   a. the first mortgage recorded
   b. unpaid real estate taxes
   c. mechanics lien
   d. home equity loan

6. The agreement signed by the owners of two adjacent houses to share a common driveway is a form of
   a. an encroachment.
   b. an emblement.
   c. an easement.
   d. a homestead.

7. A parcel of land fronts Pine Lake and is selling for $10,000 per front-foot. What will it cost to purchase this parcel if the dimensions are 100 feet wide by 150 feet deep?
   a. $500,000
   b. $1,500,000
   c. $10,000
   d. $1,000,000

8. All are common components of an adjustable rate mortgage EXCEPT
   a. that usually the interest rate is the index rate plus a premium, called the margin.
   b. that rate caps limit the amount the interest rate may change.
   c. that the borrower is protected from unaffordable individual payments by a payment cap.
   d. a fixed interest rate for the life of the loan.

9. Using the cost approach to value, the land is valued at $30,000. Replacement cost of the building is $100,000, and depreciation is $20,000. What is the indicated value?
  a. $120,000
  b. $80,000
  c. $110,000
  d. $100,000

10. A buyer wants to make an offer to purchase a house that he suspects has an electrical problem. The buyer is afraid the house may be sold to someone else before he has a chance to get information about the electrical system. What should he do?
  a. He should make an offer to purchase that is contingent on an electrical inspection.
  b. He should hire an electrical contractor to give an estimate prior to making an offer.
  c. He should ask the seller to repair the electrical system prior to making an offer.
  d. He should ask for the broker's opinion on the electrical system.

11. A quitclaim deed is often used for transfers
  a. to clear title defects.
  b. for arms-length transactions.
  c. when the grantee requires full assurances.
  d. that must go into effect immediately.

12. The amount of commission to be paid to a broker is determined by
  a. the Federal Trade Commission.
  b. negotiation between agent and client.
  c. the Sherman Anti-Trust Act.
  d. the local association of real estate professionals.

13. The Real Estate Settlement Procedures Act (RESPA) applies to
  a. all residential financing.
  b. land contracts.
  c. first mortgages only.
  d. financing of one- to four-family residences.

14. When advertising credit terms in conjunction with the sale of a house, the broker mentions the amount of the monthly payment. The broker must also include all of the following pieces of information EXCEPT
  a. the annual percentage rate (APR).
  b. the number and frequency of installments.
  c. the length of the loan.
  d. the total to be paid back over the life of the loan.

15. All of the following examples are members of a protected class EXCEPT
  a. a pregnant woman.
  b. a blind person.
  c. a senior citizen.
  d. a person with HIV.

16. Encouraging the sale of properties in a neighborhood by revealing the entry of a member of a protected class is called
  a. redlining.
  b. blockbusting.
  c. disclosure.
  d. market hysteria.

17. A tenant applicant confined to a wheelchair is interested in renting a townhome. A request is made to the landlord to allow the tenant to have an access ramp constructed. Which of the following is true in this situation?
   a. The tenant application must be rejected.
   b. The landlord must allow the tenant to make the modification at the tenant's expense.
   c. The landlord is required to fund modifications to the property to accommodate the access problem.
   d. The landlord may collect an additional deposit to assure compliance.

18. A property owner is in violation of the Fair Housing Act of 1968 if the owner
   a. refuses to rent a room in a single-family home occupied by the owner.
   b. discriminates in the rental of a building of four or fewer units, one of which is occupied by the owner.
   c. denies housing on the basis of race.
   d. denies nonmembers of a private club sleeping quarters when occupancy is limited to club members.

19. All of the following are prohibited by state licensing acts EXCEPT
   a. working for more than one party in a transaction with the knowledge and consent in writing of all parties for whom the broker acts.
   b. making distinction, for discriminatory purposes, in the location of housing or dates of availability.
   c. giving false information for the purpose of discrimination.
   d. accepting listings that illegally discriminate against certain persons or groups in the sale or rental of property.

20. With regard to a lease agreement, which is true?
   a. When a property is sold, the lease agreement terminates.
   b. Upon sale of the property, the lease agreement transfers to the new owner.
   c. The lease agreement is renegotiated between the new owner and the lessee.
   d. The lessee can continue the lease only if the new owner allows.

21. In the cost approach to value, the replacement cost is
   a. cost at current prices to construct improvements similar to the subject property.
   b. the construction cost at current prices of an exact duplicate of the subject improvement.
   c. the cost per square foot.
   d. an estimate of all material and labor on a unit cost basis.

22. The Fair Housing Act of 1988, which addresses accessibility in new multifamily buildings for people with physical disabilities, mandates all of the following EXCEPT
   a. elevators or power lifts.
   b. doors, kitchens, and bathrooms that are wheelchair friendly.
   c. thermostats and lighting switches within easy reach.
   d. bathroom walls strong enough to support grab bars.

23. In calculating capital gain resulting from the sale of a principal residence, all of the following are considered EXCEPT
   a. the property's purchase price.
   b. the brokerage fee.
   c. fix-up expenses within the 60 days prior to contract.
   d. closing costs.

24. Which is NOT a common element in condominium ownership?
   a. owner's driveway
   b. lobby
   c. hallway
   d. swimming pool

25. Using the income approach to value, an appraiser must do all of the following EXCEPT
   a. estimate potential gross income.
   b. compare similar sold properties.
   c. apply the capitalization rate to the property's annual net operating income.
   d. deduct an appropriate allowance for vacancy and rent loss.

26. One of the requirements of the federal lead-based paint law is that the
   a. owner is required to remove lead-based materials prior to the sale or lease of property.
   b. agent must arrange for an inspection by a certified remediator.
   c. buyer has ten days in which to arrange for an inspection to evaluate the extent of the hazardous materials.
   d. lender must warrant that the property is free from lead problems.

27. Using a cap rate of 12%, what is the value of a property with a net income of $60,000?
   a. $72,000
   b. $400,000
   c. $450,000
   d. $500,000

28. An owner of a marina wants to sell his business and real estate so that he may retire. However, the tax on the capital gains would be prohibitive. One alternative that would allow the owner to make a change in lifestyle while avoiding payment of capital gains tax is to
   a. sell, and then buy a larger, more expensive venture.
   b. do an arms-length swap with a close relative.
   c. structure a like-kind exchange involving a similar property.
   d. sell, and then buy a foreign property.

29. Homeowners may deduct all of the following expenses on their tax returns EXCEPT
   a. mortgage loan interest paid.
   b. property taxes paid.
   c. points on a purchase money mortgage.
   d. depreciation and maintenance expenses.

30. Which of the following expenses is tax deductible for homeowners?
   a. homeowners association dues
   b. utility payments
   c. interest paid on mortgages
   d. addition of children's playhouse in the yard

31. An apartment unit rents for $600 per month. This tenant has a two-year lease. Your commission is 6% of the gross lease. What is your commission?
a. $864
b. $432
c. $600
d. $1,200

32. When an owner sells a principal residence, the capital gain is calculated by
a. subtracting selling expenses from the sales price.
b. subtracting the sales price from the original purchase price.
c. reducing the net sales price by the property's adjusted cost basis.
d. subtracting the selling expenses from the original purchase price.

33. Which of the following programs would probably be of the most benefit to owners of property located in the lowlands along a river?
a. Superfund and Reauthorization Act
b. National Flood Insurance Act
c. Resources Conservation and Recovery Act
d. Interstate Land Sales Full Disclosure Act

34. A developer includes restrictive covenants in the deeds for all properties within a subdivision. These covenants may dictate all of the following EXCEPT
a. the owner's use of the property.
b. the style of architecture.
c. the appearance of outbuildings and fences.
d. the ethnic character of future owners.

35. At a general meeting of the brokers' trade association, several members begin talking about fees and business practices. This activity could be considered
a. a violation of the Sherman Anti-Trust Act.
b. an activity prohibited by the Better Business Bureau.
c. an appropriate activity within the association.
d. a good way for brokers to learn about the different practices nationwide.

36. When evaluating the priority of liens against a property, which of the following has the highest priority?
a. property taxes
b. income tax liens
c. recorded mortgages
d. judgments

37. A condo closing is to take place on March 18. The condo fee of $175 per month has been paid for March. Which of the following should be reflected on the closing statement?
a. Debit seller $101.61, credit buyer $101.61.
b. Credit seller $101.61, debit buyer $101.61.
c. Debit seller $73.39, credit buyer $73.39.
d. Credit seller $73.39, debit buyer $73.39.

38. A settlement is held on April 21 involving the purchase of a property by assumption of the loan. The interest rate is 8.5%, and the loan balance is $198,000. How is the interest on the loan payment adjusted? Prorate to the day of closing using a statutory year.
a. Debit buyer and credit seller $1,402.50.
b. Debit seller and credit buyer $467.50.
c. Debit buyer and credit seller $467.50.
d. Debit seller and credit buyer $935.

39. Which is considered a credit to a buyer on a HUD settlement statement?

    a. a mortgage loan

    b. a sales price

    c. a refund to seller of prepaid water

    d. the unearned portion of general real estate taxes if the seller paid in advance

40. Alex Garcia has just settled on his new home. He obtained a loan of $151,000 at 8% interest that requires a monthly PI payment of $7.34 per thousand. He also has an estimated annual property tax of $2,900 and an insurance premium of $560 per year, which he will pay in monthly deposits into escrow. What is the total monthly PITI payment for Mr. Garcia?

    a. $1,108.34

    b. $1,396.67

    c. $1,350

    d. $1,156

41. A homeowner has a remaining mortgage balance of $149,570.75. The interest rate is 9.5%, and the monthly payment is $1,303.55. After the next two payments, what will be the balance?

    a. $149,451.30

    b. $148,267.20

    c. $149,330.91

    d. $149,570.75

42. A property manager may legally attract prospective tenants to a building by doing all of the following EXCEPT

    a. offering generous concessions.

    b. removing troublesome tenants.

    c. undertaking an extensive remodeling effort.

    d. paying referral fees directly to salespersons.

43. All of the following are true of FHA loans EXCEPT

    a. an approved lender provides the loan.

    b. the FHA provides the insurance.

    c. the FHA loan is guaranteed by the government.

    d. the FHA sets maximum loan amounts.

44. Which of the following items should NOT be included in a manager's budget for a property?

    a. utilities

    b. cleaning services and supplies

    c. purchase of adjacent property for a parking lot expansion

    d. debt service

45. Unless otherwise stated in the sales agreement, the buyer accepts the property in its condition at the time of the

    a. settlement.

    b. contract.

    c. walk-through inspection.

    d. possession.

46. Which one of the following agencies is owned by the federal government?

    a. Freddie Mac

    b. Farmer Mae

    c. Ginnie Mae

    d. Fannie Mae

47. At a typical closing, the seller is responsible for providing all of the following EXCEPT

    a. the mortgage or deed of trust.

    b. the deed.

    c. a proof of ownership.

    d. any necessary inspection reports.

48. RESPA requires all of the following EXCEPT that the
   a. buyer receives the HUD special information booklet from the lender.
   b. lender makes a good-faith estimate of closing costs for the buyer.
   c. buyer is offered a loan that is 0.5% or less below market rate.
   d. closing will be conducted using the HUD 1 Uniform Settlement Statement.

49. A fence is being built to enclose a 100-foot-by-300-foot lot. If there will be two 5-foot-long gates, how many feet of fence will it take?
   a. 970 feet
   b. 790 feet
   c. 800 feet
   d. 810 feet

50. Which of the following is NOT usually prorated between the seller and the buyer at closing?
   a. utility bills
   b. real estate taxes
   c. prepaid rents
   d. recording charges

51. Which of the following changes in zoning should result in compensation to the owner?
   a. spot zoning
   b. down-zoning
   c. buffer zoning
   d. taking

52. What happens if one party crosses out or changes any wording in the contract during negotiations?
   a. Each party must initial the change in the margin for it to be valid.
   b. The whole contract will become void.
   c. The document must be retyped.
   d. The statute of frauds requires that the document be notarized.

53. A buyer paid $8,000 for a 150' × 160' lot. What price did she pay per front-foot?
   a. $53.33
   b. $50
   c. $3
   d. $53

54. Land can be owned apart from the buildings on it under the arrangement known as a
   a. net lease.
   b. life estate.
   c. reversion.
   d. ground lease.

55. Rents may be considered too low if
   a. there is a high vacancy level.
   b. there is a high building occupancy.
   c. the building is poorly maintained.
   d. many For Rent signs are in the general area.

56. At closing, the lending institution may ask the buyer to
   a. pay the state transfer tax.
   b. sign a disclosure of property condition.
   c. deposit money in an escrow account.
   d. reimburse the seller for prepaid property taxes.

57. If a forced sale fails to bring enough to pay off a lien on a 16-unit apartment building, the lender may seek a
  a. release deed.
  b. promissory note.
  c. deficiency judgment.
  d. right of redemption.

58. Lenders would likely purchase mortgages offered by which of the following?
  a. Office of Thrift Supervision
  b. Federal Deposit Insurance Corporation
  c. Fannie Mae
  d. HUD

59. The type of depreciation always classified as incurable is
  a. physical deterioration.
  b. fictional IRS depreciation.
  c. functional obsolescence.
  d. economic or external obsolescence.

60. The form of value estimate that takes into account the prices of houses that failed to sell is a
  a. competitive market analysis.
  b. limited appraisal.
  c. reconciliation report.
  d. cost approach.

61. Taxes on a given property are $3,726.50 per year. Taxes for the first half of 2002 have been paid. If the property closes on January 16, 2003, which of the following would be reflected on the closing statement?
  a. Credit buyer $2,041.92, debit seller $1,684.50.
  b. Credit buyer $1,684.50, debit seller $1,684.50.
  c. Debit buyer $1,684.50, credit seller $1,684.50.
  d. Credit buyer $2,041.92, debit seller $2,041.92.

62. In what type of market are prices likely to rise?
  a. buyer's market
  b. seller's market
  c. thin market
  d. broad market

63. One effect of a clause in a sales agreement that states that "time is of the essence" might be that
  a. the seller can take care of matters at his or her convenience.
  b. the buyer must deal with the details of the contract as they occur.
  c. the agent must see that the contract has been fulfilled prior to closing.
  d. all parties must comply strictly to the deadlines called for in the contract.

64. Jessie Petersen makes a written offer to buy Lee Chen's house for $120,000. She confides in Lee's agent, George Everly, that if necessary she'd pay $10,000 more, but she doesn't want Lee to know that. George should
  a. present the offer to Lee but respect Jessie's confidentiality.
  b. warn Jessie that he must pass on to Lee anything useful he knows and then do so.
  c. refuse to convey the lower offer to Lee.
  d. explain to Jessie why the house isn't worth more than $120,000.

65. A buyer and seller have each signed a written purchase agreement. The Uniform Vendor and Purchaser Risk Act states that until the buyer has either possession of, or title to, a property, responsibility for the physical condition of the property
   a. remains with the seller.
   b. is delegated to the buyer, who has equitable title to the property.
   c. is insured under errors and omissions insurance.
   d. is assumed by the seller's homeowners insurance company.

66. Carlos Flores, salesperson, is sponsored by Broker Rob O'Conner. Mr. Flores signed an agreement with Mr. O'Conner that authorizes him to sign agreements that bind the broker to perform certain services for clients. This is called
   a. broad authority agency.
   b. sub-limited agency.
   c. business agency.
   d. general agency.

67. Kelly Adams lists her house and tells her listing agent, Sheila Fabris, "I'm listing for $180,000, but I might take less." Sheila may properly
   a. advertise the property for $180,000 or less.
   b. explain Kelly's position to prospective buyers in an effort to obtain an offer.
   c. share Kelly's statement only with the buyer's broker.
   d. keep the information to herself.

68. One of the Garzas' stated requirements for their new home was that it be located in the Sunnyvale school district. The seller falsely and knowingly stated that the subject property was, indeed, in that school district. After closing, the Garzas discovered that the house was actually in an adjacent school district. The Garzas
   a. may seek to rescind the contract.
   b. can collect on their title insurance.
   c. must honor all agreements in the contract.
   d. could file a claim with the seller's insurance company.

69. Paul and John Mitchell are brothers who own a chain of auto shops. Paul Mitchell is also a real estate broker, and he has been authorized to find a buyer for their business. What does Paul have?
   a. an ostensible agency
   b. a designated agency
   c. an agency by ratification
   d. an agency coupled with an interest

70. Real estate licensees are required to disclose early in a transaction to all parties
   a. the nature of the agency relationship.
   b. the commission rate offered by the seller.
   c. possible financial arrangements for the purchase.
   d. the name of the firm's principal.

71. The federal government requires a leaflet about possible lead-paint contamination to be given to any potential purchaser or tenant of a residence built before what year?
   a. 1995
   b. 1987
   c. 1981
   d. 1978

72. The broker who is sued for an unintentional mistake can expect court costs to be paid by
a. the client in the transaction involved.
b. the local Board of REALTORS®.
c. the company underwriting the broker's errors and omissions policy.
d. his or her company's own recovery fund.

73. All the salespeople in Alison's brokerage firm work as independent contractors. Their office most likely provides them with which of the following?
a. access to the local multiple-listing service
b. stock options
c. a retirement plan
d. a business expense account

74. The listing broker's commission is earned when
a. the property is listed.
b. an offer has been accepted.
c. financing has been arranged.
d. the property is finally closed.

75. Ken Laughton's house is for sale by owner. Lia Nguyen falls in love with it during an open house, tells Ken she'll pay the full asking price, and promises to send Ken an earnest money check for $5,000. Ken accepts the offer. The contract between them is
a. enforceable by court action if either tries to back out.
b. invalid because it lacks consideration.
c. valid only if there were witnesses.
d. unenforceable.

76. Consideration to bind a contract may be in the form of
a. cash or cash equivalent only.
b. anything that the parties agree upon as long as it has monetary value.
c. money, promises, or services.
d. thoughtful treatment of the other party's feelings.

77. The Millers put their house on the market, the Blacks made a written purchase offer, and the Millers accepted the offer in writing. When is the contract valid?
a. immediately
b. as soon as the signatures are notarized
c. when the Blacks are notified of the acceptance
d. when it is placed in the public records

78. A seller receives an offer to purchase, and puts forth a counteroffer to the buyer. Until the buyer notifies the seller of her acceptance or rejection, the seller
a. is legally bound to the terms of the counteroffer.
b. may accept the buyer's original offer.
c. may produce a new counteroffer.
d. cannot accept another offer from a different buyer.

79. Which of the following statements in an advertisement would trigger full financing disclosure under the TILA Regulation Z?
a. "Priced at 350,000"
b. "Special financing available"
c. "6.75% interest rate"
d. "Low down payment"

80. Bernie Goldstein owns Home Front Realty Co. and is a business partner with Sara Ali in City-wide Mortgage Co. They refer buyers to each other for real estate and mortgage services. Under RESPA, this arrangement
   a. is illegal under federal law.
   b. serves consumers' best interests for ease of settlement service shopping.
   c. requires use of the Affiliated Business Arrangement disclosure at or prior to the time of referral.
   d. requires use of the code of ethics disclosure statement at or prior to the time of referral.

▶ **Answers**

1. **b.** Breach of contract is a violation of any term or condition on a contract without legal excuse.
2. **c.** Tenants in common have the right to devise their shares to any chosen heirs. Severalty (choice **a**) applies to single ownership, and the other two choices involve automatic inheritance by one owner if the other dies.
3. **c.** Trade fixtures, installed for use in a trade or business, may be removed by the tenant prior to the expiration of the lease if the premises are returned to their original condition.
4. **b.** The Law of Agency interprets the relationship between licensees and their clients.
5. **b.** Whether entered in the public records or not, real property taxes automatically take priority over all other liens.
6. **c.** Each owner has the right to pass over the neighbor's half of the driveway, thus owning an easement on the adjoining property.

7. **d.** 100 front-feet × $10,000 per front-foot = $1,000,000
8. **d.** Adjustable rate mortgages have the ability to raise or lower the interest rate.
9. **c.** $100,000 (building cost) minus $20,000 (depreciation) equals $80,000. Add that number to $30,000 (land value) for a total of $110,000.
10. **a.** The buyer can have the property taken off the market if the seller accepts the offer using the contingency clause on the sales agreement.
11. **a.** The signer of a quitclaim deed makes no guarantee of ownership and transfers only what interest he or she may have. Besides clearing a cloud (possible or partial claims), quitclaim deeds are often used for transfers within a family or during a divorce.
12. **b.** Anti-trust legislation forbids any community-wide standard for fees, which must be set by agreement between the parties.
13. **d.** RESPA sets requirements for all federally related mortgages and home equity loans on one- to four-family residences.
14. **d.** The total to be repaid will be recited in the loan disclosure statement but is not needed in advertising under Regulation Z.
15. **c.** A senior citizen is not a member of a protected class; a person age 62 or older can be exempt from familial status in housing for older persons only.
16. **b.** This practice is called panic peddling or blockbusting, and it is illegal under Fair Housing laws. The practice of refusing to make loans in a defined minority area or neighborhood is redlining.

17. b. As long as the tenant pays, there is no violation of building codes, and the tenant agrees to restore the property to its original condition, the landlord must approve the ramp.

18. c. Discrimination on the basis of race is a violation of all laws dealing with fair housing. The Civil Rights Act of 1866 includes no exemptions and applies to all property whether real or personal, residential or commercial. The Supreme Court upheld this in the *Jones vs. Mayer* decision in 1968.

19. a. Under licensing laws, brokers are allowed to work for more than one party in a transaction as long as it is fully disclosed and both parties give written consent.

20. b. If leased real estate is sold, the new owner takes the property subject to the rights of the existing tenants.

21. a. The replacement cost is the construction cost at current prices of a property that is not necessarily an exact duplicate of the subject property, but serves the same purpose or functions as the original.

22. a. The Fair Housing Act does not require elevators or power lifts in residential real estate.

23. c. IRS regulations permit only fees and costs paid by or on behalf of the seller to be included in the calculations.

24. a. General common elements are real estate that exist beyond the individual units and may be used by all owners in the condominium complex. Areas of the real estate limited to the use by one owner are known as limited common elements.

25. b. Comparison-sold properties are used in the sales comparison approach to value.

26. c. In the purchase of target housing—property constructed prior to 1978—the seller must disclose any known lead-paint hazards or any previous lead inspections, and the buyer is to receive an information pamphlet describing the hazards of lead in a home. The buyer has ten days in which to have the property inspected.

27. d. Income of $60,000 divided by a rate of 12% equals a value of $500,000.

28. c. A Section 1031 exchange, known as a like-kind exchange, allows the owner to trade the property for a similar one. This is applicable only to investment property and is not effective in the purchase of foreign real estate.

29. d. Maintenance, depreciation, and repair can be deducted only in commercial real estate.

30. c. The only allowable deduction on the tax return for the homeowner is for taxes and mortgage interest actually paid.

31. a. $600 per month (rent) × 24 months (2 years) = $14,400 × 6% (commission) = $864

32. c. Taxable capital gain from the sale of a principal residence is calculated by subtracting the adjusted cost basis from the net proceeds of sale.

33. b. The National Flood Insurance Act (NFIA) makes flood insurance available at reasonable rates to property owners in flood-prone areas.

34. d. Restrictive covenants, also known as deed restrictions, that dictate the ethnic character of future owners would be in violation of the law.

35. a. Any discussion of fees between competitors could be viewed as an attempt to conspire to set the cost of real estate brokerage services, a violation of anti-trust law.

36. a. In a forced sale, the property taxes are paid before any other liens.

37. b. ($175 ÷ 31) × 18 days = $101.61 credit to seller and debit to buyer

38. **d.** Interest is paid after it is earned. The seller owes 20 days of interest, which would be due on May 1. $198,000 multiplied by 0.085, divided by 360 days times 20 days equals $935.

39. **a.** A mortgage loan is a credit to the buyer toward the purchase price of the property.

40. **b.** $151,000 ÷ 1,000 × 7.34 = $1,108.34 (principal and interest)
($2,900 + $560) ÷ 12 = $288.33 (taxes and insurance)
$1,108.34 + $288.33 = $1,396.67 (payment)

41. **c.** $149,570.75 multiplied by the interest rate of 0.095, then divided by 12 (months in a year), equals $1,184.10 in monthly interest. $1,184.10 subtracted from $1,303.55 monthly payment equals $119.45 principal. $119.45 subtracted from the remaining balance of $149,570.75 equals $149,451.30. $149,451.30 multiplied by 0.095, divided by 12 equals $1,183.16 in monthly interest. $1,183.16 subtracted from $1,303.55 equals $120.39 in principal. $120.39 subtracted from $149,451.30 equals $149,330.91.

42. **d.** It is illegal to pay referral fees to anyone except a principal broker.

43. **c.** VA loans, not FHA loans, are guaranteed by the government.

44. **c.** The purchase of adjacent property may be an objective of the owner but is not a part of the manager's job.

45. **b.** Properties are generally accepted in the condition as of the time the contract is executed (signed). That is why it is important that a thorough inspection be made by the buyer or designee prior to the time of closing. The seller is responsible for any changes to the condition of the property between contract and closing.

46. **c.** Farmer Mae (choice **b**) doesn't exist. Ginnie Mae (Government National Mortgage Association) is owned by the federal government.

47. **a.** The seller provides proof of ownership, a proper deed, and any required inspections.

48. **c.** The RESPA regulations have nothing to do with rates.

49. **b.** 100 feet + 100 feet + 300 feet + 300 feet = 800 total linear feet of fence. Subtract the two 5-foot-long gates for a total of 790 feet of fencing.

50. **d.** Recording of the mortgage and deed is typically the buyer's responsibility.

51. **d.** When property is rezoned so that it severely limits land use, it may be considered the same as being condemned or taken. This is a legal issue.

52. **a.** Any changes should be initialed by all parties to the contract, including both the person making the change and the person accepting it.

53. **a.** $8,000 divided by 150' (frontage) equals $53.33.

54. **d.** A ground lease, usually for a period of many years, allows the tenant to erect and own buildings on rented land.

55. **b.** Whenever the occupancy level of an apartment house or office building exceeds 95%, serious consideration may be given to raising the rents.

56. **c.** If the lender is to handle the homeowner's insurance premiums and property tax bills, the escrow account is established at closing.

57. **c.** The lender who does not receive full payment after foreclosure of a loan on this type of property may seek a deficiency judgment against the borrower to force payment of the debt.

58. c. The OTS, FDIC, and HUD are not players on the secondary mortgage market. Fannie Mae buys large packages of mortgages that meet its particular specifications and has great influence on the primary mortgage market.

59. d. Economic obsolescence is caused by factors outside the property and is considered incurable.

60. a. The competitive market analysis (CMA), which assists sellers in setting an asking price, analyzes nearby properties that failed to sell, as well as competing property presently on the market and recently sold properties.

61. d. 184 days in the second half of 2002 plus 16 days in January 2003 equals 200 days. $3,726.50 divided by 365 (days in a year) multiplied by 200 equals $2,041.92 of credit to buyer and debit to seller.

62. b. In a seller's market, buyers are competing for the few homes on the market and are likely to offer more for them.

63. d. Any party who fails to take care of his or her responsibilities in a specific, timely manner is subject to being held in default of the contract.

64. b. Jessie is entitled to honest treatment, so George should explain that he owes her no confidentiality, and that he does owe a duty of notice to Lee.

65. a. When a contract for sale is ratified, by virtue of equitable and insurable title being conveyed to the buyer, responsibility for any hazard damage to the property rests with the seller if the state has adopted the Uniform Vendor and Purchaser Risk Act.

66. d. Two types of agency are special and general. Special agency is usually for one transaction and the agent has no authority to sign for the principal (client), while general agency gives the agent the authority to sign for the principal within the scope of the business agreement.

67. d. The duty of confidentiality forbids Sheila from sharing any information that might damage her client's bargaining position.

68. a. Contracts made under fraud are subject to being rescinded at the option of the innocent party.

69. d. Paul not only is an agent, but also has an interest (part ownership) in the property and should disclose this to potential buyers.

70. a. Every state has now enacted mandatory agency disclosure laws.

71. d. Lead paint was banned nationwide in the United States in 1978.

72. c. An E & O (errors and omissions) insurance underwriter will defend the broker and pay legal costs and judgments when the mistake was not deliberate.

73. a. An independent contractor can receive nothing that resembles an employee benefit.

74. b. Although most commissions may not be paid until the closing, the listing agent's assignment has actually been completed when a buyer is produced who is willing and able to purchase on the seller's terms.

75. d. According to the statute of frauds, all contracts for the sale of real estate must be in writing to be enforceable.

76. c. If the parties agree, consideration need not be valuable in order to be considered good enough.

77. **c.** Acceptance of an offer must be communicated to the offeror.

78. **c.** Counteroffers may be withdrawn or changed at any time prior to notice of acceptance. The property is still available for purchase at any time prior to a ratified contract.

79. **c.** Under the Truth-in-Lending Act, Federal Reserve Board's Regulation Z, only the asking price or the APR may be stated in an ad without triggering full disclosure of all the financing details.

80. **c.** It is not illegal for settlement service providers to be business partners and refer business from one to the other if the AfBA is timely delivered.

▶ Scoring

Remember that this practice exam is not correlated exactly to your state's real estate broker exam; your official test will also include state-specific questions. In general, to evaluate how you fared on this practice exam, find the number of questions you got right, and divide by 80 (the number of questions on this exam). This will give you your score as a percentage. A passing score would be about 75% on this practice exam.

For now, what's much more important than your overall score is how you did on each of the areas tested by the exam. You need to diagnose your strengths and weaknesses so that you can concentrate your efforts as you prepare. The question types are mixed in the practice exam, so in order to tell where your strengths and weaknesses lie, you'll need to compare your answer sheet with the following Thomson Prometric Practice Exam 1 for Review, which shows which of the categories each question falls into.

Use your score in conjunction with the Learning-Express Test Preparation System in Chapter 2 of this book to help you devise a study plan using the Real Estate Broker Refresher Course in Chapter 7, the Real Estate Broker Math Review in Chapter 8, and the Real Estate Glossary in Chapter 9. You should plan to spend more time on the sections that correspond to the questions you found hardest and less time on the lessons that correspond to areas in which you did well.

Once you have spent some time reviewing, take the second Thomson Prometric practice exam in Chapter 12 to see how much you've improved.

Thomson Prometric Practice Exam 1 for Review

Topic	Question Numbers
Agency and Listing	4, 12, 60, 64, 66, 67, 69, 70, 71, 72, 73, 74
Business Practices and Ethics	15, 16, 17, 18, 19, 22, 23, 26, 28, 29, 30, 32, 33, 35, 79, 80
Closing/Settlement and Transferring of Title	11, 13, 37, 38, 39, 47, 50, 61
Financing Sources	8, 14, 40, 41, 43, 46, 48, 56, 57, 58
Property Characteristics, Descriptions, Ownership Interests, and Restrictions	2, 3, 5, 6, 7, 20, 24, 34, 36, 49, 51, 53
Property Management	31, 42, 44, 55
Property Valuation and the Appraisal Process	9, 21, 25, 27, 59, 62
Real Estate Sales Contracts	1, 10, 45, 52, 54, 63, 65, 68, 75, 76, 77, 78

6 ▶ PSI Practice Exam 1

CHAPTER SUMMARY

This is the first of the two PSI practice exams in this book. Take this exam to see how you would do if you took the exam today and find out where your strengths and weaknesses lie.

I f you prefer to take a practice exam on a computer, refer to the insert at the end of this book to see how you can take a free PSI practice test on our website. Taking exams on the computer is good practice for the real exam. However, if you don't have access to the Internet, taking the exams on paper will accomplish the same goal—letting you know in which areas you are strong and in which areas you need more work.

Take this exam in as relaxed a manner as possible, without worrying about timing. You can time yourself on the second PSI practice exam. You should, however, make sure that you have enough time to take the entire exam in one sitting. Find a quiet place where you can work without interruptions.

The answer sheet is on the following page, and then comes the exam. After you have finished, use the answer key and explanations to determine your strengths and weaknesses. Then use the scoring section at the end of this chapter to see how you did overall.

1.	(a)	(b)	(c)	(d)
2.	(a)	(b)	(c)	(d)
3.	(a)	(b)	(c)	(d)
4.	(a)	(b)	(c)	(d)
5.	(a)	(b)	(c)	(d)
6.	(a)	(b)	(c)	(d)
7.	(a)	(b)	(c)	(d)
8.	(a)	(b)	(c)	(d)
9.	(a)	(b)	(c)	(d)
10.	(a)	(b)	(c)	(d)
11.	(a)	(b)	(c)	(d)
12.	(a)	(b)	(c)	(d)
13.	(a)	(b)	(c)	(d)
14.	(a)	(b)	(c)	(d)
15.	(a)	(b)	(c)	(d)
16.	(a)	(b)	(c)	(d)
17.	(a)	(b)	(c)	(d)
18.	(a)	(b)	(c)	(d)
19.	(a)	(b)	(c)	(d)
20.	(a)	(b)	(c)	(d)
21.	(a)	(b)	(c)	(d)
22.	(a)	(b)	(c)	(d)
23.	(a)	(b)	(c)	(d)
24.	(a)	(b)	(c)	(d)
25.	(a)	(b)	(c)	(d)
26.	(a)	(b)	(c)	(d)
27.	(a)	(b)	(c)	(d)
28.	(a)	(b)	(c)	(d)
29.	(a)	(b)	(c)	(d)
30.	(a)	(b)	(c)	(d)

31.	(a)	(b)	(c)	(d)
32.	(a)	(b)	(c)	(d)
33.	(a)	(b)	(c)	(d)
34.	(a)	(b)	(c)	(d)
35.	(a)	(b)	(c)	(d)
36.	(a)	(b)	(c)	(d)
37.	(a)	(b)	(c)	(d)
38.	(a)	(b)	(c)	(d)
39.	(a)	(b)	(c)	(d)
40.	(a)	(b)	(c)	(d)
41.	(a)	(b)	(c)	(d)
42.	(a)	(b)	(c)	(d)
43.	(a)	(b)	(c)	(d)
44.	(a)	(b)	(c)	(d)
45.	(a)	(b)	(c)	(d)
46.	(a)	(b)	(c)	(d)
47.	(a)	(b)	(c)	(d)
48.	(a)	(b)	(c)	(d)
49.	(a)	(b)	(c)	(d)
50.	(a)	(b)	(c)	(d)
51.	(a)	(b)	(c)	(d)
52.	(a)	(b)	(c)	(d)
53.	(a)	(b)	(c)	(d)
54.	(a)	(b)	(c)	(d)
55.	(a)	(b)	(c)	(d)
56.	(a)	(b)	(c)	(d)
57.	(a)	(b)	(c)	(d)
58.	(a)	(b)	(c)	(d)
59.	(a)	(b)	(c)	(d)
60.	(a)	(b)	(c)	(d)

61.	(a)	(b)	(c)	(d)
62.	(a)	(b)	(c)	(d)
63.	(a)	(b)	(c)	(d)
64.	(a)	(b)	(c)	(d)
65.	(a)	(b)	(c)	(d)
66.	(a)	(b)	(c)	(d)
67.	(a)	(b)	(c)	(d)
68.	(a)	(b)	(c)	(d)
69.	(a)	(b)	(c)	(d)
70.	(a)	(b)	(c)	(d)
71.	(a)	(b)	(c)	(d)
72.	(a)	(b)	(c)	(d)
73.	(a)	(b)	(c)	(d)
74.	(a)	(b)	(c)	(d)
75.	(a)	(b)	(c)	(d)
76.	(a)	(b)	(c)	(d)
77.	(a)	(b)	(c)	(d)
78.	(a)	(b)	(c)	(d)
79.	(a)	(b)	(c)	(d)
80.	(a)	(b)	(c)	(d)

▶ PSI Practice Exam 1

1. Which of the following is the primary factor in a dispute as to whether an item is personal property (chattel) or real property (real estate)?
   a. method of attachment (annexation)
   b. adaptation
   c. intent of the parties (agreement)
   d. none of the above

2. The land characteristic that states no two parcels of land are ever exactly alike is
   a. scarcity.
   b. nonhomogeneous.
   c. improvements.
   d. permanence.

3. Which type of lien has both a dominant and a servient tenement?
   a. easement in gross
   b. easement appurtenant
   c. easement by prescription
   d. easement by implication

4. Which of the following would NOT be part of a rectangular or government survey legal description?
   a. townships
   b. sections
   c. principal meridians
   d. blocks

5. What type of lien that would attach to all property that is not exempt from forced sale?
   a. general lien
   b. specific lien
   c. voluntary lien
   d. mechanic's lien

6. Charlotte Tran conveys her property to the city "as long as" the property is used as a public park. What kind of ownership does the city have?
   a. fee simple
   b. fee simple absolute
   c. defeasible fee
   d. fee with a condition precedent

7. Liz Hampton conveys a home to her mother for her mother's lifetime. Upon her mother's death, the property is then to pass to Liz's daughter Carol. What kind of ownership does Carol receive upon the death of Liz's mother?
   a. remainder estate
   b. life estate
   c. reversionary estate
   d. fee simple

8. A property owner dies testate but without heirs. The government would then obtain ownership through which government right in land?
   a. police power
   b. eminent domain
   c. escheat
   d. none of the above

9. By what right does a city impose requirements in construction materials and methods used when building within the jurisdiction of the city?
   a. police power
   b. building codes
   c. city ordinance
   d. enactment

10. Mona lives in an area that until recently was zoned as residential. New industry is moving into the area, bringing jobs and economic development. The city has decided to expand the local industrial zone to include Mona's land. Mona's use is now said to be
a. an illegal, non-conforming use.
b. a legal, non-conforming use.
c. a preexisting use.
d. a zoning exception.

11. Felix Davidson is considering selling a half-section of his farm. He wants to ensure that the property will always be used for agricultural purposes. One of the ways he could accomplish this is to
a. sell the property to another farmer only.
b. put a statement to that effect in the sales contract.
c. place a restriction in the deed limiting the land use to agricultural.
d. obtain an oral agreement from the buyer to limit the use to agricultural.

12. When a government takes private property for a public use under the right of eminent domain, what must the government pay the property owner for the loss?
a. The government has no obligation to pay a property owner for the loss.
b. market value
c. fair market value
d. just compensation

13. Subdivision regulations imposed on an area by a city would be an example of
a. police power.
b. deed restrictions.
c. condemnation.
d. public restrictions.

14. A city places a greenbelt or park between an area zoned as industrial and another that is zoned as residential. This area is known as a
a. dividing ground.
b. buffer zone.
c. green border.
d. division zone.

15. The Financial Institutions Reform, Recovery, and Enforcement Act (FIRREA) requires that a licensed or certified appraiser be used to appraise property in all
a. federally related transactions.
b. commercial transactions.
c. federally related transactions above $250,000.
d. transactions with a total value more than $1,000,000.

16. Which of the following would NOT be part of market value?
a. the highest price
b. willing buyer and willing seller
c. neither party under pressure
d. property exposed in the open market

17. What is an opinion of value prepared by a real estate broker for pricing purposes that does NOT follow the Uniform Standards of Professional Appraisal Practices (USPAP) guidelines?
a. broker appraisal
b. informal appraisal
c. marketing appraisal
d. competitive market analysis

18. Which approach to appraisal takes into consideration an improvement's physical deterioration, functional obsolescence, and external obsolescence?
   a. market data approach
   b. cost approach
   c. income approach
   d. component approach

19. Jill McDonald is an appraiser with Do It Right Appraisal Associates. She has been assigned the job of appraising an office building in the central business district. Which approach to value would be the most appropriate for Ms. McDonald to use in estimating the value of this property?
   a. sales comparison approach
   b. cost approach
   c. market data approach
   d. income approach

20. What is the basic formula used in estimating value under the income approach?
   a. potential gross income divided by the capitalization rate
   b. net operating income divided by the before tax cash flow
   c. gross operating income divided by the after tax cash flow
   d. net operating income divided by the capitalization rate

21. George and Jeanette Cosakis had always wanted a lakefront home to use as a vacation retreat. They find a two-bedroom cottage on the water that is fully furnished and has a sailboat that comes with the property. The Cosakises obtain a single loan that pledges the house, furnishings, and the sailboat. What kind of loan did they receive?
   a. combination mortgage
   b. blanket mortgage
   c. chattel mortgage
   d. package mortgage

22. What is a loan that has a series of steady, even, periodic payments made up of part interest and part principal in an amount sufficient to retire the loan at maturity?
   a. balloon loan
   b. graduated payment loan
   c. fully amortized loan
   d. segmented loan

23. Which of the following is NOT a source of lending in the primary money market?
   a. savings associations
   b. commercial banks
   c. Fannie Mae
   d. pension funds

24. Which of the following attributes do the Federal Housing Administration (FHA) and the Department of Veterans Affairs (DVA) have in common?
  a. They both insure loans.
  b. They are both overseen by the Department Housing and Urban Development (HUD).
  c. Neither type of loan may be sold into the secondary market.
  d. Neither one lends money.

25. Carla Hoffman bought a small retail center. After making a substantial down payment, she borrowed slightly less than one million dollars. In the mortgage documents, Carla would be identified as the
  a. mortgagor.
  b. mortgagee.
  c. trustee.
  d. beneficiary.

26. Which federal statute requires every lender to identify its market's geographical boundaries, specify the types of credit offered, and make reports on its efforts to meet local credit needs?
  a. Equal Credit Opportunity Act
  b. Community Reinvestment Act
  c. Home Mortgage Disclosure Act
  d. Federal Lending Disclosure Act

27. Which of the following does NOT apply to the Truth-in-Lending Act (Regulation Z)?
  a. loans made to individuals for personal, family, or household uses when the amount of credit is $25,000 or less
  b. any loan that is secured by a residence
  c. a three-day right of rescission on any loan covered by the regulations
  d. the language in advertising financing terms including the Annual Percentage Rate (APR)

28. An agency relationship may be formed by all the following methods EXCEPT
  a. express agency.
  b. implied agency.
  c. agency by default.
  d. agency by ratification.

29. An agent that may act for a principal in a broad range of matters within the scope of a trade or business and with the authority to bind the principal is a
  a. general agent.
  b. special agent.
  c. universal agent.
  d. business agent.

30. Carol Patel is working with Malcolm and Estelle Jackson. Although Carol has shown the Jacksons the property they want to purchase and has put them in touch with a lender, she has not been hired to represent the Jacksons. In fact, the Jacksons have made it clear that they do not wish to be represented. What kind of agent is Carol?
   a. special agent
   b. subagent
   c. implied agent
   d. all of the above

31. Lester Oliver is a broker representing the seller of a parcel of land. Under the agreement, only Lester may sell the property unless the seller finds a buyer without assistance. What kind of listing agreement would this be?
   a. exclusive right to sell
   b. exclusive agency
   c. open listing
   d. net listing

32. What is a formal, legal relationship between a principal and an agent that imposes the duties of obedience, loyalty, disclosure, confidentiality, accounting, and reasonable care upon the agent?
   a. formal relationship
   b. fiduciary relationship
   c. statutory relationship
   d. expressed relationship

33. Three brokers in town get together at their regular monthly breakfast. One broker laments the fact that his salespeople are having trouble getting sellers to sign listings for more than 90 days. The other two brokers share the same complaint, and all three agree to take listings for not less than 180 days with a commission of not less than 6%. These brokers would be guilty of price fixing under which law?
   a. Federal Fair Housing
   b. Sherman Anti-Trust Act
   c. Federal Real Estate Control Act
   d. Coleman Anti-Trust Act

34. Which of the following duties is NOT owed to a customer?
   a. honesty
   b. fairness
   c. disclosure
   d. confidentiality

35. When should an agent make clear who he or she represents?
   a. at the time an offer is made
   b. prior to closing
   c. prior to a contract being executed
   d. at all times

36. What is a listing agreement that may be signed between a single property owner and multiple brokers?
   a. exclusive right to sell
   b. open listing
   c. net listing
   d. general listing

37. A broker has a listing with a seller. While showing the property to a buyer, the broker comments that the seller is in financial trouble and must sell quickly. The seller never authorized the broker to make such disclosure, and is not aware the broker has made this statement to the buyer. The broker is now acting as a(n)
   a. buyer agent.
   b. dual agent.
   c. undisclosed dual agent.
   d. universal agent.

38. Which properties are covered by the federal lead-based paint regulations?
   a. all properties built before 1978
   b. most residential properties built before 1978
   c. all residential properties built before 1978
   d. any residential property built before 1978 and sold with the assistance of a real estate broker

39. What is the rule concerning the disclosure of the presence of HIV or AIDS in a dwelling?
   a. Federal Fair Housing law does not permit such disclosures.
   b. Federal Fair Housing law does not prohibit such disclosures.
   c. State law controls this issue and will vary from state to state.
   d. Federal health regulations require the disclosure of HIV or AIDS.

40. What is an intentional deception designed to deprive someone of something of value such as money, property, or rights?
   a. misrepresentation
   b. puffing
   c. misrepresentation by commission
   d. fraud

41. What is a broker's duty with regard to disclosure of known material defects in a property?
   a. Such defects must be disclosed only if the broker represents the buyer.
   b. Such defects must be disclosed only if the broker represents the seller.
   c. Such defects must be disclosed no matter which party the broker represents.
   d. It is up to a buyer to discover any material defects under the legal concept of "let the buyer beware."

42. When is the best time to present to the buyer any seller property disclosure form?
   a. at closing
   b. before a purchase contract is signed by all parties
   c. within ten days of a buyer's request for such disclosure form
   d. after a buyer is approved for financing

43. Which of the following is NOT required to be disclosed to a prospective buyer by an agent representing the seller?
   a. environmental issues
   b. which party the broker is representing
   c. the seller's motivation for selling
   d. the proposed condemnation of the property

44. Under IRS regulations, what must be disclosed to a purchaser of real property in the United States?
   a. if the seller is a "foreign person" under IRS rules
   b. if cash over a specified amount changes hands in the transaction
   c. both of the above
   d. none of the above

45. A contract was signed between a seller and a buyer. Thirty days later, all promises by both parties have been fulfilled and the transaction has closed to the satisfaction of all. At this point, the contract is said to be
   a. executed.
   b. executory.
   c. valid.
   d. executable.

46. Which of the following is NOT an essential element of a real estate purchase contract?
   a. offer and acceptance
   b. earnest money
   c. competent parties
   d. legality of object

47. Mike McBride is a buyer purchasing the home of Maybelle Ude. Mike decides not to buy after all and transfers his right to purchase to David Goldberg. However, Mike is not released from liability under the contract. What would this transfer of the right to purchased be called?
   a. transferal
   b. novation
   c. assignment
   d. substitution

48. Ellen Duprey is a salesperson with Midtown Realty. She has listed a shopping center for sale for Shopwell Corporation. She has received four offers on the property while the asset manager at Shopwell has been out of town and unreachable. She is to meet with the asset manager tomorrow afternoon. In what order should she present the offers?
   a. in any order, as long as she presents all the offers
   b. one at a time in the order they were received
   c. from lowest to highest offer
   d. present only the offer that came in first

49. A buyer has signed a contract to purchase a home. The closing will not take place for 90 days. Until closing, what kind of title is held by the buyer?
   a. none
   b. bare title
   c. legal title
   d. equitable title

50. What kind of lease requires a tenant to pay a flat amount of rent plus some or all of the property expenses such as taxes, insurance, or maintenance?
   a. gross lease
   b. percentage lease
   c. extracted lease
   d. net lease

51. What type of contract cancellation is used when both parties agree to the cancellation and both parties are restored to their original positions?
a. refundment
b. withdrawal
c. mutual rescission
d. bilateral reliction

52. The Tillman Corporation signs a contract to sell an office building to its competitor International Partners. Tillman fails to disclose that the property has asbestos and lead-based paint. What legal effect would the contract have?
a. invalid
b. null and void
c. unenforceable
d. voidable

53. What is a lawsuit to compel action called for in a contract?
a. specific performance
b. general performance
c. forcible performance
d. injunctionable performance

54. Which of the following events would terminate a purchase contract?
a. death of the seller
b. destruction of the property
c. bankruptcy of the buyer
d. none of the above

55. If a buyer is more interested in being reimbursed for a loss of title on a property, which of the following would best accomplish that goal?
a. a general warranty deed
b. an abstract of title
c. title insurance
d. an attorney's opinion of title

56. Which type of deed states that the grantor will only defend against claims that arise from the grantor's period of ownership?
a. general warranty deed
b. special warranty deed
c. quitclaim deed
d. bargain and sale deed

57. A closing in which the seller has signed and delivered a deed to a disinterested third party and a buyer deposits the money with the same disinterested third party, whose function is to make the exchange at closing, is called
a. a third-party closing.
b. title company closing.
c. deposit closing.
d. closing in escrow.

58. What is the requirement for homeowners to receive the full benefit of the tax-free capital gains on the sale of their principal residence?
a. One of the owners must be at least 55 years of age.
b. They must have occupied the home as their principal residence for at least two years.
c. They must have occupied the residence for at least two years and not have leased the property at any time.
d. They must have owned and occupied the home as their principal residence for at least two out of the last five years.

59. When a person dies intestate, when does title to real property pass to the deceased's heirs?
a. at the instant of death
b. upon filing of the death certificate
c. upon completion of probate
d. when the will is recorded in public record

60. What is a foreclosure called that has been conducted under a "power of sale" clause?
a. judicial foreclosure
b. nonjudicial foreclosure
c. strict foreclosure
d. automatic foreclosure

61. The Civil Rights Act of 1866 prohibits which of the following acts?
a. discrimination in the sale, lease, or purchase of real or personal property because of a person's ancestry
b. discrimination in the sale, lease, or purchase of real or personal property because of a person's color
c. discrimination in housing because of a person's race, religion, color, sex, or national origin
d. discrimination in the sale or lease of housing for any reason

62. Which of the following is NOT a protected class under the Fair Housing Act?
a. handicap
b. familial status
c. religion
d. marital status

63. A broker sends letters to area homeowners informing them of a proposed group home for teenagers with severe learning disabilities. He tells the homeowners to sell quickly before the project is approved and finalized. This broker could be found guilty of
a. steering.
b. less favorable treatment.
c. blockbusting.
d. nothing, because there is no fair housing issue in this scenario.

64. What statement must be included in all advertisements placed by a broker on behalf of the broker's clients?
a. that the firm does business in accordance with fair housing laws
b. that the person placing the advertisement as a licensed broker or agent
c. that real estate commissions are negotiable under anti-trust law
d. all of the above

65. What is an exaggeration often referred to as "salesperson talk"?
a. misrepresentation by commission
b. misrepresentation by omission
c. puffery
d. fraud

66. Which of the following statements is true concerning a broker's duty to supervise the professional acts of salespeople sponsored by the broker?
a. A broker is responsible for the professional acts of the salespeople sponsored by the broker but has no specific duty to supervise their activities on a daily basis.
b. A broker must supervise all professional acts performed by salespeople sponsored by the broker.
c. A broker has no duty to supervise the acts of salespeople sponsored by the broker and has no liability for their actions, as long as the salespeople are associated with the broker as independent contractors.
d. A broker must supervise the professional acts of employees, but not of independent contractors.

67. Handicap is defined in federal Fair Housing law as

a. a physical impairment that substantially limits one or more major life activities.

b. a physical or mental impairment that substantially limits one or more major life activities.

c. a physical or mental impairment that substantially limits a person's mobility.

d. any impairment that limits any of a person's five senses.

68. Creating the independent contractor status requires all the following EXCEPT

a. pay must be related to sales, not hours worked.

b. broker may not direct the salesperson's daily activities.

c. a contract must be signed between the broker and salespeople, stating that the salespeople are independent contractors.

d. an affidavit must be filed with the IRS, confirming the independent contractor status.

69. Failure of a broker to have the Fair Housing Poster prominently displayed in the office where the public will see it may result in which of the following?

a. a fair housing complaint filed by HUD or a member of the public

b. an assumption in law that the lack of the poster is, by itself, an act of discrimination

c. a shift of the burden of proof in any fair housing lawsuit from the plaintiff (consumer) to the defendant (broker)

d. all of the above

70. James Hart is a broker. He has just signed a listing on a $5,000,000 estate. This is the highest-priced listing James has ever had. Two days after taking the listing, James receives an offer from a competing company and an offer from a buyer he is working with personally. Which offer should James recommend to his clients?

a. whichever offer best meets the clients' goals, no matter which offer it may be

b. the offer from the other company, so as not to put his firm in a dual agent position

c. the offer from his buyer, so that he has more control in the transaction

d. the offer from his buyer, so that he can offer a discounted commission to the clients

71. Barbara Tete, a real estate broker, is discussing goals with her seller client. The seller indicates that he must pay off a $170,000 loan, do about $8,000 in repairs, pay closing costs of $6,500, have the property treated for termites at a cost of $3,500, and pay Barbara her commission of 7%. In addition, the seller wishes to net at least $120,000 from the sale. What would the property need to sell for in order to meet this goal?

a. $308,000

b. $329,560

c. $331,182.80

d. $344,768.20

72. What would be the annual property tax bill on a property assessed for $873,000 (after all exemptions) in an area where the city's tax rate is $0.37 per hundred of valuation, the county charges $0.23 per hundred, and the school district collects $1.02 per hundred?
  a. $11,381.76
  b. $1,178.55
  c. $14,142.60
  d. $2,336.17

73. A property is valued and sold for $363,500. The buyer makes a 20% down payment. What would the total principal, interest, tax, and insurance payment be on a 6.5%, 30-year loan (use a loan factor of $6.32) with an *ad valorem* tax rate of $2.17 per hundred of valuation per annum, hazard insurance rate of 1.5% of the value each year, and flood insurance of $1,650 annually?
  a. $3,087.07
  b. $2,949.57
  c. $4,599.57
  d. $3,144.88

74. What is the indicated value of an income-producing property that has a potential gross income of $400,000, assuming a vacancy rate of 5% of gross potential income, operating expenses totaling $210,000 and using a capitalization rate of 8%?
  a. $2,375,000
  b. $2,125,000
  c. $3,100,000
  d. $3,375,000

75. What is the total interest paid on a $188,500, 30-year, fully amortized loan with an interest rate of 10%, using a payment factor of $8.78?
  a. $595,810.80
  b. $504,650.10
  c. $488,294.80
  d. $407,310.80

76. How many acres are there in a parcel of land that is 3,600 feet across the front and 8,150 feet deep?
  a. 500 acres
  b. 543.20 acres
  c. 673.55 acres
  d. 682.33 acres

77. Which of the following is NOT a common function of a professional property manager?
  a. advising the owners on the best tax strategy for their investment
  b. generating income for the owner
  c. preserving and/or improve the condition of the property
  d. meeting the owner's objectives

78. In calculating the capital gain on an apartment complex, an investor would depreciate the improvements over how many years?
  a. 27.5
  b. 30
  c. 39
  d. 40.5

79. Subdivision regulations such as setback lines and lot sizes are most commonly imposed by what level of government?
   a. federal
   b. state
   c. county
   d. city

80. What level of law is most landlord-tenant law?
   a. federal common law
   b. state statutory law
   c. county civil law
   d. city ordinance

▶ Answers

1. c. In case of a dispute, it is the intent or agreement of the parties that will be the deciding factor. Often, the contractual agreement between the parties is what a court uses in making this determination.

2. b. Every piece of land is unique or nonhomogeneous if for no other reason than its location. Two parcels next to each other, both 60 feet wide and 120 feet deep, are still different because of their locations.

3. b. An easement appurtenant has a dominant tenement, which is the parcel that uses the easement, and a servient tenement, which is the parcel that has the easement on it. An easement in gross has only a servient tenement; the other two are methods of creating easements.

4. d. Blocks are used in a recorded plat description and not on a rectangular survey.

5. a. A general lien attaches to all property (in general), and a specific lien is against only the specific property on which the debt is owed.

6. c. The city holds a defeasible fee estate that may be defeated if the city violates the restriction that the property be used only as a public park.

7. d. Carol's interest is a remainder as long as Liz's mother lives, but it converts to a full fee simple ownership upon the life tenant's death.

8. d. The answer is none of the above. The answer would have been escheat had the property owner died intestate and without heirs.

9. a. Police power is the right of government to pass laws, rules, and regulations to protect the health, safety, morals, and welfare of the public, which includes building codes. However, building codes are a process, not a right.

10. b. Because Mona's residential use of the property predates the zoning change, her use is said to be a legal, non-conforming use.

11. c. Placing a deed restriction, or restrictive covenant, will accomplish Mr. Davidson's goal. A deed restriction is a private covenant in a deed that may restrict the future use of land.

12. d. The Fifth Amendment to the U.S. Constitution requires the government to pay a property owner "just compensation."

13. a. A city may place subdivision regulations through its right of police power. Police power is the right of government to pass laws, rules, and regulations (including subdivision regulations) to protect the health, safety, morals, and welfare of the public.

14. b. This green area between two differently zoned land uses is known as a buffer zone.

15. c. FIRREA requires that a licensed or certified appraiser be used in federally related transactions above $250,000.

16. a. Market value is the most probable price, not the highest price a property would bring.

17. d. A competitive market analysis (CMA) is used to determine a listing price for a property for marketing purposes and is not an appraisal that follows USPAP guidelines.

18. b. The cost approach starts with an estimate of the replacement or reproduction cost of an improvement and then adjusts the cost according to the three types of depreciation mentioned in the question.

19. d. Although any or all three of the approaches could be used, the income approach would probably be the most accurate for an office building.

20. d. The net operating income (income left after operating expenses are paid) divided by the capitalization rate (the rate of return based on purchase price that would attract capital) would equal the indicated or estimated value.

21. d. They received a package mortgage. A blanket mortgage has more than one parcel of real estate as collateral, and a chattel mortgage has only personal property as collateral.

22. c. This type of loan is a fully amortized loan.

23. c. Fannie Mae does not make loans and is not a part of the primary money market. Fannie Mae buys loans made in the primary market and is part of the secondary market.

24. d. FHA insures loans and DVA guarantees loans. Only FHA is overseen by HUD. Both loans insured by FHA and loans guaranteed by DVA may be sold into the secondary market. Neither one lends money.

25. a. The borrower is the mortgagor and the lender is the mortgagee. A mortgage is not a loan but rather a pledge of property as collateral. It is the borrower who must pledge the property.

26. b. The Community Reinvestment Act requires lenders to reinvest in the communities from which they take deposits and to report on those efforts.

27. c. The three-day right of rescission does not apply to a residential first mortgage loan for acquisition or initial construction.

28. c. Express agency is created by words, whether oral or written. Implied agency is created by the parties' actions. Agency by ratification is an agency created after the fact when a principal accepts a previously unauthorized action and benefits from such act.

29. a. This kind of agent is a general agent. A good example would be a property manager. A special agent cannot bind the principal, and a universal agent may bind the principal in all matters.

30. d. Carol is all of the above. She is representing the seller indirectly through the listing firm, making her a subagent. Her actions have implied that she represents the seller, and she cannot bind the principal, making her a special agent as well.

31. b. Under an exclusive agency listing, the property must be sold through the listing agent unless the seller finds a buyer without the assistance of any broker.

32. b. Such relationships are called fiduciary relationships; they include all the listed duties, which may be remembered with the acronym of OLD CAR (Obediance, Loyalty, Disclosure, Confidentiality, Accounting, Reasonable care).

33. b. The Sherman Anti-Trust Act of 1895 prohibits price fixing. Price fixing is agreeing with competitors to fix, set, or limit prices or terms.

34. d. Confidentiality is not owed to a customer. If a buyer whom you do not represent tells you, "Offer $250,000, but I'll pay as much as $300,000," then your duty is to disclose to your seller-client what the buyer-customer said.

35. d. A real estate licensee must make it clear at all times the licensee's agency relationship.

36. b. An open listing may be signed between a single property owner and as many brokers as the property owner pleases. The commission will be paid to whichever broker brings the buyer.

37. c. The broker is acting in the best interest of the buyer without the knowledge of the seller while holding a listing agreement with the seller. This would make the broker not simply a dual agent, but an undisclosed dual agent.

38. b. Most residential properties built before 1978 are covered by these regulations. Exceptions include properties leased for fewer than 100 days and zero bedroom units.

39. a. Under federal Fair Housing law, such disclosures would be prohibited under handicap status.

40. d. Fraud goes further than misrepresentation and includes an element of intention or premeditation.

41. c. Material defects must be disclosed to a buyer no matter whom the broker represents. "Let the buyer beware" is an outmoded legal concept in real estate.

42. b. Although not always required, it is best to have any seller disclosure of property condition form in the buyer's hands before there is a signed purchase contract between the parties.

43. c. The seller's motivation for selling is not material to the transaction. If a seller is moving because of defects in the property, the defects must be disclosed, but the fact that the defects are motivating the seller to sell need not be disclosed.

44. c. A "foreign person" is defined by the law as a nonresident alien, foreign corporation, foreign partnership, or foreign trust. The IRS regulations also require filing certain reports if currency in excess of specified amounts is received in the transaction.

45. a. When all the promises in a contract have been fulfilled, it is said to be executed. All the promises have been executed.

46. b. Earnest money is not an essential element of a real estate purchase contract. The consideration is often thought to be the earnest money, but it is not required. The consideration may be other property, services, or an exchange of promises. The other three elements listed must be present.

47. c. Assignment transfers rights under a contract to a third party but does not release the first party of liability under the contract. In this scenario, if David does not show for closing, then Mike will still be required to purchase the property. Novation would be the complete substitution of one party or contract for another thereby releasing the first party of liability.

48. a. All the offers must be presented, and their order is not important. No offer has priority over any other.

49. d. Until closing, the buyer holds equitable title. Equitable in this context means "in fairness."

50. d. A net lease requires the payment of at least some of the property expenses along with a flat rental fee.

51. c. Mutual rescission releases both parties and restores them to their original positions.

52. d. The contract would be voidable by International Partners. International Partners may hold Tillman to the contract if it believes that the benefits of the contract would outweigh the loss in value because of the undisclosed environmental issues. On the other hand, International Partners may void the contract if it so pleases, but the contract is not automatically void.

53. a. Specific performance is a lawsuit to force the other party to fulfill a promise or promises made in a contract.

54. b. Destruction of the property would terminate a contract. In case of the seller's death, the heirs must perform, and bankruptcy of the buyer may make it impossible for the buyer to close but does not terminate the contract.

55. c. Title insurance pays for a covered loss of title up to the policy limit. None of the other items listed is required to have money to pay for a loss or, in the case of a grantor under a general warranty deed, may simply not have the assets to pay.

56. b. A special warranty deed, also known as a limited warranty deed, promises defense only against defects in title that arise from the grantor's period of ownership.

57. d. A closing wherein the seller deposits the deed and the buyer deposits the funds with a disinterested third party, such as a title company or lawyer, is called closing in escrow or an escrow closing.

58. d. The owners must have owned and occupied the home as their principal residence for at least two out of the last five years. They may have leased the home out for part of that time as long as they occupied it for two years out of the last five.

59. a. Ownership or title would pass at the instant of death, although the heirs may not receive full control of the property until probate is complete.

60. b. When a property is sold in foreclosure under a "power of sale" clause, no judge is involved. The process does not take place in a courtroom and is, therefore, known as a nonjudicial foreclosure.

61. b. The Civil Rights Act of 1866 states that "All citizens of the United States shall have the same right in every state and territory, as is enjoyed by white citizens thereof, to inherit, purchase, lease, sell, hold, and convey both real and personal property." This effectively prohibits discrimination based upon a person's race.

62. d. Although marital status is a protected class under equal lending law, it is not a protected class under the Fair Housing Act.

63. c. Blockbusting is the act of inducing panic in an effort to induce property owners to sell because of the entry, or prospective entry, of a protected class. In this scenario, the protected class could be handicap and/or familial status.

64. b. All advertisements placed by a broker on behalf of the broker's clients must disclose that the ad has been placed by a licensed broker. Although a fair housing statement is a good idea for any residential firm, it is not required.

65. c. Puffery is an exaggeration and may or may not be considered misrepresentation by a court.

66. a. Although brokers would be wise to supervise the professional acts of the salespeople they sponsor, they are generally not required to do so.

67. b. A handicap may be physical or mental and limits a major life activity such as the ability to walk, see, hear, think, or communicate.

68. d. No such filing is required.

69. **d.** The lack of the Fair Housing Poster may result in all three of the listed consequences.

70. **a.** Ethically, James should recommend the offer that best fits his client's needs.

71. **c.** Add all the items that must be covered and then divide by the percentage that is not the commission (100% − 7% = 93%).
$170,000 + $120,000 + $8,000 + $6,500 + $3,500 = $308,000
$308,000 ÷ 93% = $331,182.80

72. **c.** $873,000 ÷ 100 × 1.62 = $14,142.60
The $1.62 total tax rate is arrived at by simply adding the three tax rates together.

73. **a.** $363,500 − 20% ÷ 1,000 × 6.32 = $1,837.86 monthly principal and interest
$363,500 ÷ 100 × 2.17 ÷ 12 = $657.33 per month for taxes
$363,500 × 1.5% ÷ 12 = $454.38 per month for hazard insurance
$1,650 ÷ 12 = $137.50 per month for flood insurance
The monthly PITI payment totals $3,087.07.

74. **b.** $400,000 − 5% − $210,000 ÷ 8% = $2,125,000

75. **d.** $188,500 ÷ 1,000 × 8.78 = $1,655.03 monthly principal and interest
$1,655.03 × 360 = $595,810.80 total principal and interest
$595,810.80 − $188,500 = $407,310.80 total interest paid

76. **c.** 3,600 × 8,150 ÷ 43,560 = 673.55 acres

77. **a.** Such tax advice should be left to a professional accountant or CPA.

78. **a.** The IRS makes the distinction between residential and nonresidential property, not residential and commercial. Therefore, the apartment complex, as a residential property, would be depreciated over 27.5 years.

79. **d.** Cities or municipalities are primarily responsible for placing and enforcing subdivision regulations such as these.

80. **b.** State statutory law is the most common source of landlord-tenant law.

▶ Scoring

Remember that this practice exam is not correlated exactly to your state's real estate broker exam; your official test will also include state-specific questions. In general, to evaluate how you fared on this practice exam, find the number of questions you got right, and divide by 80 (the number of questions on this exam). This will give you your score as a percentage. A passing score would be about 70% on this practice exam.

For now, what's much more important than your overall score is how you did on each of the areas tested by the exam. You need to diagnose your strengths and weaknesses so that you can concentrate your efforts as you prepare. The question types are mixed in the practice exam, so in order to tell where your strengths and weaknesses lie, you'll need to compare your answer sheet with the following PSI Practice Exam 1 for Review, which shows which of the categories each question falls into.

Use your score in conjunction with the Learning-Express Test Preparation System in Chapter 2 of this book to help you devise a study plan using the Real Estate Broker Refresher Course in Chapter 7, the Real Estate Broker Math Review in Chapter 8, and the Real Estate Glossary in Chapter 9. You should plan to spend more time on the sections that correspond to the questions you found hardest and less time on the lessons that correspond to areas in which you did well.

Once you have spent some time reviewing, take the second PSI practice exam in Chapter 13 to see how much you've improved.

PSI Practice Exam 1 for Review

Topic	Question Numbers
Property Ownership	1, 2, 3, 4, 5, 6, 7
Land Use Control and Regulations	8, 9, 10, 11, 12, 13, 14
Valuation and Market Analysis	15, 16, 17, 18, 19, 20
Financing	21, 22, 23, 24, 25, 26, 27
Laws of Agency	28, 29, 30, 31, 32, 33, 34, 35, 36, 37
Mandated Disclosures	38, 39, 40, 41, 42, 43, 44
Contracts	45, 46, 47, 48, 49, 50, 51, 52, 53, 54
Transfer of Property	55, 56, 57, 58, 59, 60
Practice of Real Estate	61, 62, 63, 64, 65, 66, 67, 68, 69, 70
Real Estate Calculations	71, 72, 73, 74, 75, 76
Specialty Areas	77, 78, 79, 80

7 ▶ Real Estate Broker Refresher Course

CHAPTER SUMMARY

In order to succeed on your exam, you'll need a solid foundation of knowledge about essential real estate concepts. Using this chapter, you can review just what you need to know for the test.

How you use this chapter is up to you. You may want to proceed through the entire course in order, or perhaps, after taking the first practice exam, you know that you need to brush up on just one or two areas. In that case, you can concentrate only on those areas.

Following are the major sections of the real estate refresher course and the page on which you can begin your review of each one.

▶ Real Estate Principles and Practices

Note: Mathematics will be covered in Chapter 5.

▶ Real Estate Principles and Practices

Property Characteristics

Classes of Property

All property that can be owned and subsequently inherited is legally known as hereditaments. Land and that which is permanently attached to the land are identified as real property. Items not attached to land are known as personal property or chattels.

When an item of personal property or a chattel is permanently attached to real estate, it becomes real property and is identified as a fixture. Fixtures become appurtenances and remain with the property when ownership transfers to a new owner. An exception occurs when a commercial tenant installs a business fixture to be used in the business for which the space has been leased. Trade fixtures remain the property of the tenant and may be removed by the tenant at the end of the lease. The tenant is obligated to repair any damage caused by the removal of a trade fixture.

The determination of a fixture is made by asking and answering the following questions.

1. How is the item attached?
2. Have the improvements been modified to accommodate the item?
3. What was the intent of the attachor?
4. Is there a contractual agreement that defines the item as a fixture or as a chattel?

Land Characteristics

Land is the earth's surface (surface rights), the minerals and water below the surface (subsurface rights), and the air space above the surface (air rights). Ownership of land has long been regarded as the basis of all wealth.

From a physical standpoint, each parcel of land is unique. It is immobile. Although its features can be modified by humans and by the forces of nature, it is indestructible. Each parcel is unique and unlike any other, which makes it nonhomogeneous.

Land also has four economic characteristics.

1. **Scarcity**—There is a limited amount of the earth's surface. Value comes to land when people want to live on it, work on it, or develop it for recreational purposes.
2. **Modification**—The value of land is increased or decreased by the changes made to surrounding parcels of land.
3. **Fixity**—Investment permanence is created by the fact that land and improvements require long periods of time to pay for themselves.
4. **Situs**—Location preference is the single most important economic characteristic that influences the value of any given parcel of land.

Encumbrances

Anything that obstructs or impairs the use of a property is known as an encumbrance and creates a cloud on title of the fee simple holder's rights in the property. Common encumbrances include, but are not limited to, encroachments, easements, or liens.

Encroachments are unauthorized intrusions of the improvements of one property on the surface or in the air space of an adjoining parcel.

Easements grant a right to use a portion of a property owner's land for a specific purpose. An easement appurtenant may grant ingress and egress to an adjoining parcel of land, thus creating a dominant estate (the parcel that benefits from the easement) and a servient estate (the parcel across which the easement passes).

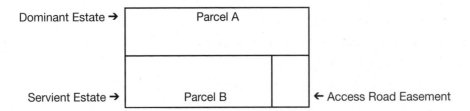

An easement in gross does not benefit any one parcel of real estate, but rather benefits a number of parcels to bring such things as utilities.

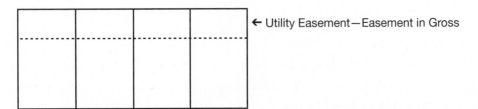

Liens are claims against property that secure payment of a financial obligation owed by the property or the property owner. They come in many varieties.

Liens may be created voluntarily or by operation of law. A lien on real property is voluntary if it is imposed with the consent of the property owner. It is involuntary if it can be imposed without the consent of the property owner.

A mechanic's lien is an example of an involuntary lien. State law specifies the requirements for creating and enforcing a mechanic's lien. In general, a mechanic's lien is available to anyone who provides material or labor for an improvement to real estate, including design services. An architect, surveyor, contractor, carpenter, plumber, electrician, landscaper, and many other participants in the construction process are all entitled to a mechanic's lien if they have not been paid for their services or materials.

There are statutory time periods for

- providing notice to the property owner of the right to file a mechanic's lien.
- filing the lien.
- foreclosing on the lien in the event that the underlying debt is not repaid.

When a mechanic's lien is properly created, it takes priority over all other subsequent liens, except for tax liens.

Foreclosure (sale) of the real estate may be postponed by the property owner during a court hearing on the merits of the case, provided the property owner posts a bond to ensure payment to the claimant. Foreclosure will also be covered in the section on Qualifying the Buyer for Financing on page 139.

A judgment is a determination of a court that may impose an obligation for payment on a property owner. If the judgment is unpaid, a writ of attachment specifies the property that the sheriff will be ordered to sell by a writ of execution.

Tax liens are available to federal, state, and local taxing authorities. Enforcement is usually by tax sale; after the sale, the purchaser receives a tax deed. Tax liens take precedence over all other liens.

A federal tax lien is imposed by the Internal Revenue Service for nonpayment of federal income tax, gift tax, or other taxes.

A state tax lien is imposed for nonpayment of state income tax, sales tax, use tax, or other tax.

A property tax or special assessment tax lien is imposed for nonpayment of state or local tax.

Other encumbrances might include

- marital rights
- rights of parties in possession
- outstanding option to purchase
- judgments against the owner
- unpaid tax liens

Types of Ownership

The primary responsibility of a property seller is to convey marketable title, an ownership interest that a well-informed buyer can reasonably be expected to accept and that the buyer can transfer in a future transaction. There are several ways in which the buyer can be assured of acceptable title.

A title search will reveal the chain of title, the history of conveyances and encumbrances that can be found in the public records. The title search begins with the name of the present owner and the instrument that establishes title in that owner as the grantee. Working back through what is called the grantee index, the name of the grantor to the present owner is found on the deed in which that owner is the grantee. In this way, the person examining the title can go back to the first recorded document of the property. Subsequently, as a method of checking the validity of the search through the grantee index, the searcher moves forward through the grantor index from the first recorded document, verifying that the chain is complete and accurate.

There are many different entities that can acquire ownership in real property: an individual, a group of individuals, a large corporation, a government entity (at any level of government), and others. In addition, there are many different forms of ownership. Estate in severalty (sole ownership) occurs when property is held by one person or a single legal entity. The individual's interest is severed from everyone else's. Tenancy in common involves two or more individuals who own an undivided interest in real property without rights to survivorship (the right of a surviving joint tenant to receive a co-owner's share of interest upon the death of the co-owner). Undivided means that each tenant has an interest in the entire property.

The interest in the estate can vary among the tenants. One party can have 40%, another 25%, and another 35%. If a deed conveying property is made out to two people but does not stipulate their relationship, they are presumed (as in many states) to be tenants in common with equal interest. A party can freely dispose of his or her interest by sale, gift, devise, or descent.

Joint tenancy also involves two or more people but includes a right of survivorship. Four unities must exist to create a valid joint tenancy.

1. **Unity of time.** All tenants must acquire their interests at the same moment. Thus, no new tenants can be added at a later time.
2. **Unity of title.** All tenants must acquire their interest from the same source—the same deed, will, or other conveyance.
3. **Unity of interest.** Each tenant has an equal percentage ownership.
4. **Unity of possession.** Each tenant enjoys the same undivided interest in the whole property and right to occupy the property.

Joint tenancy also includes the right of survivorship. Upon the death of a joint tenant, the tenant's interest in the property is extinguished and is absorbed by the remaining joint tenant(s). The last survivor becomes the sole owner.

Tenancy by the entirety is a form of joint tenancy specifically for married couples in noncommunity property states. Tenancy by the entirety requires the previous four unities, and one more: unity of person. The legal premise is that a husband and wife are an indivisible legal unit. Thus, neither can dispose of the property independently; both must sign the deed in order to transfer the property. Tenancy by the entirety, like tenancy in common, provides the right of survivorship for the remaining spouse.

Partnerships are very popular forms of ownership, especially for properties held as investments. There are two main types of partnerships.

In a general partnership (or regular partnership), all the partners have joint and severable liability for any and all debts of the partnership.

In a limited partnership, the limited partners are not liable for the obligations of the partnership. However, there must be one or more general partners who carry the personal liability for the financial obligations of the partnership. In both types of partnerships, the partners may have differing interests depending on their contribution to the partnership. A limited liability company (LLC) also provides some protection for owners and managers as well as offering some tax benefits.

A partnership is different from a joint venture. In a joint venture, two or more entities join together to develop a real estate project. For example, a landowner, a developer, a lender, and a major tenant participate in a joint venture to develop an office building or a shopping center. A joint venture is created to accomplish a single business venture. Partnerships are created to pool resources and conduct business for profit on an ongoing basis.

Corporations can hold title to real estate, but a corporation is not a popular vehicle for holding investment property because the income is effectively taxed twice. The corporation pays taxes on any income from the property, and then the stockholders pay taxes again when the after-tax income is distributed to them in the form of dividends. Partnerships, on the other hand, do not pay income taxes. They simply file an information return and distribute all of the pretax income to the partners. The partners then pay taxes according to their individual tax brackets.

To avoid double taxation but retain some of the benefits of a corporation, investors may use a Real Estate Investment Trust (REIT). Passive investors—those who do not participate in the management of their properties— are likely to use REITs. A REIT will typically hold a wide variety of investment properties: office buildings, shopping centers, apartments, warehouses, and even raw land. A REIT does not have to pay corporate income tax as long as 90% of its income is distributed to shareholders. At least 75% of the trust's income must come from real estate. Certain other conditions must also be met.

There are other important types of trusts. For instance, an *inter vivos* trust is created during the lifetime of one individual for the benefit of another. (*Inter vivos* means "during the lifetime" in Latin.)

A land trust is often created to conceal the identity of the owner(s). Land is the only asset of the trust; the title is conveyed to the trustee. A land trust is usually used when investors want to speculate on land but would prefer that their identities not be revealed. When you acquire real estate, you get a bundle of rights that constitute your interest in real property. The highest and best form of ownership in real property is called a fee simple estate. The owner of a fee simple estate has the right to

- occupy, rent, or mortgage the property
- sell, dispose of, or transfer ownership of the property
- build on the property (or destroy buildings already part of the property)
- mine or extract oil, gas, and minerals
- restrict or allow the use of the property to others

A leasehold estate gives the holder of the estate a right to occupy the property until the end of the lease when the right will revert to the fee simple holder.

Descriptions of Property

In order to convey real property, the deed must include an unmistakable description of the property. To satisfy the requirement for legal description in the deed, one of four methods may be used.

1. Metes and Bounds. A metes and bounds land description identifies a parcel by specifying its shape and boundaries. Typically, a convenient natural or artificial object is identified to locate the beginning corner of the subject tract, and a compass direction is specified. The surveyor, moving in a clockwise direction from the point of beginning, sets the center of a circle compass on each corner of the parcel to find the direction of travel to each successive corner of the subject tract.

A legal description of a property using the metes and bounds method might read something like: "From the pecan tree ten inches in diameter on the west bank of Salado Creek N 4° 11¢ 18° E, 139.58¢ to a point of beginning." This description would instruct the surveyor on how to begin the metes and bounds survey.

A reference like the pecan tree is seldom used anymore. Surveyors now use permanent monuments. At the corner where the survey begins, a monument in the form of an iron pipe or bar one or two inches in diameter is driven into the ground. Concrete or stone monuments may also be used.

To guard against the possibility that the monument might later be destroyed or removed, it is referenced by means of a connection line to a nearby permanent reference mark established by a government survey agency.

2. Rectangular Survey System. The rectangular survey system (also known as the government survey system or U.S. public lands survey system) was authorized by Congress in order to divide the land systematically north and west of the Ohio River into six-mile squares, now called congressional townships.

This method is based on the system of mapping lines first imagined by ancient geographers and navigators: the east-west latitude lines and the north-south longitude lines that encircle the earth.

Certain longitude lines were selected to act as principal meridians. For each of these, an intercepting latitude line was selected as a baseline. Land is referenced to a principal meridian and a baseline. Every six miles east and west of each principal meridian, parallel survey lines are drawn. The resulting six-mile wide columns are called ranges and are numbered consecutively east and west of the principal meridian.

Every six miles north and south of a baseline, township lines are drawn. They intersect with the range lines and produce six-mile-by-six-mile, mapped squares called townships. Each tier or row of townships thus created is numbered with respect to the baseline. Each 36-square mile township is divided into 36 one-square mile units called sections, which are numbered 1 through 36, starting in the upper right corner of the township. Any two sections with consecutive numbers share a common boundary.

Each square mile section contains 640 acres (43,560 square feet). Any parcel of land smaller than a full 640-acre section is identified by its position in the section. This is done by dividing the section into quarters and halves.

This is an example of a legal description using the rectangular survey system method: "The E $\frac{1}{2}$ of the SE $\frac{1}{4}$ of the NE $\frac{1}{4}$ of Section 28."

3. Recorded Plat. Reference by recorded plat provides the simplest and most convenient method of land description. The vast majority of residential properties are described by this method. When a tract of land is ready for subdividing into lots for homes and businesses, a plat, or map, that shows the location and boundaries of individual building lots is filed in the map records at the courthouse of the county where the property is located.

When the surveyor's plat is filed in the public records office, it becomes notice that a metes and bounds survey has been made and a map has been prepared to show in detail the boundaries of each parcel of land. Each parcel is then assigned a lot number. Each block in the tract is given a block number, and the tract itself is given a name or number. A large subdivision may be further divided into sections.

The following diagram is an example of a legal description using the recorded plat method: "Lot 13, Blk. 4, Sec 3 of Briargrove Hills Subdivision."

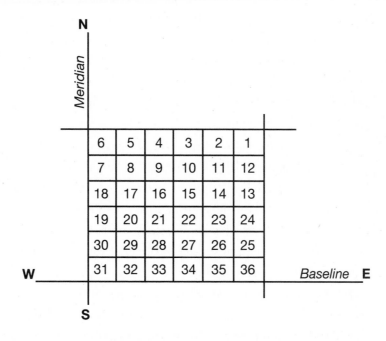

Numbered sections of the township
that is located at Tier 1 North, Range 1 East

Land can also be described by reference to documents other than maps. For instance, if a tract of land was conveyed by deed some years ago and the deed was recorded, the reference can be made to that recorded deed when the property is to be conveyed again. An example of this kind of legal description is, "All the land described in the deed from Abraham Jacobs to Regina Murrow recorded in Book 5106, page 146, county of Kent, state of Oregon, at the public recorder's office for said county and state."

4. Assessor's Parcel Number. In some states, the assessor's parcel number, also known as the appraisal district's account number, is used to describe land. An appraisal district is responsible for determining the appraised (or market) value of every parcel of real estate in a county. The appraisal district assigns a parcel number to each parcel of land in the county to aid in the assessment of property for tax purposes. These parcel numbers are public information, so real estate brokers, appraisers, and investors can and do use them extensively to assist in identifying real properties.

Although the appraisers' maps are public records, they should not be relied upon as the final authority. The appraisal district's parcel number is never used as a legal description in a deed.

Government Rights in Land

Escheat

When a person dies and leaves no heirs and no instructions as to how to dispose of his or her real and personal property, or when property is abandoned, the ownership of the property reverts to the state. This reversion to the state is called *escheat*, from the Anglo-French word meaning "to fall back."

Taxation

The government has the right to collect property taxes from property owners to provide funds for services such as schools, fire and police protection, parks, and libraries. The federal government does not tax property, relying on income taxes for operating revenues, but cities, counties, and, in some cases, the state, do levy taxes on real property. These taxes are levied according to the value of the property and are called *ad valorem* taxes. The tax rate, or millage, is determined through the governing institutions budgetary process, in order to meet its financial requirements. (A mill is one-tenth of a penny.) The amount of the tax will vary based on the value of the property. An owner can appeal the valuation if he or she believes it is unfair, and hopefully lower the taxes due.

To encourage property owners to pay their taxes in full and on time, the government retains the right to seize ownership of real estate upon which taxes are delinquent and to sell the property to recover the unpaid taxes. The taxing authority must depend upon a judicial foreclosure to collect delinquent taxes.

Property taxes are calculated as

$$\text{Taxes} = \text{Assessed value} \times \text{Millage}$$

In some states, tax rates are established as an amount per \$100 of assessed valuation. The assessed value is established by the County Appraisal District (CAD).

The federal government (and, in some cases, state governments and even city governments) raises money through income taxes. Real property is affected by these taxes in several ways:

- taxation of cash flows from investment properties (passive activity income)
- taxation of profits from the sale of real properties (capital gains income)
- depreciation deductions on investment properties

Capital gains on the sale of a principal residence are treated differently from profits on the sale of investment property. The first \$250,000 (\$500,000 for a married couple filing jointly) of capital gain on the sale of a principal residence is tax exempt. There are ownership and residence requirements that apply for both single and married filers. The owner needs to keep records of home improvements. In calculating the capital gain, the value of these improvements is added to the original purchase price. That amount is then subtracted from the sale price to determine the actual profit. In theory, a homeowner could sell a residence every two years, and, as long as no sale produced more than $250,000 (or $500,000 for married couples filing jointly) in profits, no capital gains tax would be due.

Depreciation, a loss in the estimated value of a property, is another factor that affects property taxes. If you own an investment property, you deduct all operating expenses and interest on the mortgage from your income. Then you also are allowed to take another deduction for depreciation, which is now called cost recovery in the tax code. The premise is that the real property's improvements are deteriorating and losing value.

If the property is an apartment or residential property, you can deduct the value of the structure over a life of 27.5 years. Only the building and other improvements can be depreciated; land cannot be depreciated, because the land does not deteriorate physically. Assuming the building is valued at $850,000, one year's depreciation would be $850,000 divided by 27.5 years, or $30,909 per year. Suppose you had an income (minus expenses and interest) of $20,000 last year. Your investment lost value in the amount of $30,909 and netted you only $20,000. $30,909 − $20,000 = $10,909 negative income. You owe no taxes. In fact, you can even carry over the negative amount into subsequent tax years. To review your math skills, see Chapter 5.

When the property is sold, you will have to recapture cost recovery deductions taken. The recapture will be subtracted from the adjusted basis and affect the capital gains calculation.

The cost recovery deduction is allowed on investment properties, but not on residences. However, if you changed your residence and rented your old house, you could then consider the old house an investment property.

Public Controls

Police Power
The government's right to control the owner's use of private property is called police power. The government may enact laws and enforce them to protect the safety, health, morals, and general welfare of the public. Examples of the government's exercise of police power applied to real estate include

- planning and zoning laws
- building, health, and fire codes
- rent controls

Often, these laws restrict the type of use of a property. For example, a zoning ordinance can restrict the construction of an industrial facility in a residential area, protecting the homeowners from excessive noise or noxious odors. Another restriction may require that all homes a developer builds in a location conform to a historic style.

These laws restrict property owners' use of their land but do not constitute a taking (see "Eminent Domain"). Consequently, there is no payment to the property owner who suffers a loss of value through the exercise of police power.

Eminent Domain

The right of government to take ownership of privately held land is called eminent domain. Typically, land is taken for schools, freeways, parks, public housing, urban renewal, and other social and public purposes. Because of its broad definition, many states have placed restrictions on the definition of "social and public purposes" in order to protect property owners. Certain nongovernment entities, such as public utilities, may also take ownership of private property for public benefit.

When direct negotiations with the property owner are unsuccessful, the legal proceeding involved in exercising the right of eminent domain is called condemnation. The property owner must be paid the fair market value of the property taken.

When only a portion of a parcel of land is being taken, severance damages may be awarded in addition to payment for land actually being taken. This is called a partial taking.

An inverse condemnation is a proceeding brought about by a property owner demanding that a government entity purchase his or her land. A property owner might choose this proceeding if his or her land has been adversely affected by the taking of neighboring land. For instance, homeowners at the ends of airport runways may try to force airport authorities to buy their homes because of the noise of aircraft during takeoffs.

Damage awards may also be made when land is not taken but its usefulness is reduced because of a nearby condemnation. The award would be considered consequential damages. An example of this would be when land is taken for a sewage treatment plant. Privately owned land downwind suffers a loss in value owing to the prevalence of foul odors, so the property owner might be awarded consequential damages.

Environmental Hazards and Regulations

Environmental regulations exist at both federal and state levels. Some of the most important federal laws in this area include

- Clean Water Act
- Clean Air Act
- National Environmental Policy Act
- Toxic Substances Control Act
- Safe Drinking Water Act
- Residential Lead-Based Paint Hazard Reduction Act

Private Controls

The government is not the only entity that can control land. Developers often create restrictive covenants or deed restrictions to control everything from the type and size of the homes built in a subdivision to landscaping requirements. Developers can also control what can be parked in a driveway, how high a fence can be built, and whether a property owner can run a home-based business on the premises.

Homeowners associations may be created that require every homeowner to maintain membership. Homeowners can be required to pay assessments to the association and may be subject to foreclosure if they become delinquent.

Private restrictions are designed to preserve a quality of life and to enhance the value of residential properties. Many of the issues addressed in zoning laws, such as building lines and single-family occupancy versus multifamily occupancy may be addressed by the deed restrictions or restrictive covenants placed on the property by the developer. Restrictions are also termed conditions, covenants, and restrictions (CC&Rs). In practice, the term restriction can refer to any condition, covenant, or restriction.

- A condition stipulates an action that a property owner must perform or refrain from performing.
- A covenant is a promise of a property owner.
- A restriction stipulates a forbidden activity or property use.

Water Rights

Water rights are defined by state law and depend on the water source and use. On a navigable body of water, the property owner's boundary will extend to the water's edge or the mean (average) high water line. On a non-navigable body of water, the property owner's boundary will extend to the center of the body of water.

Littoral rights are defined as the rights of a landowner whose property borders on a non-flowing body of water, such as a lake, ocean, or other body of still water. Owners of riparian land (property bordering a flowing stream) may have riparian rights, the rights to use the flowing water.

According to the natural flow doctrine, the owner of riparian land is entitled to the ordinary flow of water but may not impede the use of the ordinary flow by a downstream owner.

According to the doctrine of reasonable use, individual owners of riparian land have the right to reasonable use of the water that does not prevent use by other owners. States following this principle usually assign a higher priority to some uses, such as the domestic use of water on a residential property.

The doctrine of prior appropriation has been used by many western states to give priority to the first users of water for economic reasons. A requirement of prior appropriation is that the water be put to beneficial use. There can be conditions placed on the appropriation that can limit the use. For example, some states require that all users get some water during time of drought.

Water permits issued by the state are used to ration scarce water resources in areas of growing population, particularly in western states.

Use of underground (subterranean) water is vital in many states that have insufficient water from surface sources for residential, agricultural, and commercial uses.

Percolating water drains from the surface to underground strata. States have modified the traditional English rule that there was no limitation on the amount of water a landowner could remove.

The doctrine of correlative rights limits the amount of water that can be taken to a proportionate share based on each owner's share of the surface area.

Underground streams confined to well-defined channels can be difficult to establish. If the location of an underground stream can be determined by a non-invasive method, the type of distribution applied to surface water will be followed.

Property Condition Disclosure Forms

Many states have adopted various property disclosure forms that real estate sellers and their agents are required to furnish to prospective buyers either prior to signing a purchase agreement or at some point prior to closing. Failure to provide the required disclosure may result in a voidable or unenforceable purchase contract.

Licensees should always remember to refrain from making any representations about the physical condition of the property and should always recommend that purchasers have the property evaluated by professional inspectors selected and hired by the purchaser.

Need for Inspection

Many conditions (latent structural defects) can exist and may go undetected by the untrained eye. At a minimum, a purchaser should have a professional evaluation done to determine the condition of the structure and the mechanical systems of the property. Failure to do so could result in a buyer facing expensive unexpected repairs soon after closing, and a seller and the real estate agents facing legal action brought by an unhappy buyer.

Material Facts

In every jurisdiction, agents have a duty to disclose all known material facts about a property being offered for sale. A material fact is any piece of information that a purchaser would take into consideration when making a decision about whether to purchase or about how much to pay.

▶ Property Valuation/Appraisal

Value

Value is ever changing and its movement up and down is influenced by basic economic truths. The actions of buyers and sellers dictate values.

Value, Price, and Cost

Appraisals are most often used to estimate a property's market value. Market value can be defined as the price that a buyer will be likely to pay and that a seller will be likely to accept, when

- both parties are aware of the condition of the property
- neither party is acting under duress
- financing for the transaction is typical of what is available locally

Market value is an estimate of value only. The estimate is not necessarily equal to what a property will actually sell for.

A property's cost is the expense to its owner of buying or improving it. A property's sales price is what someone else pays for it. The sales price can be less than the cost of the land and improvements. This happens when a property owner over-customizes or over-improves a property, failing to take into account the likely needs of a prospective purchaser.

There are a number of other types of property value, including the following ones listed.

Assessed value: determination by the County Appraisal District (CAD) for property tax purposes

Book value: depreciated cost basis used for accounting and tax purposes

Insurance value: the maximum amount that an insurer will be willing to pay for an insured loss

Investment value: the amount that an investor is willing to pay for the right to receive the cash flow produced by the property

Loan value: the maximum loan that can be secured by the property

Salvage value: what the component parts of a building or other improvements will be worth following demolition or removal

Characteristics of Property That Affect Value

Any factor in the climate, terrain, or other natural feature of an area that affects value is called an environmental factor. The effects of environmental factors, such as high pollution from fires following a drought, can be global or local.

Externalities are factors outside of the property that affect property value. An example of an externality is any government action, such as the mortgage interest deduction for homeowners, taken to increase housing affordability, and thus purchases. The life cycle of a property also affects value. The term *life cycle* applies both to individual properties and to neighborhoods.

The initial period of development (growth or integration) becomes a period of equilibrium (when properties are at their highest and best use). Equilibrium is followed by decline (disintegration), when property values go down as maintenance requirements increase and are not met. In areas that undergo the substantial expense of building renovation, a period of revitalization may occur.

Finally, value is affected by supply and demand. As the number of properties available for sale goes up relative to the number of potential buyers, prices will fall. As the number of properties declines while the number of potential buyers remains the same or increases, prices will rise.

Principles of Value

Many principles of value underlie the appraisal process, including the following:

Anticipation: the expectation that property value will rise over time

Assemblage: combining two or more parcels together

Pottage: combining two or more parcels to make them more valuable for a particular purpose, such as construction of a residential or commercial development

Change: forces to which all property is subject, including

Physical: changes caused by the elements, which can occur gradually or over a brief period of time

Political: regulations that affect property use

Economic: employment level, business start-ups, expansions, and failures, and other factors that influence the level of prosperity of a region

Social: demographic and other trends that affect the demand for property

Conformity: individual properties in a residential neighborhood tend to have a higher value when they are of similar architecture, design, age, and size; the same principle applies generally to commercial properties

Competition: a result of increased demand as well as a cause of increased demand. For example, even though a regional mall may offer many stores selling similar products, it will benefit all store owners by bringing more shoppers to the area

Highest and best use: the legally allowed property use that makes maximum physical use of a site and generates the highest income

Principle of diminishing marginal returns: the relationship between additional improvements to a property and the value added. There is a point at which these changes no longer provide additional value equal to the investment

Progression: the benefit to a property of being located in an area of more desirable properties; a small, plain house on a street of mansions will benefit from proximity to them

Regression: the detriment to a property of being located in a neighborhood of less desirable properties; a large, over-improved house on a street of small, plain houses will have a lower value than it would in a neighborhood of comparable houses

Substitution: the principle that the typical buyer will want to pay no more for a property than would be required to buy another, equivalent property; this principle, when applied to income-producing property, is called opportunity cost. In addition, an investor will want to pay no more for real estate than for another investment offering the same likely risk and potential reward

Methods of Estimating: Value/Appraisal Process

Typically, an appraiser uses three different approaches in developing a final estimate of the value of a property: market data approach, cost approach, and income approach. In the final reconciliation, the appraiser gives the most weight to the value that would be most appropriate for that property.

Market Data Approach (Direct Sales Comparison)

If the property being appraised is a single-family residence, the most important determinant of value is the price that other similar properties have commanded in the open market. In using the market data approach, the appraiser will select comparables (comps) to compare to the subject property (the property being appraised). For example, if several comparable properties sold for $100,000, the subject would most likely sell for about $100,000 as well. An appraiser would prefer to have at least three comps for a market data appraisal.

Features that should be considered in choosing comps include

- size
- proximity to the subject
- quality of construction

- age
- number of bedrooms, bathrooms, and total rooms
- date of sale, preferably within the last six months
- similarity of features such as fireplaces, pools, spas, and patios

The ideal comparable would be a house that sold very recently and is the same size; in the same condition; the same age; on the same block in the same subdivision; with the same number of bedrooms, bathrooms, and total rooms; and with all of the same features as the subject. Typically, an appraiser will use sales within the last six months only.

Obviously the chances of finding such a comparable are not very good. So the appraiser must secure the best comparables available and make adjustments to bring the comparables as close to the subject as possible. For example, Comparable A has three bedrooms and sold for $100,000. The subject has four bedrooms. In this subdivision, historically, one more bedroom has added $6,000 to the purchase price of a home. So the appraiser would assume that Comparable A, if it had had four bedrooms instead of three, would have sold for $6,000 more, or $106,000.

In analyzing the adjusted comparable sales, the appraiser would give the most weight to the comparable with the fewest adjustments.

Cost Approach

When the property is not an income-producing property and it is difficult to find a market comparable, the cost approach to value is often used. This approach is most often used with unique properties. For instance, if you had to appraise a mosque located in Nacogdoches, Texas, you would have a hard time finding three comparable properties in the same area. The cost approach would also be useful in appraising properties such as a college campus, an abandoned fire station, or a state capitol building.

The formula for determining value using the cost approach is as follows:

$$\text{Value} = \text{Replacement or Reproduction Cost} - \text{Accrued Depreciation} + \text{Land Value}$$

The appraiser begins by estimating the replacement cost of the improvements. Replacement cost is the cost, at today's prices and using today's methods of construction, for an improvement having the same or equivalent usefulness as the subject property. Or, the appraiser may estimate the reproduction cost, the cost of creating an exact replica of the improvements.

This would show the value of a new building. Because the subject property is not new, adjustments must be made for depreciation. The amount of adjustment depends on the amount and type of depreciation. There are three types of depreciation.

1. Physical deterioration results from wear and tear through use, such as wall-to-wall carpet that has been worn thin, or a dishwasher, garbage disposal, or water heater that must be replaced. Nature, neglect, vandalism, and other factors contribute to physical deterioration.

2. Functional obsolescence results from outmoded equipment, faulty or outmoded design, inadequate structural facilities, or over-adequate structural facilities.

3. Environmental or economic depreciation results from factors outside of the property over which the owner has no control.

Physical and functional obsolescence can be either curable or incurable. Curable obsolescence can be fixed at reasonable cost. Examples include worn carpeting or outdated kitchen appliances. Incurable obsolescence cannot be fixed at a reasonable cost. For example, an illogical room layout or a kitchen that is too small for the size of the house would be considered incurable obsolescence.

The value of the land must also be considered in determining value by the cost approach. The value of the land is established as though it were vacant, using the market data approach. While land value can decrease, land does not depreciate in the sense that it is subject to physical or functional obsolescence.

Income Approach

If a property produces income in the form of rent and other revenues, its value is estimated by analyzing the amount and stability of the income it can produce. The income approach, used to value properties such as apartment complexes, shopping centers, and office buildings, considers the monetary returns a property can be expected to produce and then converts that amount into a value the property should sell for if placed on the market. This is called capitalization of the income stream. To capitalize means to convert future cash flows to a present value.

The formula for determining value by the income approach is

$$\text{Value} = \text{Net Operating Income} \div \text{Capitalization Rate}$$

The income is the net income that the property produces after paying all maintenance and operating expenses of the building. The capitalization rate (cap rate) is determined by the appraiser as a function of the market and the type and location of the property.

Purpose and Use of Appraisal

An appraisal is defined under federal law as "a written statement used in connection with a federally related transaction that is independent and impartially prepared by a licensed, certified appraiser that states an opinion of the defined value of an adequately described property as of a specific date that is supported by the presentation and analysis of relevant market information." The real estate practitioner defines appraisal more simply as "the act or process of estimating value."

Market value or fair market value is the highest price that a property will bring if all of the following apply:

1. The payment is made in cash or its equivalent.
2. The property is exposed on the open market for a reasonable length of time.
3. The buyer and seller are fully informed as to market conditions and the uses to which the property may be put.

4. Neither buyer nor seller is under abnormal pressure to conclude a transaction.

5. The seller is capable of conveying marketable title.

Role of Appraiser

There are seven major steps in the appraisal process:

1. **State the problem.** The nature of the appraisal assignment must be clearly understood. The assignment may be to find a market value of the subject property. If so, that should be stated.

2. **Determine the kinds and sources of data necessary.**
   - What are the characteristics of the subject property?
   - What economic or other factors will play a role in determining property value?
   - What approach(es) will be most appropriate in this appraisal, and what kind of data will be necessary?

3. **Determine the highest and best use of the site.**

4. **Estimate the value of the site.**

5. **Estimate the property's value by each of the appropriate approaches** (market data, cost, and/or income).

6. **Reconcile the different values reached by the different approaches to estimate the property's most probable market value.** This process is called *reconciliation* or *correlation*.

7. **Report the estimate of value to the client in writing.** There are several types of documents that may be prepared.
   - The narrative appraisal report provides a lengthy discussion of the factors considered in the appraisal and the reasons for the conclusion of value.
   - The form report is used most often for single-family residential appraisals. A Uniform Residential Appraisal Report (URAR) is required by various agencies and organizations. Computerized appraisal generation is possible and is increasingly expected by banks and other lenders.
   - Reports may be written in other formats, which are defined by the Uniform Standards of Professional Appraisal Practice (USPAP). The self-contained report is as complete as the narrative appraisal report and should include explanations of the methods used during appraisal and the appraiser's conclusion. The summary report is less detailed than the self-contained report, and the restricted report, which reveals only minimal information and should be used only by clients, is less detailed than the summary report. Using either of the two latter types of reports will require the consent of the client.

Competitive Market Analysis

Real estate licensees do not generally prepare appraisals, although licensed brokers are permitted to do so provided they follow the uniform standards. Licensees must be careful to state that a competitive market analysis (CMA) is not an appraisal and should not be regarded as such. All CMAs must include a notice to this effect.

The CMA is a tool used by the licensee to enable prospective sellers or buyers to identify a range of value in a given neighborhood. It identifies the properties currently listed, those that have been on the market without success and have expired, and those that have sold.

The client can then choose an asking or offering price that is realistic and within the range. Sellers who establish an asking price above the upper end of the range will make their property invisible to many of the best potential buyers for their properties. Buyers who offer too little, or lowball, will often insult the sellers and make it impossible to negotiate with them.

▶ Financing

General Concepts

Mortgages, Deeds of Trust, and Their Provisions

A mortgage is a pledge of property to secure the repayment of a debt. If the debt is not repaid as agreed between the lender and borrower, the lender can force the sale of the pledged property and apply the proceeds to repayment of the debt.

Leaving the borrower in possession of the pledged property is known as *hypothecation*. The borrower conveys title to the lender but retains the use of the property. This conveyance of title in the mortgage agreement is conditional. The mortgage states that if the debt is repaid on time, title returns to the borrower. This is known as a defeasance clause.

Lenders require that borrowers pledge the real estate as collateral for a mortgage loan. If the borrower defaults on the loan, the lender can terminate the borrower's interest in a property through a judicial process called foreclosure. Traditionally, because the borrower had possession of the property, this process was the only way for a lender to seek satisfaction in the event of a default. However, a judicial foreclosure requiring court action can be time-consuming and very costly.

Some states provide for an alternative to traditional foreclosure in order to avoid the typical drawbacks of the process. One form of mortgage document is the deed of trust, sometimes called a trust deed. In a deed of trust, a third party is given the power of sale by the borrower. The deed provides for a nonjudicial foreclosure when all statutory requirements are followed. The process of nonjudicial foreclosure is smoother and less time-consuming than traditional foreclosure, and is therefore appealing to a lender.

The other major document that a borrower signs, besides the deed of trust, is the promissory note. This is a promise to pay the loan off according to a schedule of payments at a certain interest rate over a specified period of time.

The two documents are closely related. The deed of trust stipulates what will happen in the event of a default in the terms of the promissory note. In fact, it is standard practice to record only the deed of trust because it is tied so closely to the promissory note.

Real estate can be pledged as collateral for a loan using any of the following four methods.

1. The standard or regular mortgage is the most common type used today. The borrower conveys title to the lender as security for the debt. The mortgage contains a statement that the mortgage will become void if the debt it secures is paid in full and on time.

2. An equitable mortgage is a written agreement that does not follow the form of a regular mortgage, but is still considered by the courts to be one. An equitable mortgage can arise in a number of ways. For example, a prospective buyer generally gives the seller a monetary deposit along with an offer to purchase property. If the seller refuses the offer and also refuses to return the deposit, the court will hold that the purchaser has an equitable mortgage in the amount of the deposit against the seller's property.

3. In some cases, the borrower may convey the deed to the pledged property to the lender as a deed as security for a loan. If the loan is repaid in full and on time, the borrower can force the lender to convey the real property back to him or her. Like the equitable mortgage, a deed used as security is treated according to its intent, not its label.

4. A deed of trust is a three-party agreement including a borrower, a lender, and a neutral third party. The key aspect of this method is that the borrower executes a deed to the trustee rather than to the lender. If the borrower pays the debt in full and on time, the trustee delivers a release of liability to the borrower.

Qualifying the Buyer for Financing

In commercial loans, lenders look only to the income from the property for repayment, so they are not particularly concerned about the borrower's income. However, in residential loans, the borrower's income is of prime importance because that is what will be used to repay the loan. The borrower's income is analyzed from the standpoint of its quantity and durability. Also, the borrower's willingness to pay is of prime importance.

To evaluate the borrower's quantity of income, the lender calculates the front ratio: the ratio of the requested monthly payment to the borrower's gross income. The monthly payment is the sum of all housing costs: principal, interest, taxes, and insurance (PITI). Most conventional lenders will not let the front ratio exceed 28%. For example, if a borrower's monthly income is $5,000, the monthly housing costs could not be more than 28% of $5,000, or $1,400.

The lender is also concerned about other fixed obligations the borrower may already have. Fixed obligations include any payments that the borrower is required to make on a regular basis, such as car payments, bank loans, credit cards, open charge accounts, and so on. The lender calculates the ratio of housing cost plus other fixed obligations to gross monthly income. Most lenders will not let this ratio exceed 36%. So if the borrower makes $5,000 a month, the amount of housing costs plus fixed obligations could not exceed 36% of $5,000, or $1,800.

Lenders want to be assured that a borrower will be able to pay back the loan in a timely manner. Depending on the kind of property for which the loan is being sought, lenders make various analyses to determine the creditworthiness of the borrower.

Unimproved land is the most difficult loan to underwrite because it produces little or no income to use to pay back the loan. Also, because the borrower does not occupy the property, there may be little incentive to pay back the loan in the event of financial difficulties.

Income-producing properties are analyzed on their ability to generate enough cash flow to pay back the loan. The property's net operating income must cover the debt service (the amount of money required to make regular payments on the loan).

The lender typically requires a certain debt coverage ratio, depending on the type of property and the quality of the income. The debt coverage ratio is equal to the net operating income of the property divided by the debt service on the loan. For instance, if a property had a net operating income of $120,000 and the lender required a debt coverage ratio of 1.2, the maximum debt service the lender would allow would be $100,000.

$$\$120,000 \div 1.2 = \$100,000$$

To review your math skills, see Chapter 8.

Types of Loans

The most common residential loan is amortized, or paid off, in equal monthly installments that include principal and interest. During a time of reasonable interest rates, the borrower will most often choose a fixed interest rate for the life of the loan.

The most popular time period for fixed rate loans is 15 or 30 years; however, other loan terms are also available. Borrowers who choose a shorter time frame save a sizable amount of money in interest payments.

In some instances, a loan will be structured as an amortized loan with a term of 30 years, but the loan will balloon after a certain period. That is, the loan becomes due and payable before the end of the amortization term. The loan may balloon in five, seven, or ten years, or however long the lender stipulates. A balloon loan usually charges a lower interest rate than a regular fixed-rate loan. Because the lenders don't have to wait 30 years to get their money back, they can afford to charge a lower interest rate because the inflation risk is reduced.

Balloon loans are frequently used in seller financing, because the seller typically does not want to wait for 30 years to be paid in full. Buyers may find a balloon loan attractive if they know that they are going to be selling the property before the loan is due.

During times of high interest rates, a borrower may prefer an adjustable rate loan. The lender will give the borrowers a lower-than-market interest rate for a certain period of time, typically a year. Then, the rate is adjusted each year (or whatever time period is agreed upon) to adjust for inflation. The most common type of adjustable rate loan is a one-year adjustable plan.

The rate is adjusted at the specified time based on some predetermined indicator, such as Treasury bill rates. For the borrower's protection, there is usually a cap, or limit, on the amount the rate can be increased in any given year or over the life of the loan.

Sources

The sources of loanable funds and the financing arrangements available to a prospective borrower increase each year. Loans can even be arranged on the Internet and by brokers and real estate salespersons.

Even though the choices grow daily, there are two major types of loans:

1. loans that are insured or guaranteed by an agency of government
2. loans that are funded in the private sector

The loans that are neither insured nor guaranteed by an agency of government (loans funded in the private sector) are known as conventional loans.

A significant number of residential loans are originated by mortgage bankers and mortgage brokers. Regulated financial institutions, including commercial banks, savings and loans, mutual savings banks, and credit unions, provide a significant amount of funds for residential loans.

Whether the loan is from a bank or a mortgage company, the loan will most likely be sold to investors through the secondary mortgage market. The major purchasers of home loans are

- Federal National Mortgage Association (Fannie Mae)
- Federal Home Loan Mortgage Corporation (FHLMC or Freddie Mac)
- Government National Mortgage Association (GNMA or Ginnie Mae)

The loans purchased are most often pooled and used to back securities that are sold to other investors. The money is then available to invest in additional mortgages.

These entities buy so many loans that they have a great deal of influence on the operation of the loan origination or primary market. A loan that meets Fannie Mae's guidelines is called a *conforming loan*. Most conventional loans will use uniform instruments for

- loan applications
- appraisal reporting forms
- closing statements

In addition, there is a limit to the loan amount of a conforming loan. This limit changes from year to year. In 2006, the maximum amount of a conforming loan for a property in the continental United States was $417,000.

Government Programs

Decades ago, the federal government established a number of programs to get as many people into homes as possible. Two examples are the Federal Housing Administration (FHA) and the Department of Veteran Affairs (VA) loans. Both are designed to reduce the lender's risk when low down payment loans are made.

FHA mortgage insurance requires the payment of a premium, a sum of money paid in addition to the amount of the loan. In 2006, the premium was 1.5% of the loan amount, payable at the time the loan is funded. In addition, an annual premium of 0.5% of the loan balance is payable over the life of the loan. However, once the mortgage reaches the point in its schedule of payments where the loan-to-value (LTV) ratio is approximately 80%, the annual premium will be automatically canceled. If the borrower makes principal curtailments, he or she can request cancellation of the premium once the LTV is 80%. (These requirements are for 30-year, fixed rate mortgages. Other terms and types differ.) FHA insurance covers the entire loan balance for the life of the loan.

The VA program is designed to encourage lenders to make loans to veterans. Basically, the VA guarantees a portion of the loan in sufficient amount to entice lenders to make loans. Depending on eligibility, a veteran may be able to borrow 100% of the purchase price up to approximately $200,000. Rather than a premium, the VA charges a funding fee. The amount of the funding fee for purchase and construction loans ranges from 1.25% to 3.3%, depending on the amount of down payment and the veteran's service status.

Private Mortgage Insurance (PMI)

There are more than a dozen private mortgage companies, which offer protection to the lender similar to that offered by FHA. They do not offer protection for the entire loan, only for the top 20% to 25%. This allows lenders to make higher LTV loans without increasing their risk. Like FHA, the borrower pays both an up front and an annual premium. The 1999 Home Owners Protection Act requires that when the principal reaches 78% of the property's original value, the PMI is automatically cancelled, subject to certain restrictions.

Mortgages

A mortgage is a pledge of property made by a mortgagor (the borrower) to pledge collateral (the property) that may be sold at auction (foreclosure) when the borrower defaults and fails to fulfill the promises made in the mortgage instrument. The mortgage (pledge of the collateral) is given for the benefit of the mortgagee (the lender). Remember that in real estate terminology, words ending in *or* refer to the person giving something (the borrower gives the pledge), and the words ending in *ee* refer to the person receiving something (the lender receives the benefit of the pledge of the collateral). Forget about the fact that the lender gives the money; it is the pledge of collateral that is important in this discussion.

When a lender makes a loan, the borrower signs a promissory note that promises to repay the loan and defines the terms of the repayment.

A mortgage pledges the property as collateral when duly executed by the borrower. When all payments have been made per the terms of the note, the lender (mortgagee) will issue a Release of Lien that should be recorded to remove the encumbrance affecting the title to the property.

A defaulting borrower faces penalties of varying severity. Late charges will be incurred if the borrower is late in making a payment. If the borrower remains in default, an acceleration clause may be invoked by the lender. An acceleration clause gives the lender the right to collect the balance of the loan immediately. Finally, if the debt remains unpaid, the formal process of foreclosure will begin.

The process of foreclosure will depend on the terms of the mortgage instrument. If it contains a "Power of Sale" clause, a nonjudicial foreclosure may take place providing all statutory requirements are followed. In the absence of a "Power of Sale" clause, a judicial process will be required.

On a default by the borrower, the traditional remedy for the holder of a mortgage was strict foreclosure in which the property could be sold immediately. The modern requirement is a foreclosure action that must be brought in court following statutory notice and other requirements unless a deed of trust instrument provides for a nonjudicial foreclosure.

If the security instrument is a mortgage with power of sale (deed of trust), the property may be sold without a court hearing. In this case, state law still applies, and there will be specific notice and procedural requirements. Even after the property has been sold at public auction, there may be a right of redemption for the borrower within a statutory time period.

If the proceeds of the foreclosure sale do not cover the amount owed on the loan, some states allow the lender to obtain a deficiency judgment against the borrower. This means that other assets can be claimed by the lender to satisfy the remaining indebtedness. Other states provide homeowners with anti-deficiency protection in the event that the proceeds of sale on loan default do not cover the amount owed. This means that the lender has no recourse except the real estate.

In the case of a deed of trust, the trustee is authorized to sell the property in the event of a default to pay off the remaining debt. When the property is sold, a trustee's deed is given to the new owner. As with a mortgage foreclosure, state law will dictate whether or not the lender is entitled to seek a deficiency judgment in the event that the proceeds of a forced sale do not cover the amount owed.

If the existing mortgage does not include a due-on-sale clause, its benefits can be passed to the buyer. The buyer can purchase property **subject to the existing loan**. In this case, the seller remains responsible for the loan, even thought the buyer pays the remaining payments.

In an **assumption**, the buyer has a written agreement with the seller to pay the loan and is therefore obligated to the seller. However, the seller is still responsible to the lender.

The best route for the seller is to request the lender to substitute the buyer's liability for theirs. This is called **novation**.

Financing/Credit Laws

Truth-in-Lending Act and Regulation Z

The Federal Consumer Credit Protection Act, also known as the Truth-in-Lending Act (TIL), went into effect in 1969. It is implemented by the Federal Reserve Board. As implemented by Regulation Z, the act requires that borrowers be clearly shown how much they are paying for credit in both dollar terms and percentage terms before committing to the loan. The borrower is also given the right to rescind the transaction under certain conditions.

The act requires certain disclosures in advertising anything that involves financing. If an advertisement contains any one of the TIL list of financing terms (called trigger terms), the ad must also include five disclosures. The following are some of the trigger terms:

- amount of down payment
- amount of any additional payments
- number of payments
- period of payments
- dollar amount of any finance charge
- statement that there is no financing

If the ad contains any of the trigger terms above, then the ad must also include these disclosures:

- cash price or the amount of the loan
- amount of down payment or a statement that none is required
- number, amount, and frequency of repayments
- annual percentage rate
- deferred payment price or total payments

Equal Credit Opportunity Act

The Equal Credit Opportunity Act, a federal law that has been in effect since 1975, prohibits discrimination in the granting of credit on the basis of age, sex, race, color, marital status, religion, or national origin. It also prohibits discrimination against applicants who receive all or part of their incomes from public assistance.

Factors that can legitimately be considered are the applicant's income, stability of the source of the income, total assets and liabilities, and credit rating (history of use of credit).

Fair Credit Reporting Act

Congress enacted the Fair Credit Reporting Act (FCRA) in 1970 to protect consumers from the reporting of inaccurate credit information to credit reporting agencies. This legislation is administered by the Federal Trade Commission. It requires that if a buyer of real estate is denied credit because of an unfavorable credit report, the lender refusing to make the loan must reveal to the buyer the identity of the credit agency reporting the information that was the basis of the rejection. Most negative items are to be dropped from the report after a period of seven years; an exception is bankruptcy information, which may be held for ten years. In underwriting the mortgage, a complex calculation is performed to produce a score. The credit score is used to determine the risk to the lender, It influences eligibility for credit and the interest rate charged.

The three major credit agencies are Equifax, TransUnion, and Experian. Under the terms of the FCRA, consumers are entitled to a free copy of their credit report annually from each agency.

Commercial Financing

Financing for commercial properties is different from residential. Funding sources include insurance companies, pension funds, mortgage banking firms, savings banks, and regional banks. There are also specialized firms that channel investment monies by issuing securities to investors (commercial mortgage backed securities, or CMBS). The commercial funding process may be lengthy and requires significant documentation, including

- an income and expense statement which reflects a solid income stream, or a business plan which predicts such
- tenant profiles (if applicable), with a copy of all leases
- financial statements for all the principals
- the property appraisal
- complete plans and surveys of the property, if available

When fixtures like manufacturing machinery are purchased on credit, the creditor can record a chattel mortgage. If the borrower defaults, the creditor can seize the mortgaged items.

▶ Contracts/Agency Relationships

General

A contract is a legally enforceable agreement between two parties to do something (performance) or to refrain from certain acts (forbearance). To create a real estate contract, there are seven requirements. A contract must

1. involve legally competent parties
2. be in writing as required by the Statute of Frauds (one notable exception is a lease for one year or less)
3. be signed by the parties to the agreement
4. have a lawful objective
5. include consideration (this does not need to be money)
6. mention offer and acceptance and notification of the acceptance
7. contain a legal description of the property

Listing Agreements

A real estate transaction that makes use of the services of one or more real estate licensees usually begins with an agreement between property owner and licensee (on behalf of their company) to list the property for sale, lease, or trade.

The listing agreement includes

- identity of the parties
- legal description of the property
- object of the agreement (property sale, exchange, lease)
- term (length of time) of the agreement
- definition of the agent's role and list of the agent's obligations
- statement of compensation to which the agent is entitled on fulfilling his or her obligations
- safety clause stipulating that the agent's compensation is to be paid if a sale is transacted with a buyer who was introduced to the property owner by the agent, within a stated period after termination of the listing agreement
- authorization for the agent to use the local multiple-listing system, Internet-listing system, or other marketing forum
- authorization for the use of subagents or for the broker to function as an intermediary
- authorization for the agent to retain a key to the property, or to use a lock box or other means of property entry in the owner's absence
- authorization to receive a deposit or other funds on behalf of the buyer and stipulation as to how those funds are to be handled
- arbitration or mediation provision to be used in the event of a contract dispute
- statement of compliance with all applicable fair housing laws
- any other provision required by law
- signature of seller and signature of broker or the broker's sales associate (general agent)

Legal Requirements

In order to be enforceable, a listing agreement must be signed by both the real estate licensee and the property owner (or the property owner's representative acting under a power of attorney or a court order).

Fiduciary Duties and Representations

Once a listing is signed, the broker is obligated to all of the fiduciary duties that an agent owes to a principal. The owner owes the agent honesty, availability, indemnification, and compensation.

Terminating a Listing

A listing agreement is terminated under the same conditions as other contracts. Those conditions include

- performance of the agreed-upon terms
- mutual rescission of the parties
- passage of the agreed-upon time
- death of the seller or broker
- abandonment
- breach of a fiduciary duty

Buyer-Broker Agreements

In recent years, it has become common for buyers to appoint exclusive agents to represent them in real estate transactions. The contract that appoints an exclusive buyer agent should contain the basic elements found in a listing agreement with a few minor changes. The subjects to be addressed include, but are not limited to,

- the names of the client and the agent
- a definition of the market area
- how the agent will be compensated
- the term of the agreement
- the authority of the agent
- the duties of the agent
- the duties of the client
- provisions for dispute resolution
- notices relating to Fair Housing, anti-trust, and other legal disclosures
- signatures of the parties

Offers/Purchase Agreements

The sales contract (sometimes called an earnest money contract) is arguably the most important document used in a real estate transaction. Because a defective contract can allow either buyer or seller to end the transaction, real estate practitioners must be thoroughly familiar with contract law.

A contract is a legally enforceable agreement to do or not do a certain thing. Most contracts are based on promises by the parties involved to act in some manner. Examples of such acts would be to pay money, to provide services, or to deliver title. However, a contract can also contain a promise to forbear (not to act) by one or more of its parties. For example, a lender may agree not to foreclose on a delinquent mortgage loan if the borrower agrees to a new payment schedule.

A contract may be either **express** or **implied**.

- An express contract occurs when the parties to the contract declare their intentions either orally or in writing. Leases and contracts to purchase real estate are examples of express contracts. The Statute of Frauds requires that all documents affecting title to or an interest in real estate be expressed in writing, except for a lease of one year or less.
- An implied contract is created by the actions of the parties rather than by words. An example of an implied contract is the agreement between you and a restaurant when you walk in and sit down. The presence of tables, silverware, and menus implies that you will be served food. When you order, you imply that you are going to pay the bill.

A contract may be **bilateral** or **unilateral**.

- A bilateral contract results when a promise is exchanged for a promise. A bilateral contract is essentially an agreement that says, "I will do this, and you will do that." A real estate sales contract is a good example of a bilateral contract.
- A unilateral contract results when a promise is exchanged for performance. It is essentially an agreement that says, "I will do this if you do that." If the sales manager offers a bonus if you sell $3,000,000 worth of real estate, you are not obligated to sell $3,000,000 worth of real estate—but the sales manager is obligated to pay you the bonus if you do.

A contract can be construed by the courts to be **valid, void, voidable,** or **unenforceable**.

- A valid contract meets all the requirements of law. It is binding upon its parties and legally enforceable in a court of law. For a contract to be valid, it must meet five requirements:
  1. The parties must be legally competent.
  2. There must be mutual agreement.
  3. The objective must be lawful.
  4. There must be consideration given (value exchanged).
  5. The contract must be in writing when required by law.
- A void contract has no legal effect and, in fact, is not a contract at all. Even though the parties may have intended to enter into a contract, no legal rights are created and no party is bound. The word *void* means the absence of something.
- A voidable contract binds at most one party. For example, when one party is guilty of fraud, the other party may void the contract. But if the offended party wishes to fulfill the contract, then the party who committed fraud is still bound to the terms of the contract. A contract with a minor is voidable at the option of the minor party.
- An unenforceable contract is one in which neither party can enforce the obligations. There are a number of reasons that a contract may be unenforceable, such as if there were coercion.

Counteroffers/Multiple Counteroffers

Purpose of Offer and Counteroffer

The real estate sales contract begins as a written offer from buyer to seller and will typically include

- identities of all parties to the transaction
- full legal description of the real estate, as well as a listing of any personal property to be included
- sales price, including the amount of down payment and an indication of how the remainder of the price will be paid at closing
- financing contingency giving details of the type of financing the buyer hopes to obtain and stipulating a deadline for release of the contingency
- statement that the transaction is contingent on a sale of other property of the buyer (the seller will want a deadline for release of the contingency, particularly if a noncontingent offer is made while the transaction is pending)
- name of the escrow agent for the transaction, by whom the fee for this service will be paid
- list of property inspections to be made and by whom, including deadlines for the inspections as well as the appropriate notifications to buyer and/or seller (the seller will want a limit on expenditures for any pest control treatment or necessary repairs)
- list of applicable categories of disclosure required by state and federal law, which may include location in a flood, earthquake, or other zone, and the presence of hazardous materials, such as lead-based paint
- provision for arbitration or mediation of disputes that may arise between the parties
- remedies, including suit for specific performance, money damages, or acceptance of liquidated damages, in the event that one of the parties breaches the agreement
- statement of compliance with the federal Foreign Investment in Real Property Tax Act (FIRPTA)
- statement of compliance with all applicable fair housing laws
- statement of compliance with any other state or federal law not already mentioned
- provision for a final walk-through by the buyer to ensure that the property has been adequately maintained before closing
- statement of who will bear the risk of loss in the event of property damage or destruction between the time the contract is signed and the transaction is closed
- statement of the agency representation and commission owed
- signature of the buyer(s) and space for signature of the seller(s)

An offer will expire (end) if it is not accepted by the deadline specified in its terms. If no deadline is specified, a reasonable time period will be implied. An offer can be withdrawn at any time prior to the offeror being notified of its acceptance.

Any change to the terms of an offer is a counteroffer and has the effect of rejecting the initial offer and making a new offer. The offer and acceptance must both be made voluntarily (without coercion) and without misrepresentation.

Valid Methods of Communicating Offers

Although verbal negotiations may appear to save time and to be efficient, a licensee needs to remember that agreements for the sale of real estate must be reduced to writing to be enforceable. The Statute of Frauds requires that there be a written offer and written acceptance. As soon as the written acceptance is obtained, the offeror must be notified of the acceptance. The notification is accomplished by delivering a copy of the accepted document to the offeror.

Remember that a party making an offer or a counteroffer may revoke that offer or counteroffer at any time prior to acceptance by the other party. Revocation of a written offer or counteroffer must be made in writing to be effective.

When one party fails to perform as required by the contract, a breach of contract or default has occurred. The wronged or innocent party has six possible remedies.

1. **Accept partial performance.** If the purchaser is expecting 25 acres to be conveyed, but the survey shows that there are only 23.57 acres in the tract, the purchaser may accept the property as is.
2. **Rescind the contract unilaterally.** The wronged party can simply rescind or cancel the contract and return to the status prior to executing the contract.
3. **Sue for specific performance.** Specific performance means doing exactly what the contract requires. The party seeking specific performance must have acted in good faith and not committed a material breach of the contract.
4. **Sue for money damages.** For example, if a seller cannot perform, but the buyer has already spent a large amount of money on inspections, appraisals, and so on, the buyer could sue to recover the money spent.
5. **Accept liquidated money damages.** This remedy, available only to the seller, means retaining the earnest money.
6. **Mutually rescind the contract.** Sometimes both parties are better off just walking away from the contract and canceling the agreement. A mutual rescission must be expressed in writing.

Before closing a real estate transaction, the parties involved must be assured that certain conditions are met. By signing a contract, the parties affirm their mutual agreement. Once they are bound to the terms of the agreement, they can then take the time to ensure that these conditions are met. If there was no contract, and the parties were not bound to honor their agreement, one or both of the parties might spend considerable time and money on a transaction that could fall through.

There are three basic contingencies.

1. **Buyer's ability to obtain suitable financing.** When buyers start looking at properties, they typically meet with a lender to determine what loan amount they would likely qualify for. Once they have selected a specific property, they must get lender approval for a loan on that property. This takes time, so it is important to have the property tied to a specific contractual agreement.
2. **Buyer's approval of title matters.** Buyers generally will not take the time and effort to examine the title until they have a firm agreement from the seller.

3. **Buyer's acceptance of the property condition.** A property may appear to be in good condition when the buyer initially views it, but the buyer will likely require a thorough inspection of the property after negotiating with the seller. The inspection, too, will take time to complete.

Leases as Contracts

A lease is a contract wherein a property owner (lessor) transfers the rights of possession, quiet enjoyment, and use to the tenant (lessee) for a period of time, thus creating a leasehold estate. When property ownership transfers during the term of a lease, the lease remains binding upon the new owner.

This topic will be discussed in more detail under "Property Management" on page 165.

Options

An option is a unilateral contract. An option to purchase enables a purchaser to purchase a property at a set price within a given time frame. An option to terminate grants a purchaser the unrestricted right to terminate a contract without penalty within a given time frame.

To create a valid option, the property owner must be paid some cash (valuable consideration), and time is of the essence.

Rescission and Cancellation Agreements

Contracts usually come to an end by completion of the objective of the contract or by expiration of the term specified in the agreement. On occasion, the parties will decide to end the agreement and to restore each other to the position enjoyed prior to entering into the agreement. This is identified in legal terms as mutual rescission.

Agency appointments may be ended early by termination or withdrawal. If a property owner has entered into an exclusive right to sell listing agreement and decides to terminate, he or she may withdraw the listing and request that the agent stop marketing the property. If the owner then sells the property during the term of the listing, the broker is still entitled to receive the agreed-upon compensation.

The seller may terminate with the agreement and consent of the agent. To effect a termination, the broker may require some compensation to cover expenses incurred through the date of the termination. If all parties can reach agreement, the termination becomes a mutual rescission. When an agreement cannot be reached, the property owner should seek legal counsel before attempting to fire the agent, and the agent should seek legal counsel before quitting or renouncing the agency appointment.

With regard to leases and purchase agreements, the parties may cancel an agreement through mutual rescission or may create a substitute agreement to replace the original contract. The substitution of a new agreement for an existing contract is known as a novation. The new agreement should reference the agreement that it is replacing and clearly state that it replaces the original agreement.

Broker-Salesperson Agreements

Most salespersons function as independent contractors rather than as employees of the broker. The federal tax code requires that the broker and salesperson enter into a written contract to create the working relationship. The agreement should clearly stipulate that the salesperson is an independent contractor and that

- he or she has paid his or her own licensing fees
- he or she is free to work on his or her own time schedule
- he or she may perform the tasks of the business where he or she wishes
- compensation is based solely on production and that no salary, hourly wages, or benefits are paid or provided
- the salesperson is responsible for paying quarterly federal income tax payments and the full 15.3% of gross wages for FICA taxes

The agreement also needs to define compensation amounts and issues such as payment of commissions generated prior to termination of the agreement but not yet paid.

Law, Definition, and Nature of Agency Relationships, Type of Agencies, and Agents

When one person agrees to act on behalf of another, an agency relationship is established. Agency relationships are regulated by a body of laws collectively known as the Law of Agency. An agency is a legal, fiduciary relationship in which the agent works for and under the direction and control of a principal or client. Two kinds of agency relationships are common in real estate practice.

1. **General agency**—Real estate brokers typically have licensees who act as their agents in working with their principals.
2. **Special agency**—A principal to a transaction (the seller or buyer) secures the advice and assistance of a real estate broker and the broker's associates.

Creation of Agency and Agency Agreements

An agency relationship is established when a buyer or seller delegates authority to a broker, and the broker accepts the authority to act on behalf of the principal. Although the delegation may be given orally, the best method of establishing an agency relationship is by an express written agreement called a listing agreement or a buyer representation agreement. There is more information about listing agreements under "Contracts" on page 144.

There are four basic types of listing agreements in common use.

1. **Exclusive right to sell**, from the broker's point of view, is the best type of listing. During the period set out in the listing agreement, the listing broker has the exclusive right to produce a ready, willing, and able buyer at the price and terms agreed upon in the listing agreement. If any other person—including the seller or another broker—procures a buyer, the listing broker is still entitled to the commission stipulated in the listing agreement. However, if another broker procures a buyer, most listing brokers are happy to

share the commission with the procuring broker. With this type of listing, brokers will exert maximum effort in marketing property, because they have strong assurance that they will be compensated.

Under the exclusive right to sell agreement, the listing broker is entitled to a commission when the broker procures a buyer who will meet the seller's price and terms, even if the seller then refuses to sell the property.

2. An **exclusive agency listing** is similar to an exclusive right to sell listing, except that it gives the seller the right to sell the property without paying the broker a commission. This agreement is nevertheless an exclusive agency agreement because the seller cannot give the listing to another broker.

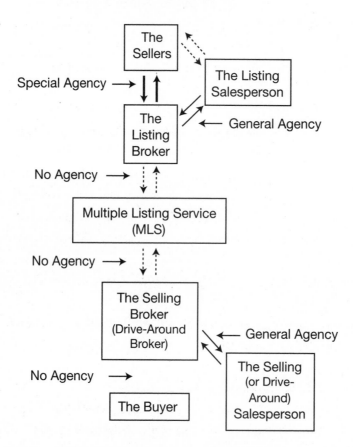

The Residential Real Estate Transaction
Listing Broker and Subagent

3. An **open listing** is simply an agreement that a commission will be paid if the broker is the procuring cause in producing a ready, willing, and able buyer. A seller may enter into an open listing with an unlimited number of brokers. The only real benefit to the brokers is that they know they will be compensated if they are the procuring cause of the sale. In residential transactions, brokers rarely accept open listings, because there is a strong possibility that another broker or the seller will find a buyer. However, the seller of a multimillion dollar commercial property is not as likely to give an exclusive listing. So a commercial real estate broker would be more likely to accept an open listing, because such a broker typically has a group of clients with whom he or she has worked in the past to whom the broker can present the property.

The Residential Real Estate Transaction
Listing Broker and Buyer's Broker

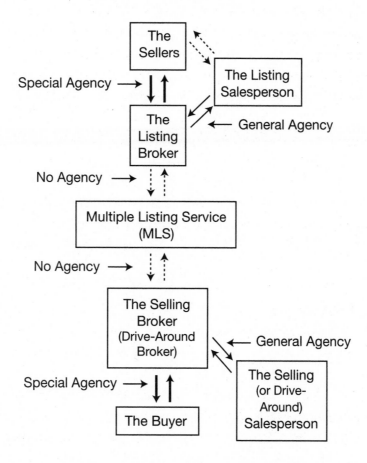

4. A **net listing** can be an exclusive or a nonexclusive listing. It offers the property owner a guaranteed net amount at closing, with the listing broker taking any part of the purchase price over that amount. Net listings often leave brokers open to charges of fraud or misconduct and should, therefore, be avoided if possible. In many states, they are illegal.

For example, the owner might say to a broker, "I want $100,000 for my property. You can keep anything over that amount that the property sells for." The broker knows that the property will sell for $120,000 in this market, so she feels she has a great opportunity. But when the broker brings in an offer for $120,000 and the transaction closes, the broker may be sued for violating her fiduciary duty of loyalty to the client. The broker should have informed the seller of the true market value of the property.

So the broker might instead present the property at $106,000, thinking she will then earn a reasonable commission. A prospective buyer offers $98,000. Complying with the legal requirement to present all offers, the broker submits the offer and the seller accepts. The broker is then left without a commission and wondering why she ever took a net listing.

Listing Procedures

Disclosing Agency Relationships

The law requires that when an agent first has substantive dialogue with a prospective buyer or seller for the purposes of discussing, listing, or showing property, the agent must present the statutory information concerning possible agency relationships and available brokerage services. This is critical if the agent is acting as a subagent of the seller, so that the buyer will not reveal any information that would give an advantage to the seller.

Evaluating Property

An agent needs to be totally honest with the client who is getting ready to sell or purchase a property. A competitive market analysis (CMA) should be prepared to help the seller client or buyer client identify the right asking or offering price. The agent should advise the seller on how to get the property ready to show to its best advantage and to be attractive to buyers. Although the agent must never take on the role of property inspector, an agent should also point out potential problem areas relating to the structural and mechanical systems of the property improvements.

Disclosure of Property Conditions

Both property owners and real estate licensees are required to reveal any material facts about the property that may be known to one or the other, but may not easily be observed by an untrained person. These deficiencies are known as latent structural defects or property defects.

In a growing number of states, a real estate licensee is responsible for conducting a reasonable visual inspection of property to be listed, noting any defects or conditions that could affect the property's value or desirability (called red flags) and revealing those facts to prospective buyers. Part of this process includes questioning the property owner about conditions that may not be apparent in a visual inspection.

In some states, the owner of a previously occupied single-family residential dwelling unit must complete a statement disclosing the condition of the property to the best of the owner's knowledge.

Fraud and Misrepresentation

A broker or salesperson commits fraud when the licensee deliberately deceives the consumer. For instance, a broker might encourage a consumer to part with something of value or to enter into a contract that the consumer would not have entered into had truthful information been provided. Misrepresentation, more correctly called innocent misrepresentation, is unintentional rather than deliberate.

Often, real estate professionals are found guilty of fraud or misrepresentation because of what they fail to reveal. Failure to disclose a property defect constitutes fraud or misrepresentation by omission. Giving wrong information constitutes fraud or misrepresentation by commission.

Brokers and salespersons must avoid making any representation when they do not have the correct answer. Instead, real estate professionals should guide buyers and sellers to sources from which the buyers or sellers may obtain the information they need to make intelligent and informed decisions.

Authority

Ostensible authority or apparent authority may establish an agency relationship. This occurs when a principal gives a third party reason to believe that another person is the principal's agent even though that person is unaware of the appointment. If the third party accepts the principal's representation as true, the principal may have established ostensible authority and, therefore, may be bound by the acts of his agent.

Agency can also be established by ratification. For example, a broker might bring an offer to a property owner who had no knowledge of the broker's attempt to sell his property. If the owner accepts the offer (which generally entitles the broker to a commission), then it could be held that an agency was created when negotiations started.

An agency by estoppel can result when a principal fails to maintain due diligence over an agent and the agent exercises powers not granted to her. If this causes a third party to believe that the agent has these powers, an agency by estoppel has been created.

Within any agency relationship, implied authority can sometimes be exercised. Implied authority can arise, for example, from custom in the industry. If a broker lists a house, there may not be an express agreement concerning advertising the property in the newspaper. However, because this is a customary practice, the broker may have the implied authority to advertise. In some states, express authority in writing is required to be able to erect a For Sale sign or to share one's agency with another licensee.

Responsibilities of the Agent to the Seller/Buyer as Principal

Accepting an appointment as a seller's or buyer's agent imposes obligations and creates liabilities. A licensee who fails to fulfill his or her fiduciary duties or oversteps the bounds of the agent's authority may face disciplinary action by the state's licensing authority or even a civil suit brought by an unhappy buyer or seller. The agent appointed by a listing agreement or a buyer representation agreement is a special agent and has not been granted the authority to speak or sign on behalf of the principal or client.

It is very important to know when and if an agency relationship has been created. When someone becomes an agent for another person, a dramatic change in duties and obligation occurs. The agency creates a fiduciary relationship, requiring that the agent exhibit trust, honesty, and good business judgment when working on behalf of the principal. This fiduciary relationship imposes the following duties:

- **Obedience** (also called faithful performance). The agent must obey all legal instructions given by the principal, applying best efforts and diligence in carrying out the objectives of the agency (for example, selling the property).
- **Loyalty.** The agent must put the interests of the principal above his or her own interests. This is perhaps the most difficult duty for the agent, which may be why failure of the agent to uphold this duty causes so many lawsuits.
- **Disclosure.** The agent must keep the principal informed of all pertinent facts. Because just about anything relating to the transaction could be pertinent to a principal, the agent is basically obligated to investigate and disclose everything related to the situation.
- **Confidentiality.** The agent must keep confidential information about the principal and the principal's motivations and financial interests.

- **Accounting.** The agent may not place the principal's funds in the agent's own account. This practice, called commingling, is grounds for suspension or revocation of the broker's real estate license.
- **Reasonable care.** The agent must exercise competence and expertise. The agent must not be party to any fraud or misrepresentation likely to affect the sound judgment of the principal.

Termination of Agency

Agencies are created when the principal or client delegates authority to the agent and the agent accepts the appointment. Most agencies come to a successful, happy conclusion through completion of the purpose of the agency—the property sells and the transaction closes. On occasion, the agent is not successful within the time established in the listing or buyer representation agreement, and the agency ends because the agreement expires. Other events that can terminate an agency are

- destruction of the property
- condemnation of the property
- mutual agreement (rescission) by the parties
- bankruptcy of the owner
- death or incapacity of the principal or the agent (Note: The death of a subagent would not affect the status of the agency)

Commission and Fees

Compensation paid by sellers and buyers is always negotiable between the parties and can be calculated and paid in a variety of ways.

1. **Success fees** (**contingent fees**) are usually paid at the closing of the transaction and are usually a percentage of the sales price or a flat fee. The agent gets paid only if the transaction closes.
2. **Noncontingent fees** may be calculated on an hourly basis or on a fee for specific or limited services basis. Some brokers require a nonrefundable retainer fee before beginning work for the principal.

Federal anti-trust laws prohibit price fixing. Licensees should exercise caution to make certain that they do not say anything about fees that might give someone the idea that fees are standard or fixed in a particular market.

▶ Settlement/Transfer of Property

The real estate agent does not create the instruments that transfer title. The real estate agent does assist the buyer and the seller in defining and setting down when and how the title of the property will be transferred in an agreement of purchase. Most real estate closings involve transferring title from the seller (grantor) to the buyer (grantee) by the delivery of a general warranty deed, executed by the seller and delivered to the buyer. A general warranty deed is an instrument by which the grantor guarantees the grantee that the title being conveyed is free from other claims or encumbrances.

Title Insurance

Title insurance has become the most common method of protecting the property buyer. A title company issues a preliminary title report or title commitment. It will indicate the present condition of the title based on examination of the documents contained in the public records, as well as any exceptions to the coverage that the title company is willing to provide. The title company will defend the buyer's title in a title dispute covered by the policy.

Title insurance is necessary to indemnify the new owner against financial loss in the event an error was made when the title was searched and examined. There is no guarantee that the finished abstract, or its certification, is completely accurate. Many problems can arise in the recorded chain of ownership.

- What if a recorded deed in the title chain is a forgery?
- What if a minor or an otherwise legally incompetent person executed a deed?
- What if a document was misfiled, or there were undisclosed heirs, or a missing will later came to light, or there was confusion because of similar names on documents?

These situations can result in substantial losses to property owners and lenders, yet the fault may not lie with the title closer, abstracter, or attorney, so there is no one to sue for damages. The solution has been the organization of private companies to sell insurance against losses arising from title defects such as those previously mentioned, as well as from errors in title examination.

Essentials of Title Insurance

Numerous details must be handled between the time a buyer and seller sign a sales contract and the day the title is conveyed to the buyer. Ask yourself:

- What is the status of the title? It must be checked thoroughly.
- What is the property tax status? Are the taxes up to date? Are there any special assessments? What is the tax bill for the current year?
- Are there any judgments against the seller that may encumber the property? Are there any liens that must be paid off?

The most expeditious method of preparing for the closing is to place all of these matters in the hands of a neutral third party. Because the title insurance provider has a high level of interest in having these matters handled correctly, it makes sense that it should be chosen as the closing agent or escrow agent, as noted previously.

Deeds

A deed is a written document that conveys property from the grantor (owner) to the grantee (buyer). State law dictates the form that a deed must take. There are a number of requirements for a valid deed.

- It must be in writing.
- The grantor(s) must be of sound mind (legally capable).

- It must identify the parties, preferably by full name and marital status (single, married, widow, and so on).
- It must identify the property by legal description.
- It must contain a granting clause—also called words of conveyance—that contains the appropriate words ("I hereby grant and convey").
- It must be signed by the grantor(s).
- It must be delivered to and accepted by the grantee. A deed held by a third party until the grantor dies, for instance, will have no effect during the grantor's life and on the grantor's death will be invalid. Even after a valid delivery, the fact that the deed is in the hands of the grantee does not mean that it is accepted. Many charitable donations of real estate have ultimately been rejected because of the high cost of their maintenance or remediation (as in the case of contaminated property).

There are many different types of deeds.

- A bargain and sale deed states the consideration paid by the grantee. There may or may not be a warranty that the grantor actually has an interest in the described property.
- A gift deed requires no consideration to be paid by the grantee.
- A grant deed (using the words "I grant and convey" or similar) carries three implied promises of the grantor:
  1. The grantor has good title.
  2. There are no encumbrances other than those noted.
  3. The grantor will convey any after-acquired title (ownership interest received after the grant deed is delivered) to the grantee.
- A quitclaim deed transfers whatever interest the grantor may own, but does not warrant that the grantor actually has any interest in the described property.
- A sheriff's deed conveys title to property sold at public auction following a judicial foreclosure sale or other court action.
- A tax deed conveys title to property sold at public auction to cover unpaid taxes.
- A trust deed (deed of trust) is used to make real estate security for the repayment of a debt. The trust deed conveys conditional title from the trustor (property owner) to the trustee to be held for the benefit of the named beneficiary (the lender).

Recording Title

In most states, a deed must be acknowledged (signed before a notary public or other official) in order to be recorded (made a part of the public records of the county in which the property is located).

A recorded deed provides constructive notice or legal notice of the conveyance. Recording establishes the priority of interests in or claims against a property.

Settlement Procedures

Each person attending the closing, the point in a real estate transaction when the buyer receives a deed and the seller receives the purchase price, is responsible for bringing certain documents.

The seller is typically responsible for some or all of the following:

- the deed
- recent property tax certificates
- insurance policies
- termite inspections
- survey maps
- keys, garage door openers, and the like

If an income-producing property is being sold, then the seller may also need to bring

- leases
- operating statements
- estoppel letters from the tenants
- maintenance contracts

The buyer needs to bring adequate monies in the form of a cashier's check or other form of good funds and may need to provide a(n)

- survey
- insurance policy
- flood insurance policy
- termite certificate

As the closing proceeds, many signatures are required. Both the buyer and the seller sign a closing statement. The seller signs the deed, and the buyer signs the note, the deed of trust, and numerous other documents required by the lender.

The closing agent or closing officer has several responsibilities at the closing or settlement meeting, including

- monitoring all the signatures and making copies of the documents for the buyer, seller, and brokers
- distributing checks, if so authorized by the lender (in a process called table funding, because funds are distributed at the closing table); table funding is now authorized in the majority of real estate closings
- sending the deed and deed of trust for recording to the county court house of the county in which the property is located

Most lenders require that termite inspections be made prior to closing. Because the property is their collateral, they want to be assured that the property will not be destroyed by termites. Lenders also insist on an appraisal to ensure that their collateral is sufficient value to cover the loan. Finally, lenders typically require insurance policies to cover the property from fire, casualty, flood, or wind damage.

Also at the closing, documents may have to be presented on mandatory disclosures, such as the presence of lead-based paint in a house built before 1978.

Purpose of Closing/Settlement

Immediately before closing, buyers typically do a final walk-through of the property they are about to purchase. The buyer's broker (if any) will typically accompany the client. The purpose of the walk-through is to verify the condition of the property after the sellers have moved out and to determine if any items have been improperly removed.

In addition to the buyer and seller, the following people usually attend a closing:

- attorneys for the seller and buyer, to ascertain that everything promised in the sales contract has been carried out
- real estate brokers
- title company closer (serving as the escrow agent), who will conduct the closing

Legal Requirements (includes RESPA)

Congress passed the Real Estate Settlement and Procedures Act (RESPA) in response to consumer complaints regarding real estate closing costs and procedures. The purpose of RESPA is to regulate and standardize real estate settlement practices when federally related first-mortgage loans are made on one- to four-family residences, condominiums, and cooperatives.

Almost all residential transactions come under RESPA because most home loans are sold in the secondary mortgage market to federally related organizations. The most important of these are

- Federal National Mortgage Association (Fannie Mae)
- Government National Mortgage Association (GNMA or Ginnie Mae)
- Federal Home Loan Mortgage Corporation (FHLMC or Freddie Mac)

One of the most important provisions of RESPA is a prohibition of kickbacks and fees for services not performed during the closing. Prior to the act, attorneys and closing agents in some areas routinely channeled title business to certain title companies in return for a fee. This increased closing costs to the buyer without adding services. RESPA requires that there be a justifiable service rendered for each closing fee charged. The act also prohibits the seller from requiring that the buyer purchase title insurance from a particular title company.

Finally, RESPA places restrictions on the amount of advance property tax and insurance payments a lender can collect and place in an impound or reserve account. The amount that may be collected in advance is limited to one-sixth, or two months' worth, of annual property taxes.

Tax Aspects

In many jurisdictions, a transfer tax is assessed when ownership of real estate occurs. The tax is based on the sales price and is calculated in mills or in dollars per $100, $500, or $1,000.

Legal versus Equitable Title

Equitable title is an interest held by a purchaser (vendee) under a purchase contract or a contract for deed. The vendee may demand that legal title be transferred upon full payment of the contract purchase price.

Legal title is title that is fully vested in the owner as evidenced by a deed, will, or court document. Legal title to land and its appurtenances encompasses the entire bundle of rights that an owner possesses. The best title or greatest bundle of rights that an individual can own and hold is fee simple ownership.

Special Processes

Probate

Probate is the legal process of finalizing the affairs of a deceased person and distributing the real and personal property left by the decedent. A person who dies with a will (testate) will have his or her property distributed as specified in the will. A person who dies without having written a will (intestate) will have his or her property administered and distributed by the probate court under the provisions of the state's law of decent and intestate succession.

Foreclosure

Foreclosure is covered in "Financing" on page 143.

▶ Business Practices

Fair Housing and Anti-Discrimination Laws

In addition to the U.S. Constitution, there are two major federal laws that prohibit discrimination in housing.

The Civil Rights Act of 1866 states that "all citizens of the United States shall have the same right in every State and every Territory, as is enjoyed by the white citizens thereof to inherit, purchase, lease, sell, hold, and convey real and personal property." In 1968, the Supreme Court affirmed that the 1866 act prohibits "all racial discrimination, private as well as public, in the sale of real property." The 1866 law prohibits discrimination based on skin color. Later laws and rulings prohibit discrimination based on race.

The Federal Fair Housing Act (Title VIII of the Civil Rights Act of 1968) makes it illegal to discriminate on the basis of race, color, religion, sex, or national origin in connection with the sale or rental of housing or vacant land offered for residential construction or use. The law specifically prohibits the following discriminatory acts:

- refusing to sell to, rent to, or negotiate with any person who is a member of a protected class, or otherwise making a dwelling unavailable to such a person
- changing terms, conditions, or services for different individuals as a means of discrimination against a member of a protected class

- practicing discrimination through any statement or advertisement that restricts the sale or rental of residential property
- representing to any person, as a means of discrimination, that a dwelling is unavailable for sale or rental
- making a profit by inducing owners of housing to sell or rent by representing that persons of a protected category are moving into the neighborhood
- altering the conditions of a home loan to any person, or otherwise denying such a loan as a means of discrimination
- denying persons membership or limiting their participation in any multiple-listing service, real estate brokers' organization, or other facility related to the sale or rental of dwellings

A protected class is any group of people designated as such by the Department of Housing and Urban Development (HUD) in consideration of federal and state civil rights legislation. Protected classes currently include color, race, religion or creed, ancestry or national origin, gender, handicap, and familial status.

The Fair Housing Amendment defines a handicapped person as one who meets one of the following criteria:

- has a physical or mental impairment that substantially limits one or more major life activities
- has a record of having such an impairment
- is regarded as having such an impairment

The act also protects persons associated with a handicapped individual, such as a parent or spouse.

The current use of illegal substances is not considered a handicap under the law. However, a person undergoing treatment for drug abuse is considered handicapped. AIDS and HIV-positive status are defined as handicaps.

Protected familial status applies to any household with one or more individuals under the age of 18 living with a parent or legal guardian. This status also applies to anyone who is pregnant or is in the process of obtaining legal custody of an individual under the age of 18. In other words, it is illegal to discriminate against families with children.

The most common violations of Federal Fair Housing Laws involve steering, blockbusting, advertising, and less favorable treatment.

Steering (also called channeling) is the practice of directing home seekers to or away from particular neighborhoods based on race, color, religion, sex, national origin, handicap, or familial status. Steering includes both efforts to exclude minorities from one area of a city and efforts to direct minorities to minority or changing areas. Steering accounts for many of the complaints filed against real estate agents under the Fair Housing Act.

Examples of steering include

- showing only certain neighborhoods
- slanting property descriptions
- downgrading neighborhoods
- implying that certain properties are no longer available when in reality they are available

Blockbusting (also called panic peddling) is the illegal practice of inducing panic selling in a neighborhood for financial gain. Blockbusting typically starts when someone induces one homeowner to sell cheaply by implying that an impending change in the racial or religious composition of the neighborhood will cause property values to fall. The first home thus acquired is sold at a markup to a minority family. The process quickly snowballs as residents panic and sell at progressively lower prices.

Less favorable treatment occurs when members of a protected category are provided with fewer services and less information than other people. This violation involves the claim that a minority client received inferior service, was unable to negotiate, or was offered different terms and conditions than a comparable nonminority client. Less favorable treatment is often very subtle, but it has the same discriminatory effects as steering or blockbusting.

Two types of housing are covered by the 1968 Fair Housing Act: single-family houses and multifamily dwellings.

A single-family house is covered if one of the following is true:

- It is owned by a private individual who uses a real estate broker or other person in the business of selling or renting dwellings or who advertises the dwelling.
- It is not owned by private individuals.
- It is owned by a private individual who owns more than three such houses or who, in any two-year period, sells more than one dwelling in which the individual was not the most recent resident.

A multifamily dwelling is covered if one of the following is true:

- It consists of five units or more.
- It consists of four or fewer units, and the owner does not reside in one of the units.

The act does not cover

- rentals of rooms or units in owner-occupied multifamily dwellings of two to four units, as long as discriminatory advertising and the services of a real estate agent are not used
- restricting the sale, rental, or occupancy of dwellings owned or operated by a religious organization for a noncommercial purpose to persons of the same religion, as long as membership in that religion is not restricted on account of race, color, or national origin
- restricting the rental or occupancy of lodgings operated by a private club for its members for other than commercial purposes
- housing for the elderly that meets certain Department of Housing and Urban Development (HUD) guidelines

A person who believes he or she has been discriminated against can pursue one of three avenues. He or she can

1. file a written complaint with HUD.
2. file a civil action directly in a U.S. District Court or state or local court.

3. file a complaint with the U.S. Attorney General.

The burden of proof is on the person filing the complaint. A person found guilty of a fair housing violation may face

- an injunction to stop the sale or rental of the property to someone else, making it available to the complainant
- monetary fines for actual damages caused by the discrimination
- unlimited punitive damages
- court costs
- criminal penalties against those who coerce, intimidate, threaten, or interfere with a person's buying, renting, or selling of housing
- state penalties, including the loss of the real estate license

Antitrust Compliance

The Sherman Anti-Trust Act prohibits certain business practices that could place unfair restrictions on free competition in the marketplace. Prohibitions against restraint of trade that directly affect the real estate industry include the following:

- There can be no price fixing. Agency fees or commission are always subject to negotiation between a principal and an agent. Agents for different companies are not allowed to agree to predetermined fees or to agree on a range of fees for specific services. Even discussion of such matters could subject licensees to civil and criminal penalties including fines and/or imprisonment.
- Realty firms cannot agree to provide service only in a designated geographic area.
- Realty firms cannot agree to boycott (direct business away from) certain companies or other realty firms.
- Agents are not to form exclusive organizations (such as property listing services) that arbitrarily prevent nonmembers from gaining access to sales and marketing information. Membership criteria must be designed so as not to unfairly exclude otherwise qualified brokers from participation.

Advertising

At all times, real estate licensees must make a diligent effort to make certain that all of their advertising creates an accurate and truthful picture. There is no place in the real estate business for falsehoods and inaccuracies.

When advertising credit terms, be sure to comply with the federal Truth-in-Lending Act and give complete information including the Annual Percentage Rate (APR) whenever any trigger term is used. For a list of trigger terms, please review "Financing/Credit Laws" on page 143.

▶ Property Management

Property Management and Landlord/Tenant or Commercial/Income Property

Tenancies and Leasehold Estates

A lease is a contract that transfers a possessory interest in real estate. The leasehold estate conveys to the tenant a right to occupy the property for the term of the lease.

Leases may be oral or written, but the Statute of Frauds requires that leases of real estate, except for residential leases of one year or less, be in writing to be enforceable.

Leases must be signed by the landlord and the tenant but need not be recorded to be enforceable. An individual who wishes to notify the public of a leasehold interest may record a memorandum of lease.

A lease must include a sufficient property description. A legal description as used in a deed is appropriate, although in certain residential leases, a street address and apartment number are sufficient.

There are several kinds of leases:

- A gross lease specifies that the landlord pay all expenses: property taxes, insurance, maintenance. This kind of lease is often used for apartments and other residential properties.
- A net lease specifies that the tenant pay certain expenses. The most common arrangement requires the tenant to pay property taxes, insurance, and maintenance. This is called a net, net, net or triple net lease.
- An office-building lease is a hybrid of a gross and a net lease. The landlord pays the first portion of the expenses, and each tenant pays a pro rata share of all expenses over that.
- A percentage lease requires the tenant to pay a percentage of gross sales as rent in addition to a base rental amount specified in the lease.

Several types of tenancies can be created by a lease:

- An estate for years is given for a specified term. This common type of lease agreement includes all leaseholds that continue for a specific period of time and have a definite termination date, such as a five-year office lease or a 20-year retail lease.
- A periodic estate is initially given for a specific term and then renews automatically until notice of termination is given. It does not have a definite termination date but runs from month to month or year to year. A periodic estate is generally created when the landlord and tenant contract to rent month to month, without specifying the number of months or years the lease will run.
- A tenancy at will extends indefinitely and may be terminated at any time by either the landlord or tenant by giving a notice equal to one rental period's notice.
- Tenancy at sufferance is created when a tenant takes possession of a property lawfully and continues to hold possession of the property after the right to remain has expired. However, if the holdover tenancy exists with the consent of the landlord, then a periodic tenancy is created. When a lease is assigned to a

third party, the third party assumes all the obligations of the lessee (tenant). The right of the tenant to assign the lease must be granted in writing by the landlord.

- An assignment is the transfer of all the lessee's rights to another party. The assignor is still liable for the performance of the agreement, unless the lessor releases them.
- If a tenant subleases some or all of the space, only a portion of the rights are granted to the sublessee. The original tenant's relationship with the landlord does not change. The original lease should specify whether a sublet is allowed.

Property Manager and Owner Relationships

The range of services that the property manager can perform for the landlord (property owner) includes marketing, leasing, maintenance, and rent collection.

A major activity of the property manager will be the cost-effective marketing of vacant units, primarily by ongoing advertising in selected publications. This usually will include classified ads in local newspapers, but may also include specialty publications as well as Internet rental listing services. Use of rental listing agencies, particularly for residential property, will require compliance with specific state laws intended to safeguard the consumer. On-site posting of unit availability will help attract the drive-by prospect.

The law of supply and demand applies in the leasing as well as the sale of real estate. Continuing surveys of the number of units and vacancies available on the market and rents charged will help the property remain competitive.

Advertising through newspapers, use of billboards, and posting on Internet and other listing services should attract a steady flow of prospective tenants, provided the units have been competitively priced and offer amenities expected in the area. The applicant review process should be conducted in a personal interview on-site, for the benefit of both the property manager and the prospective tenant.

Laws Affecting Property Management

All or part of the wording of the rental application, as well as the time frame in which the applicant must be notified of acceptance or nonacceptance, may be mandated by state law. Federal law regarding the use of a credit report may also apply.

A property manager must comply with all federal and state fair housing laws to avoid charges of unlawful discrimination.

State law governs many of the provisions in a residential lease (or rental agreement). The typical lease will include

- the identity of the lessor (landlord) and lessee (tenant)
- a description of the premises to be leased
- the terms of the lease, including beginning and ending times
- the amount of rent to be paid and when payment is due—a grace period may be specified, as well as the penalty for late payment due after that time
- the obligations of the lessor, which will include compliance with an express or implied warranty of habitability

- the obligations of the lessee, which will include payment of the stated rent as well as maintenance of the premises
- a provision for arbitration or mediation clause to be enforced in the event of a dispute in the terms of the agreement
- the signature of the lessee and signature of the lessor (or agent)

In most states, the Statute of Frauds requires that a lease that will terminate one year or more from the date of its signing must be in writing.

Federal law now requires compliance with the Lead-Based Paint Disclosure Law. This law is applicable for a new or renewal lease on residential property constructed prior to 1978. States may have other laws that supersede the federal statute.

The state may require specific disclosures as part of the rental agreement, such as whether or not a smoke alarm has been installed in the rental unit. The state may require deadbolt locks on exterior doors of rental units. A sprinkler system may be a requirement in a commercial building or a fire hazard area.

Common Interest Ownership Properties

Many properties are owned by multiple owners. Here are three types of these properties.

1. **Cooperatives** are apartments owned by a corporation that holds titles to the entire cooperative property and is liable for the mortgage obligations and the ad valorem taxes for the entire property.

   Each purchaser of an apartment unit is a stockholder in the corporation and obtains the right to occupy through a proprietary lease. Each block of stock is tied to a specific right to occupy and carries a lease payment financial obligation that represents a *pro rata* share of the total cost of the operations expense and mortgage payments on the building.

2. **Condominiums** are created under state laws that permit a multi-tenant building to be divided into air lots; they are declared as separate parcels of real estate by recording a vertical and horizontal plot. The condominium declaration identifies each condominium and the percentage ownership that the individual owns in the land and the common elements of the structures. Some of the common elements will be defined as limited common elements and will be designated as for the exclusive use of a specific unit.

   An advantage of condominium ownership over cooperative ownership is that default in payment of taxes, mortgage payment, or monthly assessment affects only the specific unit. Each unit is defined as a separate parcel of real estate and is owned fee simple.

3. **Time-shares** are agreements by which multiple owners own a proportional interest in a single condominium unit with the exclusive right to use and occupy the unit for a specified period of time each year. The individual owners pay common expense and maintenance costs based on the ratio between the ownership period and the total number of ownership periods available in the property. This type of ownership can be either a fee simple or leasehold interest.

4. In **fractional ownership**, a group of individuals pool their resources to buy a property. For example, family members contribute to purchase a beachfront vacation property. The arrangements usually divide ownership by fourths, eighths, thirteenths, or another increment. The owners may buy their shares from a management company, which handles maintenance and scheduling use. They are similar to time-shares, but the contributions are much larger. Financing can be difficult to find and maintenance fees are often high.

Subdivisions

When larger tracts of land are divided into smaller parcels that will be owned by multiple owners, the tract will be converted into a subdivision. The subdivider divides the tract into smaller lots for sale. The developer will improve the land by installing utilities, building roads, and preparing the sites for the activities of the builders who will construct the buildings.

State and local governments control subdividing and land planning. A land development plan that matches their comprehensive plan must be created before subdividing can begin. Where the subdivider's plan conflicts with the comprehensive plan, a waiver must be sought.

The subdivision of the tract may be regulated by local, state, and federal regulations. The subdivision will be evidenced by the recording of a plat that shows lots, blocks, streets, and common amenities. The plat will also identify easements on each lot, easements in gross, for the purpose of bringing necessary utilities to the lots.

Zoning and comprehensive plans can require minimum lot size, population density, and open space.

When the lots are offered for sale across state lines, the Federal Interstate Land Sales Full Disclosure Act, enforced by HUD, will require the filing of various reports. This law applies only to subdivisions with more than 25 lots and lots in excess of 20 acres.

Frequently, subdividers and developers will place restrictive covenants on the lots that will control use of the land and establish standards for the improvements to be constructed on the lots.

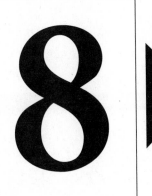

Real Estate Broker Math Review

CHAPTER SUMMARY

In most states, math accounts for almost 10% of a real estate broker exam, so you should take this topic seriously. But even if math is not your favorite subject, this chapter will help you do your best. It not only covers arithmetic, algebra, geometry, and word problems, but also has practice problems for each of the real estate math topics.

ere are some types of math questions you may encounter on your exam.

- percents
- areas
- property tax
- loan-to-value ratios
- points
- equity
- qualifying buyers
- prorations
- commissions
- sale proceeds

- transfer tax/conveyance tax/revenue stamps
- competitive market analyses (CMA)
- income properties
- depreciation

Keep in mind that although the math topics are varied, you will be using the same math skills to complete each question. But before you review your math skills, take a look at some helpful strategies for doing your best.

▶ Strategies for Math Questions

Answer Every Question
You should answer every single question, even if you don't know the answer. There is usually no penalty for a wrong answer, and, if there are four answer choices, you have a 25% chance of guessing correctly. If one or two answers are obviously wrong, the odds may be even higher on selecting the correct one.

Bring a Calculator
Your state *may* allow you to bring calculator to your exam. **You must check with your exam center to find out exactly what type of calculator is permitted.** In general, permissible calculators are battery operated, do not print, are not programmable, and do not have a keypad with letters. As a precaution, you should bring an extra battery with you to your exam. Try not to rely entirely on the calculator. Although using one can prevent simple adding and subtracting errors, it may take longer for you to use the calculator than to figure it out yourself.

Use Scratch Paper
Resist the temptation to "save time" by doing all your work on your calculator. The main pitfall with calculators is the temptation to work the problem all the way through to the end on the calculator. At this point, if none of the answers provided is correct, there is no way to know where the mistake lies. Use scratch paper to avoid this problem.

Check Your Work
Checking your work is always good practice, and it's usually quite simple. Even if you come up with an answer that is one of the answer choices, you should check your work. Test writers often include answer choices that are the results of common errors, which is what you may have.

▶ Real Estate Math Review

Here's a quick review of some basic arithmetic, algebra, geometry, and word problem skills you will need for your exam.

Arithmetic Review

Symbols of Multiplication

When two or more numbers are being multiplied, they are called **factors**. The answer that results is called the **product**.

> *Example:*
> $5 \times 6 = 30$ 5 and 6 are **factors**, and 30 is the **product**.

> There are several ways to represent multiplication in this mathematical statement.

- A dot between factors indicates multiplication:

  $5 \cdot 6 = 30$

- Parentheses around any part of the one or more factors indicates multiplication:

  $(5)6 = 30 \qquad 5(6) = 30 \qquad (5)(6) = 30$

- Multiplication is also indicated when a number is placed next to a variable:

  $5a = 30$ In this equation, 5 is being multiplied by *a*.

Divisibility

Like multiplication, division can be represented in a few different ways:

$8 \div 3 \qquad 3\overline{)8} \qquad \frac{8}{3}$

In each of these expressions, 3 is the divisor and 8 is the dividend.

If the number after the one you need to round to is 5 or more, make the preceding number one higher. If it is less than 5, drop it and leave the preceding number the same. (Information about rounding is usually provided in the exam instructions or in the exam bulletin.)

Example:
0.0135 = 0.014 or 0.01

Decimals

The most important thing to remember about decimals is that the first place value to the right begins with tenths. The place values are as follows:

1	2	6	8	.	3	4	5	7
THOUSANDS	HUNDREDS	TENS	ONES	DECIMAL POINT	TENTHS	HUNDREDTHS	THOUSANDTHS	TEN THOUSANDTHS

In expanded form, this number can also be expressed as

$1{,}268.3457 = (1 \times 1{,}000) + (2 \times 100) + (6 \times 10) + (8 \times 1) + (3 \times .01) + (4 \times .01) + (5 \times .001) + (7 \times .0001)$

Fractions

To do well when working with fractions, you'll need to understand some basic concepts. Here are some math rules for fractions using variables:

$$\frac{a}{b} \times \frac{c}{d} = \frac{a \times c}{b \times d}$$

$$\frac{a}{b} + \frac{c}{b} = \frac{a + c}{b}$$

$$\frac{a}{b} \div \frac{c}{d} = \frac{a}{b} \times \frac{d}{c} = \frac{a \times d}{b \times c}$$

$$\frac{a}{b} + \frac{c}{d} = \frac{ad + bc}{bd}$$

Multiplication of Fractions

Multiplying fractions is one of the easiest operations to perform. To multiply fractions, simply multiply the numerators and the denominators, writing each in the respective place over or under the fraction bar.

Example:

$\frac{4}{5} \times \frac{6}{7} = \frac{24}{35}$

Dividing of Fractions

Dividing fractions is the same thing as multiplying fractions by their **reciprocals**. To find the reciprocal of any number, switch its numerator and denominator. For example, the reciprocals of the following numbers are:

$\frac{1}{3} \leftarrow \frac{3}{1} = 3$

$x \leftarrow \frac{1}{x}$

$\frac{4}{5} \leftarrow \frac{5}{4}$

$5 \leftarrow \frac{1}{5}$

When dividing fractions, simply multiply the dividend (what is being divided) by the divisor's (what is doing the dividing) reciprocal to get the answer.

Example:

$\frac{12}{21} \div \frac{3}{4} = \frac{12}{21} \times \frac{4}{3} = \frac{48}{63} = \frac{16}{21}$

Adding and Subtracting Fractions

To add or subtract fractions with like denominators, just add or subtract the numerators and leave the denominator as it is. For example,

$\frac{1}{7} + \frac{5}{7} = \frac{6}{7}$ and $\frac{5}{8} - \frac{2}{8} = \frac{3}{8}$

To add or subtract fractions with unlike denominators, you must find the **least common denominator**, or LCD.

For example, if given the denominators 8 and 12, 24 would be the LCD because $8 \times 3 = 24$ and $12 \times 2 = 24$. In other words, the LCD is the smallest number divisible by each of the denominators.

Once you know the LCD, convert each fraction to its new form by multiplying both the numerator and denominator by the necessary number to get the LCD, and then add or subtract the new numerators.

Example:

$\frac{1}{3} + \frac{2}{5} = \frac{5(1)}{5(3)} + \frac{3(2)}{3(5)} = \frac{5}{15} + \frac{6}{15} = \frac{11}{15}$

Percent

A **percent** is a measure of a part to a whole, with the whole being equal to 100.

- To change a decimal to a percentage, move the decimal point two units to the right and add a percent symbol.

  Examples:
  $.45 = 45\%$ $.07 = 7\%$ $.9 = 90\%$

- To change a fraction to a percentage, first change the fraction to a decimal. To do this, divide the numerator by the denominator. Then, change the decimal to a percentage.

  Example:
  $\frac{4}{5} = .80 = 80\%$

  $\frac{2}{5} = .4 = 40\%$

  $\frac{1}{8} = .125 = 12.5\%$

- To change a decimal to a percentage, move the decimal point two units to the right and add a percent symbol.
- To change a percentage to a decimal, simply move the decimal point two places to the left and eliminate the percent symbol.

  Examples:
  $64\% = .64$ $87\% = .87$ $7\% = .07$

- To change a percentage to a fraction, divide by 100 and reduce.

  Examples:
  $64\% = \frac{64}{100} = \frac{16}{25}$

  $75\% = \frac{75}{100} = \frac{3}{4}$

  $82\% = \frac{82}{100} = \frac{41}{50}$

- Keep in mind that any percentage that is 100 or greater will need to reflect a whole number or mixed number when converted.

  Examples:
  $125\% = 1.25 \text{ or } 1\frac{1}{4}$

  $350\% = 3.5 \text{ or } 3\frac{1}{2}$

Here are some conversions you should be familiar with:

Fraction	Decimal	Percentage
$\frac{1}{2}$	.5	50%
$\frac{1}{4}$	.25	25%
$\frac{1}{3}$	.333 . . .	33.$\overline{3}$%
$\frac{2}{3}$	.666 . . .	66.$\overline{6}$%
$\frac{1}{10}$	.1	10%
$\frac{1}{8}$	.125	12.5%
$\frac{1}{6}$	.1666 . . .	16.$\overline{6}$%
$\frac{1}{5}$	.2	20%

Algebra Review

Equations
An **equation** is solved by finding a number that is equal to an unknown variable.

Simple Rules for Working with Equations
1. The equal sign separates an equation into two sides.
2. Whenever an operation is performed on one side, the same operation must be performed on the other side.
3. Your first goal is to get all of the variables on one side and all of the numbers on the other.
4. The final step often will be to divide each side by the coefficient, leaving the variable equal to a number.

Checking Equations
To check an equation, substitute the number equal to the variable in the original equation.

Example:

To check the equation below, substitute the number 10 for the variable x.

$$\frac{x}{6} = \frac{x+10}{12}$$

$$\frac{10}{6} = \frac{10+10}{12}$$

$$\frac{10}{6} = \frac{20}{12}$$

$$1\frac{2}{3} = 1\frac{2}{3} \quad \frac{10}{6} = \frac{10}{6}$$

Because this statement is true, you know the answer $x = 10$ must be correct.

Special Tips for Checking Equations

1. If time permits, be sure to check all equations.
2. Be careful to answer the question that is being asked. Sometimes, this involves solving for a variable and then performing an operation.

Example:

If the question asks the value of $x - 2$, and you find $x = 2$, the answer is not 2, but $2 - 2$. Thus, the answer is 0.

Algebraic Fractions

Algebraic fractions are very similar to fractions in arithmetic.

Example:

Write $\frac{x}{5} - \frac{x}{10}$ as a single fraction.

Solution:

Just like in arithmetic, you need to find the LCD of 5 and 10, which is 10. Then, change each fraction into an equivalent fraction that has 10 as a denominator.

$$\frac{x}{5} - \frac{x}{10} = \frac{x(2)}{5(2)} - \frac{x}{10}$$

$$= \frac{2x}{10} - \frac{x}{10}$$

$$= \frac{x}{10}$$

Geometry Review

Area	the space inside a two-dimensional figure
Circumference	the distance around a circle
Perimeter	the distance around a figure
Radius	the distance from the center point of a circle to any point on the circle

Area

Area is the space inside of the lines defining the shape.

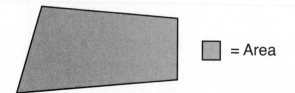

☐ = Area

This geometry review will focus on the area formula for three main shapes: circles, rectangles/squares, and triangles.

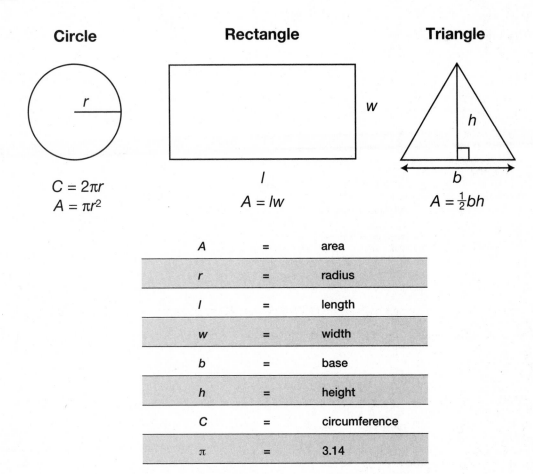

Circle	**Rectangle**	**Triangle**
$C = 2\pi r$	$A = lw$	$A = \frac{1}{2}bh$
$A = \pi r^2$		

A	=	area
r	=	radius
l	=	length
w	=	width
b	=	base
h	=	height
C	=	circumference
π	=	3.14

Perimeter

The perimeter of an object is simply the sum of all of its sides.

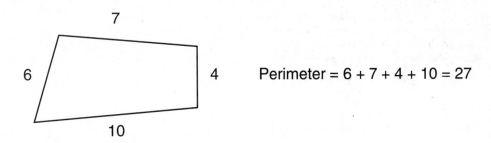

Perimeter = 6 + 7 + 4 + 10 = 27

The circumference is the perimeter of a circle.

$C = 2\pi r$

Word Problem Review

Because many of the math problems on the exam will be word problems, pay extra attention to the following review.

Translating Words into Numbers

The most important skill needed for word problems is being able to translate words into mathematical operations. The following will assist you by giving you some common examples of English phrases and their mathematical equivalents.

- "Increase" means add.

    Example:
    A number increased by five $= x + 5$

- "Less than" means subtract.

    Example:
    10 less than a number $= x - 10$

- "Times" or "product" means multiply.

    Example:
    Three times a number $= 3x$

- "Times the sum" means to multiply a number by a quantity.

    Example:
    Five times the sum of a number and three $= 5(x + 3)$

- Two variables are sometimes used together.

    Example:
    A number y exceeds 5 times a number x by 10.
    $y = 5x + 10$

- "Of" means multiply.

    Example:
    10% of 100 is 10 $= 10\% \times 100 = 10$

- "Is" means equals.

Example:
15 is 14 plus 1.
$15 = 14 + 1$.

Assigning Variables in Word Problems

It may be necessary to create and assign variables in a word problem. To do this, first identify an unknown and a known. You may not actually know the exact value of the "known," but you will know at least something about its value.

Examples:
Max is three years older than Ricky.
Unknown = Ricky's age = x
Known = Max's age is three years older.
Therefore,
Ricky's age = x and Max's age = $x + 3$.

Heidi made twice as many cookies as Rebecca.
Unknown = number of cookies Rebecca made = x
Known = number of cookies Heidi made = $2x$

Jessica has five more than three times the number of books that Becky has.
Unknown = the number of books Becky has = x
Known = the number of books Jessica has = $3x + 5$

Percentage Problems

There is one formula that is useful for solving the three types of percentage problems:

$$\underset{\text{part}}{\overset{\#}{\frac{\text{part}}{\text{whole}}}} = \underset{100}{\overset{\%}{\frac{}{100}}}$$

When reading a percentage problem, substitute the necessary information into this formula based on the following:

- 100 is always written in the denominator of the percentage sign column.
- If given a percentage, write it in the numerator position of the number column. If you are not given a percentage, then the variable should be placed there.
- The denominator of the number column represents the number that is equal to the whole, or 100%. This number always follows the word *of* in a word problem.

- The numerator of the number column represents the number that is the percent.
- In the formula, the equal sign can be interchanged with the word *is*.

Examples:

- Finding a percentage of a given number.

  What number is equal to 40% of 50?

$$\begin{array}{ccc} \# & & \% \\[6pt] \dfrac{x}{50} & = & \dfrac{40}{100} \end{array}$$

Cross multiply:

$$100(x) = (40)(50)$$
$$100x = 2{,}000$$
$$\frac{100x}{100} = \frac{2{,}000}{100}$$
$$x = 20 \quad \text{Therefore, 20 is 40\% of 50.}$$

- Finding a number when a percentage is given:

  40% of what number is 24?

$$\begin{array}{ccc} \# & & \% \\[6pt] \dfrac{24}{x} & = & \dfrac{40}{100} \end{array}$$

Cross multiply:

$$(24)(100) = (40)(x)$$
$$2{,}400 = 40x$$
$$\frac{2{,}400}{40} = \frac{40x}{40}$$
$$60 = x \quad \text{Therefore, 40\% of 60 is 24.}$$

- Finding what percentage one number is of another:

  What percentage of 75 is 15?

$$\begin{array}{ccc} \# & & \% \\[6pt] \dfrac{15}{75} & = & \dfrac{x}{100} \end{array}$$

Cross multiply:

$15(100) = (75)(x)$

$1,500 = 75x$

$\frac{1,500}{75} = \frac{75x}{75}$

$20 = x$ Therefore, 20% of 75 is 15.

Rate Problems

You may encounter a couple of different types of rate problems on your exam: cost per unit, interest rate, and tax rate. Rate is defined as a comparison of two quantities with different units of measure.

$$\text{Rate} = \frac{x \text{ units}}{y \text{ units}}$$

Examples: $\frac{\text{dollars}}{\text{square foot}}, \frac{\text{interest}}{\text{year}}$

Cost Per Unit

Some problems on your exam may require that you calculate the cost per unit.

Example:

If 100 square feet cost $1,000, how much does 1 square foot cost?

Solution:

$\frac{\text{total cost}}{\text{\# of square feet}} = \frac{1,000}{100} = \$10/\text{square foot}$

Interest Rate

The formula for simple interest is Interest = Principal × Rate × Time, or *I = PRT*. If you know certain values but not others, you can still find the answer using algebra. In simple interest problems, the value of *T* is usually 1, as in one year. There are three basic kinds of interest problems, depending on which number is missing.

▶ Practice

Now that you have reviewed some of the math skills you will need, it's time to practice real estate math questions. Following, you will find practice problems and thorough answer explanations for the real estate math topics listed.

Here are some equivalencies you may need to use to complete some questions. Generally, any equivalencies you will need to know for your exam are provided to you.

Equivalencies
12 inches (in. or ") = 1 foot (ft. or ')
3 feet or 36 inches = 1 yard (yd.)
1,760 yards = 1 mile (mi.)
5,280 feet = 1 mile
144 square inches (sq. in. or in.^{2}) = 1 square foot (sq. ft. or ft.^{2})
9 square feet = 1 square yard
43,560 feet = 1 acre
640 acres = 1 square mile

Percents

You may be asked a basic percentage problem.

Example:
What is 86% of 1,750?

Solution:
Start by translating words into math terms.
$x = (86\%)(1,750)$
Change the percent into a decimal by moving the decimal point two spaces to the *left*.
$86\% = .86$
Now you can solve.
$x = (.86)(1,750)$
$x = 1,505$

Other percentage problems you may find on the exam will come in the form of rate problems. Keep reading for more examples of these problems.

Interest Problems

Let's take a look at a problem in which you have calculate the interest rate (R). Remember, the rate is the same as the percentage.

Example:
Mary Valencia borrowed $5,000, for which she is paying $600 interest per year. What is the rate of interest being charged?

Solution:

Start with the values you know.

Principal = $5,000

Interest = $600

Rate = x

Time = 1 year

Using the formula $I = PRT$, insert the values you know, and solve for x.

$600 = 5,000(x)(1)$

$600 = 5,000x$

$\frac{600}{5,000} = \frac{x}{5,000}$

$.12 = x$

To convert .12 to a percent, move the decimal point two places to the *right*.

$.12 = 12\%$

Principal and Interest

Sometimes, you will need to know the interest rate on a loan when the only information you have is the interest portion of the current payment and the principal balance. The formula is

$$\text{Principal Balance} \times \text{Interest Rate} = \text{Annual Interest Amount}$$

Example:

If the current principal balance is $300,000 and the amount of the payment applied to interest this month is $1,500, what is the interest rate?

Solution:

Move the variables in the equation around so that it reads:

$\text{interest rate} = \frac{(\text{monthly interest} \times 12)}{\text{principal balance}}$

$\text{interest rate} = \frac{(\$1,500 \times 12)}{\$300,000}$

$\text{interest rate} = .06$

So the interest rate is 6%.

Debt Service

You may be asked to calculate the total interest paid over the life of the mortgage.

Example:

If a mortgage loan is $150,000, the annual interest rate is 6.5%, the monthly payment is $948.10, and the term is 30 years, how much interest will the borrower pay over the life of the loan?

Solution:

First, calculate the total amount paid over the life of the mortgage:

term $\times$ 12 $\times$ monthly payment = total paid

$30 \times 12 \times 948.10 = \$341,316$

Then, find the total interest paid.

total paid – principal = total interest paid

$\$341,316 - \$150,000 = \$191,316$

Private Mortgage Insurance (PMI)

Private mortgage insurance companies often charge an annual premium.

Example:

If the principal balance is $250,000 and the PMI company charges a .5% annual premium, what is the monthly PMI amount?

Solution:

The formula for the annual premium is principal balance $\times$ premium rate = annual premium.

$\$250,000 \times .005 = \$1,250$

To find the monthly PMI amount:

$$\frac{\text{annual premium}}{12} = \text{monthly PMI}$$

$$\frac{\$1,250}{12} = \$104.17$$

The monthly PMI portion of the payment is $104.17.

Discount Rate

The discount rate, or the internal rate of return, is the annual percentage increase in value of an investment.

Example:

Bob has been urged to buy a property for $150,000 because the expected value in 7 years is $350,000. Bob wants to know what the annual increase will be.

Solution:
The formula for discount rate is
$r = (\frac{FV}{PV})\frac{1}{n} - 1$
where
FV = future value
PV = present value
n = term
r = discount rate

So we set up the problem:
$r = (\frac{350,000}{150,000})\frac{1}{7} - 1$
$r = (2.33).1429 - 1$
$r = (2.33).1429 - 1$
$r = .1284$

The return is 12.84% annually.

Area
Some of the problems on your exam may ask you to figure the area of a piece of land, a building, or some other figure. Here are some formulas and how to use them.

Rectangles
Remember the formula: Area = (length)(width)

Example:
A man purchased a lot that is 50 feet by 10 feet for a garden. How many square feet of land does he have?

Solution:
Using the formula Area = (length)(width), you have
A = (50)(10) = 500 square feet

Example:
The Meyers family bought a piece of land for a summer home that was 2.75 acres. The lake frontage was 150 feet. What was the length of the lot?

Solution:

When you take your exam, you may be provided with certain equivalencies. You will need to refer to the "Equivalencies" list on page 182 to answer this question. First, find the area of the land in square feet.

(2.75)(43,560) = 119,790 square feet

In the previous example, you were given the length and the width. In this example, you are given the area and the width, so you are solving for the length. Because you know the area and the width of the lot, use the formula to solve.

Area = (length)(width)

119,790 = (x)(150)

Divide both sides by 150.

$\frac{119,790}{150} = \frac{(x)(150)}{150}$

$x = \frac{119,790}{150}$

$x = 798.6$ feet

Triangles

Although it may not be as common, you may be asked to find the area of a triangle. If you don't remember the formula, see page 177.

Example:

The Baron family is buying a triangular piece of land for a gas station. It is 200 feet at the base, and the side perpendicular to the base is 200 feet. They are paying $2 per square foot for the property. What will it cost?

Solution:

Start with the formula Area = $\frac{1}{2}$(base)(height).

Now, write down the values you know.

Area = x

Base = 200

Height = 200

If it's easier, you can change $\frac{1}{2}$ to a decimal.

$\frac{1}{2} = .5$

Now you can plug these values into the formula.

$x = (.5)(200)(200)$

$x = (.5)(40,000)$

$x = 20,000$ square feet

Don't forget that the question is not asking for the number of square feet, but for the *cost* of the property per square foot. This is a rate problem, so you need to complete one more step. (20,000 square feet)($2 per square foot) = $40,000.

Example:

Victor and Evelyn Robinson have an outlot that a neighbor wants to buy. The side of the outlot next to their property is 86 feet. The rear line is perpendicular to their side lot, and the road frontage is 111 feet. Their plat shows they own 3,000 square feet in the outlot. What is the length of the rear line of the outlot? Round your answer to the nearest whole number.

Solution:

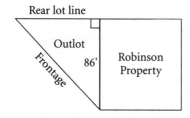

It helps to draw the figure to conceive shapes. The rear lot line is perpendicular to the side lot line. This makes the side lot line the base and the rear lot line the height (altitude).

Area = $\frac{1}{2}$(base)(height)

Area = 3,000 square feet

Base = 86 feet

Height = x

If it's easier, you can change $\frac{1}{2}$ to a decimal.

$\frac{1}{2}$ = .5

Now you can plug these values into the formula.

3,000 = (.5)(86)(x)

3,000 = (43)(x)

Divide both sides by 43.

$\frac{3,000}{43} = \frac{(43)(x)}{43}$

x = 69.767 feet

Don't forget the question says to round your answer to the nearest whole number. The answer is 70 feet.

Circles

Remember the formula Area = πr^2.

Example:

Marie Brodman, a contractor, has been awarded the job to put up a circular bandstand in the town square. The radius of the circular area for the bandstand is 15 feet. What is the area of the bandstand? Use 3.14 for π.

Solution:

Area $= \pi r^2$

Start with the values you know.

Area $= x$

$\pi = 3.14$

radius $= 15$

Now plug these values into the formula.

Area $= (3.14)(15)(15) = 706.5$ sq. ft.

Property Tax

To solve property tax questions, you will be using percents and rates.

Example:

The tax rate in your county is $4.17 per hundred of assessed valuation, and Mr. Brown, a possible client, has told you his taxes are $1,100. What is his property assessment? (Round your answer to the nearest 10 cents.)

Solution:

Start off with the values you know.

Taxes $= \$1,100$

Assessment $= x$

Tax rate $= \$4.17$ per hundred (%)

If you remember the definition of percent as being an amount per hundred, then $4.17 per hundred is actually 4.17%. To make this equation more manageable, convert this percent to a decimal by moving the decimal point two spaces to the *left*. Now the tax rate is .0417.

.0417 of the assessed value of the house is $1,100. Translate the words into math terms. This means:

$(.0417)(x) = 1,100$

To solve the equation, divide both sides by .0417.

$$\frac{.0417x}{.0417} = \frac{1,100}{.0417}$$

$x = \$26,378.896$

Remember, the question asks you round to the nearest 10 cents. That means that .896 needs to be rounded up to 90. So the answer is $26,378.90.

Example:

Ms. Sassoon knew her own taxes were $975, and her property assessment was $17,000 for the house and $6,000 for the land. She wanted to know the tax rate (%).

Tip

Note that you may be asked for monthly amounts certain problems. Most calculations are on an annual basis— unless you divide by 12.

Solution:

Start with the values you know.

Tax = $975

Assessment for house = $17,000 plus assessment for land = $6,000. Therefore, total = $23,000

Rate (%) = x

According to the question, $23,000 at a rate of x is $975. Convert this statement into an equation.

($23,000)($x$) = 975.

Solve the equation by dividing both sides by 23,000.

$$\frac{23,000x}{23,000} = \frac{975}{23,000}$$

$x = .0423913$

To make this equation more simple, round the answer to .0424.

Remember that you are looking for the rate. Therefore, you need to convert this decimal to a percent by moving the decimal point two places to the *right*. The rate is 4.24%. (This can also be expressed as $4.24 per hundred.)

Loan-to-Value Ratios

These problems often deal with percentages.

Example:

A mortgage loan for 10% is at a 75% loan-to-value ratio. The interest on the original balance for the first year is $6,590. What is the value of the property securing the loan? Round to the nearest one cent.

Solution:

First, find out the loan amount.

$6,590 is 10% of the loan amount. Let x equal the loan amount. Now, translate these words into math terms.

$6,590 = (10%)($x$)

Change 10% into a decimal by moving the decimal point two places to the *left*.

10% = .1

Rewrite the equation with the decimal.

$6,590 = (.1)($x$)

Divide both sides by (.1).

$x = $65,900

Now that you know the loan amount ($65,900), use this information to find the value of the property.

Write down the values you know.

Loan amount = $65,900

Loan-to-value ratio = 75%

Value = x

We know that 75% of the value is $65,900.

Translate this into math terms.

$(75\%)(x) = \$65,900$

Change the percent into a decimal (75% = .75) and solve.

$(.75)(x) = 65,900$

Divide both sides by .75.

$$\frac{(.75)(x)}{(.75)} = \frac{65,900}{(.75)}$$

$x = 87,866.66666$

When rounded to the nearest one cent, the answer is $87,866.67.

Points

Loan discounts are often called *points*, or loan placement fees, one point meaning 1% of the face amount of the loan. The service fee of 1% paid by buyers of government backed loans is called a *loan origination fee*.

Example:

A homebuyer may obtain a $50,000 FHA mortgage loan, provided the seller pays a discount of five points. What is the amount of the discount?

Solution:

The definition of one point is 1% of the face amount of the loan.

Therefore, five points = 5% of face of loan. First, change the percent to a decimal.

5% = .05

Now you can use these values to solve.

Amount of discount = x

Points = .05

Amount of loan = $50,000

So, $x = (.05)(50,000)$

$x = \$2,500$

Example:

A property is listed at $74,000. An offer is made for $72,000, provided the seller pays three points on a loan for 80% of the purchase price. The brokerage commission rate is 7%. How much less will the seller receive if she accepts the offer than she would have received if she sold at all cash at the original terms?

Solution:

Here are the values you know:

Sold for original terms—price	$74,000
Less 7% commission	− 5,180 (.07)(74,000) = 5,180
Seller's net	$68,820

This question becomes more difficult, because in order to find the seller's net on the offered price, you must calculate the discount. The provision is that the seller pays three points (or .03) on a loan for 80% (or .8) of the price.

Start by finding 80% of the price.

(.8)(72,000) = $57,600

Now, the points are applied to this amount. This means .03 of $57,600 is the discount.

So, (.03)(57,600) = discount = 1,728.

You know these values:

Sold at offered terms—price	$72,000
Less 7% commission	− 5,040 (.07)(72,000) = 5,040
Less discount	− 1,728
Seller's net	$65,232

$72,000	Sales price		Net at original	$68,820
× .80	Loan-to-value ratio		Net at offered	− 65,232
$57,600	Loan amount		Difference	$ 3,588
× .03	Points			
$ 1,728	Discount			

Equity

Example:

If a homeowner has a first mortgage loan balance of $48,350, a second mortgage loan balance of $18,200, and $26,300 equity, what is the value of her home?

Solution:

In this case, the value of the home is determined by the total loan balance plus the equity. Add the three numbers to find the value of the home.

$48,350 loan balance + $18,200 loan balance + $26,300 = value of the home

$92,850 = value of the home

Qualifying Buyers

Example:

A buyer is obtaining a conventional loan that requires 29/33 ratios. He earns $66,000 a year and has a $1,350 monthly car payment. What is his maximum PITI payment?

a. $1,612.50

b. $1,812.50

c. $465

d. $2,475

Solution:

$66,000 divided by 12 = $5,500 monthly income

($5,500)(.29) = $1,595 front end qualifier

($5,500)(.33) = $1,815 − $1,350 debt = $465 back end qualifier

The maximum PITI is the lower of these two qualifiers, $465.

Prorations

At the time of settlement, there must be a reconciliation or adjustment of any monies owed by either party as of that date. The important fact to bear in mind is that *the party who used the service pays for it*. If you will keep this firmly in mind, you will not have any difficulty deciding who to credit and who to debit.

Example:

Mr. Kim's taxes are $1,200 per year, paid in advance on a calendar year. He is settling on the sale of his house to Ms. Rasheed on August 1. Which of them owes how much to the other?

Solution:

Ask yourself some questions:

How many months has the seller paid for?	12	($1,200)
How many months has the seller used?	7	($700)
How many months should the seller be reimbursed for?	5	($500)
How many months will the buyer use?	5	($500)
How many months has he paid for?	0	($0)
How many months should he reimburse the seller for?	5	($500)

Credit Mr. Kim $500

Debit Ms. Rasheed $500

What would the answer be if the taxes were paid in arrears? In other words, the seller has used the service for seven months but hasn't paid anything. The buyer will have to pay it all at the end of the year. In that case, the seller owes the buyer for seven months, or $700.

In working proration problems, be sure you have the right dates when you subtract. Sometimes the termination date for the policy is not given, and the tendency is to subtract the date the policy was written from the date of settlement. This will not give you the unused portion. You must subtract the date of settlement from the date of termination of the policy, which will be exactly the same date one, three, or five years after written, depending on the term of the policy. Most problems use either a one- or three-year term.

Remember!

Use a 30-day month and a 360-day year in all calculations unless you are told otherwise. Assume a calendar year, unless a fiscal or school year is specified.

Commissions

Let's look at a commission problem. They are typically rate (percentage) problems.

Example:

Broker Roberts sold the Weisman house for $65,000. The total commission came to $4,000. What was Roberts's commission rate? Round to the nearest whole percent.

Solution:

You see the word *rate* and decide this is solved using percentages.

Start with the values you know.

Price of house = 65,000

Commission rate = x

Commission = 4,000

Now, translate the word problem into an equation.

$65,000x = 4,000$

Divide both sides by 65,000

$x = \frac{4,000}{65,000}$

$x = 0.061$

Convert the decimal to a percent by moving the decimal two places to the *right*. 0.061 becomes 6.1%.

Example:

An agent received a 3% commission on $\frac{1}{4}$ of her total sales. On the remainder, she received a 6% commission. What was her average commission for all of her sales?

Solution:

Start off by asking yourself: How many fourths (parts) were there? Four, naturally.

3%   6%   6%   6%

To find the average, you add up all the numbers, and divide by the number of items you add together. In this case, there are four numbers.

So, 3 + 6 + 6 + 6 = 21

And 21% ÷ 4 = 5.25%

Sale Proceeds

Example:

Broker Garcia was trying to list a house. The owner said he wanted to clear (net) $12,000 from the sale of the house. The balance of the mortgage was $37,000. It would cost about $1,200 to fix the house up to sell. How much would the owner have to sell the house for if the 7% commission was included? (Round your answer to the nearest cent.)

Solution:

Use a chart to clarify the problem.

Expenses	In Dollars	In Percents
Seller's net	12,000	
Loan balance	37,000	
Repairs	1,200	
Commission		7%
	50,200	7%

If the sales price is 100% and the commission is 7% of the sales price, all the remaining items added together must make 93% of the sales price. The place where most people go wrong is in not including the seller's net when they add the expenses. The seller's net has to come out of the sales price. (Where else would it come from?) Therefore, it is part of the remaining 93%. You now have a percentage problem. As always, convert your percents to decimals.

Start with the values you know:

Expenses = $50,200

Sales price = x

Seller's net, loan balance, repairs = .93 of sales price

.93 of the sales price is $50,200.

Convert this statement into an equation.

$(.93)(x) = \$50,200$

Divide both sides by .93.

$$\frac{(.93)(x)}{.93} = \frac{\$50,200}{.93}$$

$x = \frac{\$50,200}{.93}$

$x = \$53,978.4945$

Don't forget to round to the nearest cent!

$x = \$53,978.49$

Transfer Tax/Conveyance Tax/Revenue Stamps

Here is a transfer tax question.

Example:

A property is sold for \$135,800 in cash. The transfer tax is \$441.35. If transfer taxes are calculated per \$200 of value, what was the rate (per \$200) of the transfer tax?

Solution:

Start with the values you know.

Selling price = \$135,800

Transfer tax rate = x per \$200

Transfer tax = \$441.35

It's probably easiest to begin by dividing \$200 because the rate is calculated per \$200 of value.

So, $\frac{\$135,800}{\$200} = \$679$

You know that \$441.35 is some rate of \$679. Translate this into math terms.

$\$441.35 = (x)(\$679)$

Divide both sides by \$679.

$$\frac{\$441.35}{(\$679)} = \frac{(x)(\$679)}{(\$679)}$$

$.65 = x$

Therefore, the transfer tax rate is \$.65 per \$200.

Competitive Market Analyses (CMA)

To solve these problems, you will use measurements and other hypothetical features of the comparable property to arrive at a value. Remember, a CMA is not an appraisal.

Example:

If Building A measures 52' by 106' and Building B measures 75' by 85', how much will B cost if A costs \$140,000 and both cost the same per square foot to build?

Solution:

Area = (length)(width)

Area of Building A = (52)(106) = 5,512 square feet

Area of Building B = (75)(85) = 6,375 square feet

Cost of Building A per square foot = $\frac{140,000}{5,512}$ = $25.40

Cost of Building B = (6,375)($25.40) = $161,925

Example:

Carson's house (B), which is being appraised, is an exact twin of the houses on either side of it, built by the same builder at the same time. House A was appraised for $145,000, but it has a 14-by-20-foot garage, which was added at a cost of about $18 per square foot. House C was recently sold for $143,000, with central air valued at $3,000. What would be a fair estimate of the value of Carson's house?

Solution:

Comparable C	$143,000	
– Air Conditioning	– 3,000	
	$140,000	

Comparable A	$145,000	Garage: 14' × 20' = 280 sq. ft.
– Cost of Garage	– 5,040	280 sq. ft. × $18 = $5,040
	$139,960	

Answer: $140,000

Income Properties

Example:

An investor is considering the purchase of an income property generating a gross income of $350,000. Operating expenses constitute 70% of gross income. If the investor wants a return of 14%, what is the maximum she can pay?

Solution:

Gross income = $350,000

Expenses = 70% of gross income

Net income = Gross income – Expenses

Desired return = 14%

Maximum buyer can pay = x

This is a multistep problem. Start by calculating the expenses, but remember you will need to stop to calculate the net income. First, change the percent to a decimal.

70% = .70

Now, you know that expenses are 70% of the gross income of $350,000. Change the words to mathematical terms.

Expenses = $(.7)(350,000) = \$245,000$

Gross income – Expenses = Net income

$\$350,000 - \$245,000 = \$105,000$

The buyer wants the net income ($105,000) to be 14% of what he pays for the property.

Change the percent to a decimal (14% = .14) and then convert this statement to an equation.

$\$150,000 = (.14)(x)$

Divide both sides by .14.

$\frac{\$150,000}{.14} = \frac{(.14)(x)}{.14}$

$\$150,000 \div .14 = x$

$\$750,000 = x$

Depreciation

There are several methods of depreciation, but the only one you are likely to meet on your exam is the straight-line method. This method spreads the total depreciation over the useful life of the building in equal annual amounts. It is calculated by dividing the replacement cost by the years of useful life left.

$$\frac{\text{replacement cost}}{\text{years of useful life}} = \text{annual depreciation}$$

The depreciation rate may be given or may have to be calculated by the straight-line method. This means dividing the total depreciation (100%) by the estimated useful life given for the building.

$$\frac{100\%}{\text{years of useful life}} = \text{depreciated rate}$$

If a building has 50 years of useful life left, the depreciation rate would be computed as follows:

$$\frac{100\%}{50} = 2\%$$

In other words, it has a 2% depreciation rate annually.

Example:
The replacement cost of a building has been estimated at $80,000. The building is 12 years old and has an estimated 40 years of useful life left. What can be charged to annual depreciation? What is the total depreciation for 12 years? What is the present value of this building?

Solution:
Calculate the annual depreciation.

$$\frac{\text{replacement cost}}{\text{years of useful life}} = \text{annual depreciation}$$

$$\frac{\$80,000}{40} = \$2,000$$

Find the total depreciation over the 12 years.

Annual depreciation of $\$2,000 \times 12$ years $= \$24,000$

Find the current value: replacement − depreciation = current value

$\$80,000 - \$24,000 = \$56,000$

▶ Summary

Hopefully, with this review, you have realized that real estate math is not as bad as you might have imagined. If you feel you need more practice, check out LearningExpress's *Practical Math Success in 20 Minutes a Day, 3rd Edition* or *1,001 Math Problems, 2nd Edition*. Use the exams in those books to practice even more real estate math.

9 ▶ Real Estate Glossary

CHAPTER SUMMARY

One of the most basic components in preparing for your broker exam is making sure you know all the terminology. This glossary provides a list of the most commonly used real estate terms and their definitions.

T HESE TERMS WILL help you not only as you study for your broker exam, but also after you pass your exam and are on the job every day. The terms are listed in alphabetical order for easy reference.

▶ A

abandonment the voluntary surrender of a right, claim, or interest in a piece of property without naming a successor as owner or tenant.

abstract of title a certified summary of the history of a title to a particular parcel of real estate that includes the original grant and all subsequent transfers, encumbrances, and releases.

abutting sharing a common boundary; adjoining.

acceleration clause a clause in a note, mortgage, or deed of trust that permits the lender to declare the entire amount of principal and accrued interest due and payable immediately in the event of default.

acceptance the indication by a party receiving an offer that they agree to the terms of the offer. In most states, the offer and acceptance must be reduced to writing when real property is involved.

accretion the increase or addition of land resulting from the natural deposit of sand or soil by streams, lakes, or rivers.

accrued depreciation (1) the amount of depreciation, or loss in value, that has accumulated since initial construction; (2) the difference between the current appraised value and the cost to replace the building new.

accrued items a list of expenses that have been incurred but have not yet been paid, such as interest on a mortgage loan, that are included on a closing statement.

acknowledgment a formal declaration before a public official, usually a notary public, by a person who has signed a deed, contract, or other document that the execution was a voluntary act.

acre a measure of land equal to 43,560 square feet or 4,840 square yards.

actual eviction the result of legal action brought by a landlord against a defaulted tenant, whereby the tenant is physically removed from rented or leased property by a court order.

actual notice the actual knowledge that a person has of a particular fact.

addendum any provision added to a contract, or an addition to a contract that expands, modifies, or enhances the clarity of the agreement. To be a part of the contract and legally enforceable, an addendum must be referenced within the contract.

adjacent lying near but not necessarily in actual contact with.

adjoining contiguous or attached; in actual contact with.

adjustable-rate mortgage (ARM) a mortgage in which the interest changes periodically, according to corresponding fluctuations in an index. All ARMs are tied to indexes. For example, a seven-year, adjustable-rate mortgage is a loan in which the rate remains fixed for the first seven years, and then fluctuates according to the index to which it is tied.

adjusted basis the original cost of a property, plus acquisition costs, plus the value of added improvements to the property, minus accrued depreciation.

adjustment date the date the interest rate changes on an adjustable-rate mortgage.

administrator a person appointed by a court to settle the estate of a person who has died without leaving a will.

ad valorem tax tax in proportion to the value of a property.

adverse possession a method of acquiring title to another person's property through court action after taking actual, open, hostile, and continuous possession for a statutory period of time; may require payment of property taxes during the period of possession.

affidavit a written statement made under oath and signed before a licensed public official, usually a notary public.

Age Discrimination in Employment Act of 1967 a law that protects individuals 40 years of age and older from discrimination.

agency the legal relationship between principal and agent that arises out of a contract wherein an agent is employed to do certain acts on behalf of the principal, who has retained the agent to deal with a third party.

agent one who has been granted the authority to act on behalf of another.

agreement of sale a written agreement between a seller and a purchaser whereby the purchaser agrees to buy a certain piece of property from the seller for a specified price.

air rights the right to use the open space above a particular property.

alienation the transfer of ownership of a property to another, either voluntarily or involuntarily.

alienation clause the clause in a mortgage or deed of trust that permits the lender to declare all unpaid principal and accrued interest due and payable if the borrower transfers title to the property.

allodial system a system of land ownership in the United States in which land is held free and clear of any rent or services due to the government; commonly contrasted with the feudal system, in which ownership is held by a monarch.

amenities features or benefits of a particular property that enhance the property's desirability and value, such as a scenic view or a pool.

Americans with Disabilities Act (ADA) federal legislation designed to integrate people with disabilities fully into the mainstream of American life.

amortization the method of repaying a loan or debt by making periodic installment payments composed of both principal and interest. When all principal has been repaid, it is considered fully amortized.

amortization schedule a table that shows how much of each loan payment will be applied toward principal and how much toward interest over the lifespan of the loan. It also shows the gradual decrease of the outstanding loan balance until it reaches zero.

amortize to repay a loan through regular payments that are comprised of principal and interest.

annual percentage rate (APR) the total or effective amount of interest charged on a loan, expressed as a percentage, on a yearly basis. This value is created according to a government formula intended to reflect the true annual cost of borrowing.

anti-deficiency laws laws used in some states to limit the claim of a lender on default on payment of a purchase money mortgage on owner-occupied residential property to the value of the collateral.

anti-trust laws laws designed to protect free enterprise and the open marketplace by prohibiting certain business practices that restrict competition. In reference to real estate, these laws would prevent such practices as price fixing or agreements by brokers to limit their areas of trade.

apportionments adjustment of income, expenses, or carrying charges related to real estate, usually computed to the date of closing so that the seller pays all expenses to date, and then the buyer pays all expenses beginning on the closing date.

appraisal an estimate or opinion of the value of an adequately described property, as of a specific date.

appraised value an opinion of a property's fair market value, based on an appraiser's knowledge, experience, and analysis of the property and on comparable sales.

appraiser an individual qualified by education, training, and experience to estimate the value of real property. Appraisers may work directly for mortgage lenders, or they may be independent contractors.

appreciation an increase in the market value of a property.

appurtenance something that transfers with the title to land even if not an actual part of the property, such as an easement.

arbitration the process of settling a dispute in which the parties submit their differences to an impartial third party, whose decision on the matter is binding.

ARELLO the Association of Real Estate License Law Officials.

assemblage the combination of two or more parcels.

assessed value the value of a property used to calculate real estate taxes.

assessment the process of assigning value on property for taxation purposes.

assessor a public official who establishes the value of a property for taxation purposes.

asset an item of value owned by an individual. Assets that can be quickly converted into cash are considered liquid assets, such as bank accounts and stock portfolios. Other assets include real estate, personal property, and debts owed.

assignment the transfer of all the lessee's rights to another party. The assignor is still liable for the performance of the agreement, unless the lessor releases him or her.

assumption a written agreement in which the buyer will pay the mortgage and is obligated to the seller. The seller may still be liable to the lender.

assumption of mortgage the act of acquiring the title to a property that has an existing mortgage and agreeing to be liable for the payment of any debt still existing on that mortgage. However, the lender must accept the transfer of liability for the original borrower to be relieved of the debt.

attachment the process whereby a court takes custody of a debtor's property until the creditor's debt is satisfied.

attest to bear witness by providing a signature.

attorney-in-fact a person who is authorized under a power of attorney to act on behalf of another.

avulsion the removal of land from one owner to another when a stream or other body of water suddenly changes its channel.

▶ **B**

balloon mortgage a loan in which the periodic payments do not fully amortize the loan, so that a final payment (a balloon payment) is substantially larger than the amount of the periodic payments that must be made to satisfy the debt.

balloon payment the final, lump-sum payment that is due at the termination of a balloon mortgage.

bankruptcy an individual or individuals can restructure or relieve themselves of debts and liabilities by filing in federal bankruptcy court. There are many types of bankruptcies, and the most common for an individual is Chapter 7 No Asset, which relieves the borrower of most types of debts.

bargain and sale deed a deed that conveys title, but does not necessarily carry warranties against liens or encumbrances.

baseline one of the imaginary east-west lines used as a reference point when describing property with the rectangular or government survey method of property description.

bench mark a permanently marked point with a known elevation, used as a reference by surveyors to measure elevations.

beneficiary (1) one who benefits from the acts of another; (2) the lender in a deed of trust.

bequest personal property given by provision of a will.

betterment an improvement to property that increases its value.

bilateral contract a contract in which each party promises to perform an act in exchange for the other party's promise also to perform an act.

bill of sale a written instrument that transfers ownership of personal property. A bill of sale cannot be used to transfer ownership of real property, which is passed by deed.

binder an agreement, accompanied by an earnest money deposit, for the purchase of a piece of real estate to show the purchaser's good faith intent to complete a transaction.

biweekly mortgage a mortgage in which payments are made every two weeks instead of once a month. Therefore, instead of making 12 monthly payments during the year, the borrower makes the equivalent of 13 monthly payments. The extra payment reduces the principal, thereby reducing the time it takes to pay off a 30-year mortgage.

blanket mortgage a mortgage in which more than one parcel of real estate is pledged to cover a single debt.

blockbusting the illegal and discriminatory practice of inducing homeowners to sell their properties by suggesting or implying the introduction of members of a protected class into the neighborhood.

bona fide in good faith, honest.

bond evidence of personal debt secured by a mortgage or other lien on real estate.

boot money or property provided to make up a difference in value or equity between two properties in an exchange.

branch office a place of business secondary to a principal office. The branch office is a satellite office generally run by a licensed broker, for the benefit of the broker running the principal office, as well as the associate broker's convenience.

breach of contract violation of any conditions or terms in a contract without legal excuse.

broker the term *broker* can mean many things, but in terms of real estate, it is the owner-manager of a business that brings together the parties to a real estate transaction for a fee. The roles of brokers and brokers' associates are defined by state law. In the mortgage industry, *broker* usually refers to a company or individual who does not lend the money for the loans directly, but that brokers loan to larger lenders or investors.

brokerage the business of bringing together buyers and sellers or other participants in a real estate transaction.

broker's price opinion (BPO) a broker's opinion of value based on a comparative market analysis, rather than a certified appraisal.

building code local regulations that control construction, design, and materials used in construction that are based on health and safety regulations.

building line the distance from the front, rear, or sides of a building lot beyond which no structures may extend.

building restrictions limitations listed in zoning ordinances or deed restrictions on the size and type of improvements allowed on a property.

bundle of rights the concept that ownership of a property includes certain rights regarding the property, such as possession, enjoyment, control of use, and disposition.

buydown usually refers to a fixed-rate mortgage where the interest rate is bought down for a temporary period, usually one to three years. After that time and for the remainder of the term, the borrower's payment is calculated at the note rate. In order to buy down the initial rate for the temporary payment, a lump sum is paid and held in an account used to supplement the borrower's monthly payment. These funds usually come from the seller as a financial incentive to induce someone to buy their property.

buyer's broker real estate broker retained by a prospective buyer; this buyer becomes the broker's client to whom fiduciary duties are owed.

bylaws rules and regulations adopted by an association—for example, a condominium association.

▶ C

cancellation clause a provision in a lease that confers on one or all parties to the lease the right to terminate the parties' obligations, should the occurrence of the condition or contingency set forth in the clause happen.

canvassing the practice of searching for prospective clients by making unsolicited phone calls and/or visiting homes door to door.

cap the limit on fluctuation rates regarding adjustable rate mortgages. Limitations, or caps, may apply to how much the loan may adjust over a six-month period, an annual period, and the life of the loan. There is also a limit on how much that payment can change each year.

capital money used to create income, or the net worth of a business as represented by the amount by which its assets exceed its liabilities.

capital expenditure the cost of a betterment to a property.

capital gains tax a tax charged on the profit gained from the sale of a capital asset.

capitalization the process of estimating the present value of an income-producing piece of property by dividing anticipated future income by a capitalization rate.

capitalization rate the rate of return a property will generate on an owner's investment.

cash flow the net income produced by an investment property, calculated by deducting operating and fixed expenses from gross income.

caveat emptor a Latin phrase meaning "let the buyer beware."

CC&R covenants, conditions, and restrictions of a cooperative or condominium development.

certificate of discharge a document used when the security instrument is a mortgage.

certificate of eligibility a document issued by the Veterans Administration that certifies a veteran's eligibility for a VA loan.

certificate of reasonable value (CRV) a document issued by the Veterans Administration once the appraisal has been performed on a property being bought with a VA loan.

certificate of sale the document given to a purchaser of real estate that is sold at a tax foreclosure sale.

certificate of title a report stating an opinion on the status of a title, based on the examination of public records.

chain of title the recorded history of conveyances and encumbrances that affect the title to a parcel of land.

chattel personal property, as opposed to real property.

chattel mortgage a loan in which personal property is pledged to secure the debt.

city a large municipality governed under a charter and granted by the state.

Civil Rights Act of 1964 (Title VII) law that prohibits employment discrimination based on race, color, sex, or national origin.

Civil Rights Act of 1991 law that provides monetary damages for intentional employment discrimination.

clear title a title that is free of liens and legal questions as to ownership of a property that is a requirement for the sale of real estate; sometimes referred to as *just title*, *good title*, or *free and clear*.

closing the point in a real estate transaction when the purchase price is paid to the seller and the deed to the property is transferred from the seller to the buyer.

closing costs there are two kinds: (1) nonrecurring closing costs and (2) prepaid items. Nonrecurring closing costs are any items paid once as a result of buying the property or obtaining a loan. Prepaid items are items that recur over time, such as property taxes and homeowners insurance. A lender makes an attempt to estimate the amount of nonrecurring closing costs and prepaid items on the good faith estimate, which is issued to the borrower within three days of receiving a home loan application.

closing date the date on which the buyer takes over the property.

closing statement a written accounting of funds received and disbursed during a real estate transaction. The buyer and seller receive separate closing statements.

cloud on the title an outstanding claim or encumbrance that can affect or impair the owner's title.

clustering the grouping of home sites within a subdivision on smaller lots than normal, with the remaining land slated for use as common areas.

codicil a supplement or addition to a will that modifies the original instrument.

coinsurance clause a clause in an insurance policy that requires the insured to pay a portion of any loss experienced.

collateral something of value hypothecated (real property) or pledged (personal property) by a borrower as security for a debt.

collection when a borrower falls behind, the lender contacts the borrower in an effort to bring the loan current.

color of title an instrument that gives evidence of title, but may not be legally adequate to convey title.

Commercial Mortgage Backed Securities (CMBS) securities issued to investors backed by pools of commercial mortgages.

commercial property property used to produce income, such as an office building or a restaurant.

commingling the illegal act of an agent mixing a client's monies, which should be held in a separate escrow account, with the agent's personal monies; in some states, commingling also means placing funds that are separate property in an account containing funds that are community property.

commission the fee paid to a broker for services rendered in a real estate transaction.

commitment letter a pledge in writing affirming an agreement.

common areas portions of a building, land, and amenities owned (or managed) by a planned unit development or condominium project's homeowners association or a cooperative project's cooperative corporation. These areas are used by all of the unit owners, who share in the common expenses of their operation and maintenance. Common areas may include swimming pools, tennis courts, and other recreational facilities, as well as common corridors of buildings, parking areas, and lobbies.

common law the body of laws derived from local custom and judicial precedent.

community property a system of property ownership in which each spouse has equal interest in property acquired during the marriage; recognized in nine states.

comparable sales recent sales of similar properties in nearby areas that are used to help estimate the current market value of a property.

competent parties people who are legally qualified to enter a contract, usually meaning that they are of legal age, of sound mind, and not under the influence of drugs or other mind-altering substances.

competitive market analysis (CMA) an analysis intended to assist a seller or buyer in determining a property's range of value.

condemnation the judicial process by which the government exercises its power of eminent domain.

condominium a form of ownership in which an individual owns a specific unit in a multiunit building and shares ownership of common areas with other unit owners.

condominium conversion changing the ownership of an existing building (usually a multi-dwelling rental unit) from single ownership to condominium ownership.

conformity an appraisal principle that asserts that property achieves its maximum value when a neighborhood is homogeneous in its use of land; the basis for zoning ordinances.

consideration something of value that induces parties to enter into a contract, such as money or services.

construction mortgage a short-term loan used to finance the building of improvements to real estate.

constructive eviction action or inaction by a landlord that renders a property uninhabitable, forcing a tenant to move out with no further liability for rent.

constructive notice notice of a fact given by making the fact part of the public record. All persons are responsible for knowing the information, whether or not they have actually seen the record.

contingency a condition that must be met before a contract is legally binding. A satisfactory home inspection report from a qualified home inspector is an example of a common type of contingency.

contract an agreement between two or more legally competent parties to do or to refrain from doing some legal act in exchange for a consideration.

contract for deed a contract for the sale of a parcel of real estate in which the buyer makes periodic payments to the seller and receives title to the property only after all, or a substantial part, of the purchase price has been paid, or regular payments have been made for one year or longer.

conventional loan a loan that is neither insured nor guaranteed by an agency of government.

conversion option an option in an adjustable-rate mortgage to convert it to a fixed-rate mortgage.

convertible ARM an adjustable-rate mortgage that allows the borrower to change the ARM to a fixed-rate mortgage at a specific time.

conveyance the transfer of title from the grantor to the grantee.

cooperative a form of property ownership in which a corporation owns a multiunit building and stockholders of the corporation may lease and occupy individual units of the building through a proprietary lease.

corporation a type of company with multiple ownership governed by a corporate charter. Two types of corporations are C-corporations and S-corporations.

cost approach an appraisal method whereby the value of a property is calculated by estimating the cost of constructing a comparable building, subtracting depreciation, and adding land value.

counteroffer an offer submitted in response to an offer. It has the effect of overriding the original offer.

credit an agreement in which a borrower receives something of value in exchange for a promise to repay the lender.

credit history a record of an individual's repayment of debt.

cul-de-sac a dead-end street that widens at the end, creating a circular turnaround area.

curtesy the statutory or common law right of a husband to all or part of real estate owned by his deceased wife, regardless of will provisions, recognized in some states.

curtilage area of land occupied by a building, its outbuildings, and yard, either actually enclosed or considered enclosed.

▶ D

damages the amount of money recoverable by a person who has been injured by the actions of another.

datum a specific point used in surveying.

DBA the abbreviation for "doing business as."

debt an amount owed to another.

decedent a person who dies.

dedication the donation of private property by its owner to a governmental body for public use.

deed a written document that, when properly signed and delivered, conveys title to real property from the grantor to the grantee.

deed-in-lieu a foreclosure instrument used to convey title to the lender when the borrower is in default and wants to avoid foreclosure.

deed of trust a deed in which the title to property is transferred to a third party trustee to secure repayment of a loan; three-party mortgage arrangement.

deed restriction an imposed restriction for the purpose of limiting the use of land, such as the size or type of improvements to be allowed. Also called a restrictive covenant.

default the failure to perform a contractual duty.

defeasance clause a clause in a mortgage that renders it void where all obligations have been fulfilled.

deficiency judgment a personal claim against a borrower when mortgaged property is foreclosed and sale of the property does not produce sufficient funds to pay off the mortgage. Deficiency judgments may be prohibited in some circumstances by anti-deficiency protection.

delinquency failure to make mortgage or loan payments when payments are due.

density zoning a zoning ordinance that restricts the number of houses or dwelling units that can be built per acre in a particular area, such as a subdivision.

depreciation a loss in value due to physical deterioration, or functional or external obsolescence.

descent the transfer of property to an owner's heirs when the owner dies intestate.

devise the transfer of title to real estate by will.

devisee one who receives a bequest of real estate by will.

devisor one who grants real estate by will.

directional growth the direction toward which certain residential sections of a city are expected to grow.

discount point 1% of the loan amount charged by a lender at closing to increase a loan's effective yield and lower the fare rate to the borrower.

discount rate the rate that lenders pay for mortgage funds—a higher rate is passed on to the borrower.

dispossess to remove a tenant from property by legal process.

dominant estate (tenement) property that includes the right to use an easement on adjoining property.

dower the right of a widow to the property of her husband upon his death in noncommunity property states.

down payment the part of the purchase price that the buyer pays in cash and is not financed with a mortgage or loan.

dual agency an agent who represents both parties in a transaction.

due-on-sale clause a provision in a mortgage that allows the lender to demand repayment in full if the borrower sells the property that serves as security for the mortgage.

duress the use of unlawful means to force a person to act or to refrain from an action against his or her will.

▶ E

earnest money down payment made by a buyer of real estate as evidence of good faith.

easement the right of one party to use the land of another for a particular purpose, such as to lay utility lines.

easement by necessity an easement, granted by law and requiring court action that is deemed necessary for the full enjoyment of a parcel of land. An example would be an easement allowing access from landlocked property to a road.

easement by prescription a means of acquiring an easement by continued, open, and hostile use of someone else's property for a statutorily defined period of time.

easement in gross a personal right granted by an owner with no requirement that the easement holder own adjoining land.

economic life the period of time over which an improved property will generate sufficient income to justify its continued existence.

effective age an appraiser's estimate of the physical condition of a building. The actual age of a building may be different from its effective age.

emblements cultivated crops; generally considered to be personal property.

eminent domain the right of a government to take private property for public use upon payment of its fair market value. Eminent domain is the basis for condemnation proceedings.

encroachment a trespass caused when a structure, such as a wall or fence, invades another person's land or air space.

encumbrance anything that affects or limits the title to a property, such as easements, leases, mortgages, or restrictions.

Equal Employment Opportunity Commission federal agency that enforces antidiscrimination laws governing employment.

Equal Pay Act of 1963 (EPA) law that requires that men and women who perform the same work receive the same pay.

equitable title the interest in a piece of real estate held by a buyer who has agreed to purchase the property, but has not yet completed the transaction; the interest of a buyer under a contract for deed.

equity the difference between the current market value of a property and the outstanding indebtedness due on it.

equity of redemption the right of a borrower to stop the foreclosure process.

erosion the gradual wearing away of land by wind, water, and other natural processes.

escalation clause a clause in a lease allowing the lessor to charge more rent based on an increase in costs; sometimes called a pass-through clause.

escheat the claim to property by the state when the owner dies intestate and no heirs can be found.

escrow the deposit of funds and/or documents with a disinterested third party for safekeeping until the terms of the escrow agreement have been met.

escrow account a trust account established to hold escrow funds for safekeeping until disbursement.

escrow analysis annual report to disclose escrow receipts, payments, and current balances.

escrow disbursements money paid from an escrow account.

estate an interest in real property. The sum total of all the real property and personal property owned by an individual.

estate for years a leasehold estate granting possession for a definite period of time.

estate tax federal tax levied on property transferred upon death.

estoppel certificate a document that certifies the outstanding amount owed on a mortgage loan, as well as the rate of interest.

et al abbreviation for the Latin phrase *et alius,* meaning "and another."

et ux abbreviation for Latin term *et uxor,* meaning "and wife."

et vir Latin term meaning "and husband."

eviction the lawful expulsion of an occupant from real property.

evidence of title a document that identifies ownership of property.

examination of title a review of an abstract to determine current condition of title.

exchange a transaction in which property is traded for another property, rather than sold for money or other consideration.

exclusive agency listing a contract between a property owner and one broker that gives the broker the right to sell the property for a fee within a specified period of time but does not obligate the owner to pay the broker a fee if the owner produces his or her own buyer without the broker's assistance. The owner is barred only from appointing another broker within this time period.

exclusive right to sell a contract between a property owner and a broker that gives the broker the right to collect a commission regardless of who sells the property during the specified period of time of the agreement.

execution the signing of a contract.

executor/executrix a person named in a will to administer an estate. The court will appoint an administrator if no executor is named. "Executrix" is the feminine form.

executory contract a contract in which one or more of the obligations have yet to be performed.

executed contract a contract in which all obligations have been fully performed.

express contract an oral or written contract in which the terms are expressed in words.

extension agreement an agreement between mortgagor and mortgagee to extend the maturity date of the mortgage after it is due.

external obsolescence a loss in value of a property because of factors outside the property, such as a change in surrounding land use.

▶ **F**

Fair Credit Reporting Act (FCRA) federal legislation protecting consumers from the reporting of inaccurate credit information to credit reporting agencies.

Fair Housing law a term used to refer to federal and state laws prohibiting discrimination in the sale or rental of residential property.

fair market value the highest price that a buyer, willing but not compelled to buy, would pay, and the lowest a seller, willing but not compelled to sell, would accept.

Federal Fair Housing Act (Title VIII of the Civil Rights Act of 1968) federal legislation that makes it illegal to discriminate on the basis of race, color, religion, sex, or national origin in connection with the sale or rental of housing or vacant land offered for residential construction or use.

Federal Housing Administration (FHA) an agency within the U.S. Department of Housing and Urban Development (HUD) that insures mortgage loans by FHA-approved lenders to make loans available to buyers with limited cash.

Federal Interstate Land Sales Full Disclosure Act federal legislation requiring land developers to register subdivisions of 100 or more nonexempt lots with HUD and to provide each purchaser with a disclosure document called a property report.

Federal National Mortgage Association (Fannie Mae) a privately owned corporation that buys existing government-backed and conventional mortgages.

Federal Reserve System the central banking system of the United States, which controls the monetary policy and, therefore, the money supply, interest rates, and availability of credit.

fee simple the most complete form of ownership of real estate.

FHA-insured loan a loan insured by the Federal Housing Administration.

fiduciary relationship a legal relationship with an obligation of trust, as that of agent and principal.

finder's fee a fee or commission paid to a mortgage broker for finding a mortgage loan for a prospective borrower.

first mortgage a mortgage that has priority to be satisfied over all other mortgages.

fixed-rate loan a loan with an interest rate that does not change during the entire term of the loan.

fixture an article of personal property that has been permanently attached to the real estate so as to become an integral part of the real estate.

foreclosure the legal process by which a borrower in default of a mortgage is deprived of interest in the mortgaged property. Usually, this involves a forced sale of the property at public auction, where the proceeds of the sale are applied to the mortgage debt.

forfeiture the loss of money, property, rights, or privileges because of a breach of legal obligation.

Foreign Investment in Real Property Tax Act (FIRPTA) federal legislation requiring that a buyer withhold 10% of the gross sales price and send it to the IRS if the seller is a "foreign person."

fractional ownership the form of ownership that results when a group of individuals pool their resources to buy a property.

franchise in real estate, an organization that lends a standardized trade name, operating procedures, referral services, and supplies to member brokerages.

fraud a deliberate misstatement of material fact or an act or omission made with deliberate intent to deceive (active fraud) or gross disregard for the truth (constructive fraud).

freehold estate an estate of ownership in real property.

front-foot a measurement of property taken by measuring the frontage of the property along the street line.

functional obsolescence a loss in value of a property because of causes within the property, such as faulty design, outdated structural style, or inadequacy to function properly.

future interest ownership interest in property that cannot be enjoyed until the occurrence of some event; sometimes referred to as a household or equitable interest.

▶ G

general agent an agent who is authorized to act for and obligate a principal in a specific range of matters, as specified by their mutual agreement.

general lien a claim on all property, real and personal, owned by a debtor.

general partnership (GP) a type of company in which two or more persons share profits and liabilities.

general warranty deed an instrument in which the grantor guarantees the grantee that the title being conveyed is good and free of other claims or encumbrances.

government-backed mortgage a mortgage that is insured by the Federal Housing Administration (FHA) or guaranteed by the Department of Veterans Affairs (VA) or the Rural Housing Service (RHS). Mortgages that are not government loans are identified as conventional loans.

Government National Mortgage Association (Ginnie Mae) a government-owned corporation within the U.S. Department of Housing and Urban Development (HUD). Ginnie Mae manages and liquidates government-backed loans and assists HUD in special lending projects.

government survey system a method of land description in which meridians (lines of longitude) and baselines (lines of latitude) are used to divide land into townships and sections.

graduated lease a lease that calls for periodic, stated changes in rent during the term of the lease.

grant the transfer of title to real property by deed.

grant deed a deed that includes three warranties: (1) that the owner has the right to convey title to the property, (2) that there are no encumbrances other than those noted specifically in the deed, and (3) that the owner will convey any future interest that he or she may acquire in the property.

grantee one who receives title to real property.

grantor one who conveys title to real property; the present owner.

gross income the total income received from a property before deducting expenses.

gross income multiplier a rough method of estimating the market value of an income property by multiplying its gross annual rent by a multiplier discovered by dividing the sales price of comparable properties by their annual gross rent.

gross lease a lease in which a tenant pays only a fixed amount for rental and the landlord pays all operating expenses and taxes.

gross rent multiplier similar to *gross income multiplier*, except that it looks at the relationship between sales price and monthly gross rent.

ground lease a lease of land only, on which a tenant already owns a building or will construct improvements.

guaranteed sale plan an agreement between a broker and a seller that the broker will buy the seller's property if it does not sell within a specified period of time.

guardian one who is legally responsible for the care of another person's rights and/or property.

▶ H

***habendum* clause** the clause in a deed, beginning with the words "to have and to hold," that defines or limits the exact interest in the estate granted by the deed.

hamlet a small village.

heir one who is legally entitled to receive property when the owner dies intestate.

highest and best use the legally permitted use of a parcel of land that will yield the greatest return to the owner in terms of money or amenities.

holdover tenancy a tenancy in which a lessee retains possession of the property after the lease has expired, and the landlord, by continuing to accept rent, agrees to the tenant's continued occupancy.

holographic will a will that is entirely handwritten, dated, and signed by the testator.

home equity conversion mortgage (HECM) often called a reverse-annuity mortgage; instead of making payments to a lender, the lender makes payments to you. It enables older homeowners to convert the equity they have in their homes into cash, usually in the form of monthly payments. Unlike traditional home equity loans, a borrower does not qualify on the basis of income but on the value of his or her home. In addition, the loan does not have to be repaid until the borrower no longer occupies the property.

home equity line of credit a mortgage loan that allows the borrower to obtain cash drawn against the equity of his or her home, up to a predetermined amount.

home inspection a thorough inspection by a professional that evaluates the structural and mechanical condition of a property. A satisfactory home inspection is often included as a contingency by the purchaser.

homeowner's insurance an insurance policy specifically designed to protect residential property owners against financial loss from common risks such as fire, theft, and liability.

homeowner's warranty an insurance policy that protects purchasers of newly constructed or pre-owned homes against certain structural and mechanical defects.

homestead the parcel of land and improvements legally qualifying as the owner's principal residence.

HUD an acronym for the Department of Housing and Urban Development, a federal agency that enforces federal fair housing laws and oversees agencies such as FHA and GNMA.

▶ I

implied contract a contract by which the agreement of the parties is created by their conduct.

improvement human-made addition to real estate.

income capitalization approach a method of estimating the value of income-producing property by dividing its expected annual net operating income of the property by a capitalization rate.

income property real estate developed or improved to produce income.

incorporeal right intangible, nonpossessory rights in real estate, such as an easement or right-of-way.

independent contractor one who is retained by another to perform a certain task and is not subject to the control and direction of the hiring person with regard to the end result of the task. Individual contractors receive a fee for their services but pay their own expenses and taxes and receive no employee benefits.

index a number used to compute the interest rate for an adjustable-rate mortgage (ARM). The index is a published number or percentage, such as the average yield on U.S. Treasury bills. A margin is added to the index to determine the interest rate to be charged on the ARM. This interest rate is subject to any caps that are associated with the mortgage.

industrial property buildings and land used for the manufacture and distribution of goods, such as a factory.

inflation an increase in the amount of money or credit available in relation to the amount of goods or services available, which causes an increase in the general price level of goods and services.

initial interest rate the beginning interest rate of the mortgage at the time of closing. This rate changes for an adjustable-rate mortgage (ARM).

installment the regular, periodic payment that a borrower agrees to make to a lender, usually in relation to a loan.

installment contract see *contract for deed.*

installment loan borrowed money that is repaid in periodic payments, known as installments.

installment sale a transaction in which the sales price is paid to the seller in two or more installments over more than one calendar year.

insurance a contract that provides indemnification from specific losses in exchange for a periodic payment. The individual contract is known as an insurance policy, and the periodic payment is known as an insurance premium.

insurance binder a document that states that temporary insurance is in effect until a permanent insurance policy is issued.

insured mortgage a mortgage that is protected by the Federal Housing Administration (FHA) or by private mortgage insurance (PMI). If the borrower defaults on the loan, the insurer must pay the lender the insured amount.

interest a fee charged by a lender for the use of the money loaned; or a share of ownership in real estate.

interest accrual rate the percentage rate at which interest accrues on the mortgage.

interest rate the rent or rate charged to use funds belonging to another.

interest rate buydown plan an arrangement in which the property seller (or any other party) deposits money to an account so that it can be released each month to reduce the mortgagor's monthly payments during the early years of a mortgage. During the specified period, the mortgagor's effective interest rate is bought down below the actual interest rate.

interest rate ceiling the maximum interest rate that may be charged for an adjustable-rate mortgage (ARM), as specified in the mortgage note.

interest rate floor the minimum interest rate for an adjustable-rate mortgage (ARM), as specified in the mortgage note.

interim financing a short-term loan made during the building phase of a project; also known as a construction loan.

intestate the state of having died without having authored a valid will.

invalid not legally binding or enforceable.

investment property a property not occupied by the owner.

▶ **J**

joint tenancy co-ownership that gives each tenant equal interest and equal rights in the property, including the right of survivorship.

joint venture an agreement between two or more parties to engage in a specific business enterprise.

judgment a decision rendered by court determining the rights and obligations of parties to an action or lawsuit.

judgment lien a lien on the property of a debtor resulting from a court judgment.

judicial foreclosure a proceeding that is handled as a civil lawsuit and conducted through court; used in some states.

jumbo loan a loan that exceeds Fannie Mae's mortgage amount limits. Also called a non-conforming loan.

junior mortgage any mortgage that is inferior to a first lien and that will be satisfied only after the first mortgage; also called a secondary mortgage.

▶ **L**

laches a doctrine used by a court to bar the assertion of a legal claim or right, based on the failure to assert the claim in a timely manner.

land the earth from its surface to its center, and the air space above it.

landlocked property surrounded on all sides by property belonging to another.

lease a contract between a landlord and a tenant wherein the landlord grants the tenant possession and use of the property for a specified period of time and for a consideration.

leased fee the landlord's interest in a parcel of leased property.

lease option a financing option that allows homebuyers to lease a home with an option to buy. Each month's rent payment may consist of rent, plus an additional amount that can be applied toward the down payment on an already specified price.

leasehold a tenant's right to occupy a parcel of real estate for the term of a lease.

legal description a description of a parcel of real estate specific and complete enough for an independent surveyor to locate and identify it.

lessee the one who receives that right to use and occupy the property during the term of the leasehold estate.

lessor the owner of the property who grants the right of possession to the lessee.

leverage the use of borrowed funds to purchase an asset.

levy to assess or collect a tax.

license (1) a revocable authorization to perform a particular act on another's property; (2) authorization granted by a state to act as a real estate broker or salesperson.

lien a legal claim against a property to secure payment of a financial obligation.

life estate a freehold estate in real property limited in duration to the lifetime of the holder of the life estate or another specified person.

life tenant one who holds a life estate.

limited liability company (LLC) a type of company that has the limited liability advantage of a corporation with the tax status of a sole proprietor or partnership.

limited partnership (LP) a type of company that includes a general partner and one or more limited partners. The limited partners invest capital, but do not participate in day-to-day operations.

liquidity the ability to convert an asset into cash.

lis pendens a Latin phrase meaning "suit pending"; a public notice that a lawsuit has been filed that may affect the title to a particular piece of property.

listing agreement a contract between the owner and a licensed real estate broker wherein the broker is employed to sell real estate on the owner's terms within a given time, for which service the owner agrees to pay the broker an agreed-upon fee.

listing broker a broker who contracts with a property owner to sell or lease the described property; the listing agreement typically may provide for the broker to make property available through a multiple-listing system.

littoral rights landowner's claim to use water in large, navigable lakes and oceans adjacent to property; ownership rights to land-bordering bodies of water up to the high-water mark.

loan a sum of borrowed money, or principal, that is generally repaid with interest.

loan officer (or lender) serves several functions and has various responsibilities, such as soliciting loans; a loan officer both represents the lending institution and represents the borrower to the lending institution.

loan-to-value ratio (LTV) the ratio of the current loan balance to the property value.

lock-in an agreement in which the lender guarantees a specified interest rate for a certain amount of time.

lock-in period the time period during which the lender has guaranteed an interest rate to a borrower.

lot and block description a method of describing a particular property by referring to a lot and block number within a subdivision recorded in the public record.

▶ **M**

management agreement a contract between the owner of an income property and a firm or individual who agrees to manage the property.

margin the difference between the interest rate and the index on an adjustable rate mortgage. The margin remains stable over the life of the loan, while the index fluctuates.

market data approach a method of estimating the value of a property by comparing it to similar properties recently sold and making monetary adjustments for the differences between the subject property and the comparable property.

market value the amount that a seller may expect to obtain for merchandise, services, or securities in the open market.

marketable title title to property that is free from encumbrances and reasonable doubts and that a court would compel a buyer to accept.

mechanic's lien a statutory lien created to secure payment for those who supply labor or materials for the construction of an improvement to land.

metes and bounds a method of describing a parcel of land using direction and distance.

mil or mill one-tenth of one cent; used by some states to express or calculate property tax rates.

millage a tax rate on property, often expressed as mills per dollar value of the property.

minor a person who has not attained the legal age of majority.

misrepresentation a misstatement of fact, either deliberate or unintentional.

modification the act of changing any of the terms of the mortgage.

money judgment a court order to settle a claim with a monetary payment, rather than specific performance.

month-to-month tenancy tenancy in which the tenant rents for only one month at a time.

monument a fixed, visible marker used to establish boundaries for a survey.

mortgage a written instrument that pledges property to secure payment of a debt obligation as evidenced by a promissory note. When duly recorded in the public record, a mortgage creates a lien against the title to a property.

mortgage banker an entity that originates, funds, and services loans to be sold into the secondary money market.

mortgage broker an entity that, for a fee, brings borrowers together with lenders.

mortgage lien an encumbrance created by recording a mortgage.

mortgagee the lender who benefits from the mortgage.

mortgagor the borrower who pledges the property as collateral.

multi-dwelling units properties that provide separate housing units for more than one family that secure only a single mortgage. Apartment buildings are also considered multi-dwelling units.

multiple-listing system (MLS; also multiple-listing service) the method of marketing a property listing to all participants in the MLS.

mutual rescission an agreement by all parties to a contract to release one another from the obligations of the contract.

▶ **N**

negative amortization occurs when an adjustable rate mortgage is allowed to fluctuate independently of a required minimum payment. A gradual increase in mortgage debt happens when the monthly payment is not large enough to cover the entire principal and interest due. The amount of the shortfall is added to the remaining balance to create negative amortization.

net income the income produced by a property, calculated by deducting operating expenses from gross income.

net lease a lease that requires the tenant to pay maintenance and operating expenses, as well as rent.

net listing a listing in which the broker's fee is established as anything above a specified amount to be received by the seller from the sale of the property.

net worth the value of all of a person's assets.

no cash out refinance a refinance transaction in which the new mortgage amount is limited to the sum of the remaining balance of the existing first mortgage.

non-conforming use a use of land that is permitted to continue, or grandfathered, even after a zoning ordinance is passed that prohibits the use.

nonliquid asset an asset that cannot easily be converted into cash.

notarize to have a document certified by a notary public.

notary public a person who is authorized to administer oaths and take acknowledgments.

note a written instrument acknowledging a debt, with a promise to repay, including an outline of the terms of repayment.

note rate the interest rate on a promissory note.

notice of default a formal written notice to a borrower that a default has occurred on a loan and that legal action may be taken.

novation the substitution of a new contract for an existing one; the new contract must reference the first and indicate that the first is being replaced and no longer has any force and effect.

▶ O

obligee person on whose favor an obligation is entered.

obligor person who is bound to another by an obligation.

obsolescence a loss in the value of a property because of functional or external factors.

offer to propose as payment; to place a bid on property.

offer and acceptance two of the necessary elements for the creation of a contract.

open-end mortgage a loan containing a clause that allows the mortgagor to borrow additional funds from the lender, up to a specified amount, without rewriting the mortgage.

open listing a listing contract given to one or more brokers in which a commission is paid only to the broker who procures a sale. If the owner sells the house without the assistance of one of the brokers, no commission is due.

opinion of title an opinion, usually given by an attorney, regarding the status of a title to property.

option an agreement that gives a prospective buyer the right to purchase a seller's property within a specified period of time for a specified price.

optionee one who receives or holds an option.

optionor one who grants an option; the property owner.

ordinance a municipal regulation.

original principal balance the total amount of principal owed on a loan before any payments are made; the amount borrowed.

origination fee the amount charged by a lender to cover the cost of assembling the loan package and originating the loan.

owner financing a real estate transaction in which the property seller provides all or part of the financing.

ownership the exclusive right to use, possess, control, and dispose of property.

▶ P

package mortgage a mortgage that pledges both real and personal property as collateral to secure repayment of a loan.

parcel a lot or specific portion of a large tract of real estate.

partial taking in eminent domain, when only a portion of a parcel of land is taken.

participation mortgage a type of mortgage in which the lender receives a certain percentage of the income or resale proceeds from a property, as well as interest on the loan.

partition the division of property held by co-owners into individual shares.

partnership an agreement between two parties to conduct business for profit. In a partnership, property is owned by the partnership, not the individual partners, so partners cannot sell their interest in the property without the consent of the other partners.

party wall a common wall used to separate two adjoining properties.

payee one who receives payment from another.

payor one who makes payment to another.

percentage lease a lease in which the rental rate is based on a percentage of the tenant's gross sales. This type of lease is most often used for retail space.

periodic estate tenancy that automatically renews itself until either the landlord or tenant gives notice to terminate it.

personal property (hereditaments) all items that are not permanently attached to real estate; also known as chattels.

physical deterioration a loss in the value of a property because of impairment of its physical condition.

PITI principal, interest, taxes, and insurance—components of a regular mortgage payment.

planned unit development (PUD) a type of zoning that provides for residential and commercial uses within a specified area.

plat a map of subdivided land showing the boundaries of individual parcels or lots.

plat book a group of maps located in the public record showing the division of land into subdivisions, blocks, and individual parcels or lots.

plat number a number that identifies a parcel of real estate for which a plat has been recorded in the public record.

PMI private mortgage insurance.

point 1% of the loan.

point of beginning the starting point for a survey using the metes and bounds method of description.

police power the right of the government to enact laws, ordinances, and regulations to protect the public health, safety, welfare, and morals.

pottage combining two or more parcels to make them more valuable for a particular purpose.

power of attorney a legal document that authorizes someone to act on another's behalf. A power of attorney can grant complete authority or can be limited to certain acts and/or certain periods of time.

preapproval condition where a borrower has completed a loan application and provided debt, income, and savings documentation that an underwriter has reviewed and approved. A preapproval is usually done at a certain loan amount, making assumptions about what the interest rate will actually be at the time the loan is actually made, as well as estimates for the amount that will be paid for property taxes, insurance, and so on.

prepayment amount paid to reduce the outstanding principal balance of a loan before the due date.

prepayment penalty a fee charged to a borrower by a lender for paying off a debt before the term of the loan expires.

prequalification a lender's opinion on the ability of a borrower to qualify for a loan, based on furnished information regarding debt, income, and available capital for down payment, closing costs, and prepaids. Prequalification is less formal than preapproval.

prescription a method of acquiring an easement to property by prolonged, unauthorized use.

primary mortgage market the financial market in which loans are originated, funded, and serviced.

prime rate the short-term interest rate that banks charge to their preferred customers. Changes in prime rate are used as the indexes in some adjustable rate mortgages, such as home equity lines of credit.

principal (1) one who authorizes another to act on his or her behalf; (2) one of the contracting parties to a transaction; (3) the amount of money borrowed in a loan, separate from the interest charged on it.

principal curtailment an off-schedule mortgage payment applied only to the principal balance.

principal meridian one of the 36 longitudinal lines used in the rectangular survey system method of land description.

private mortgage insurance (PMI) mortgage insurance offered by private companies to mitigate the risk of the first 20–25% of the mortgage amount.

probate the judicial procedure of proving the validity of a will.

procuring cause the action that brings about the desired result. For example, if a broker takes actions that result in a sale, the broker is the procuring cause of the sale.

promissory note the debt instrument that details the terms of the loan.

property management the operating of an income property for another.

property tax a tax levied by the government on property, real or personal.

prorate to divide ongoing property costs such as taxes or maintenance fees proportionately between buyer and seller at closing.

pur autre vie a Latin phrase meaning "for the life of another." In a life estate *pur autre vie*, the term of the estate is measured by the life of a person other than the person who holds the life estate.

purchase agreement a written contract signed by the buyer and seller stating the terms and conditions under which a property will be sold.

purchase money mortgage a mortgage given by a buyer to a seller to secure repayment of any loan used to pay part or all of the purchase price.

▶ **Q**

qualifying ratio a calculation to determine whether a borrower can qualify for a mortgage. There are two ratios. The top ratio is a calculation of the borrower's monthly housing costs (principal, taxes, insurance, mortgage insurance, homeowner's association fees) as a percentage of monthly income. The bottom ratio includes housing costs as well as all other monthly debt.

quitclaim deed a conveyance whereby the grantor transfers without warranty or obligations whatever interest or title he or she may have.

▶ **R**

range an area of land six miles wide, numbered east or west from a principal meridian in the rectangular survey system.

ready, willing, and able the state of being able to pay the asking price for a property and being prepared to complete the transaction.

real estate land, the earth below it, the air above it, and anything permanently attached to it.

real estate agent a real estate broker who has been appointed to market a property for and represent the property owner (listing agent), or a broker who has been appointed to represent the interest of the buyer (buyer's agent).

real estate board an organization whose members consist primarily of real estate sales agents, brokers, and administrators.

real estate broker a licensed person, association, partnership, or corporation who negotiates real estate transactions for others for a fee.

Real Estate Settlement Procedures Act (RESPA) a consumer protection law that requires lenders to give borrowers advance notice of closing costs and prohibits certain abusive practices against buyers using federally related loans to purchase their homes.

real property the rights of ownership to land and its improvements.

REALTOR® a registered trademark for use by members of the National Association of REALTORS® and affiliated state and local associations.

recording entering documents, such as deeds and mortgages, into the public record to give constructive notice.

rectangular survey system a method of land description based on principal meridians (lines of longitude) and baselines (lines of latitude). Also called the government survey system.

redemption period the statutory period of time during which an owner can reclaim foreclosed property by paying the debt owed, plus court costs and other charges established by statute.

redlining the illegal practice of lending institutions refusing to provide certain financial services, such as mortgage loans, to property owners in certain areas.

refinance transaction the process of paying off one loan with the proceeds from a new loan using the same property as security or collateral.

Regulation Z a Federal Reserve regulation that implements the federal Truth-in-Lending Act.

release clause a clause in a mortgage that releases a portion of the property upon payment of a portion of the loan.

remainder estate a future interest in an estate that takes effect upon the termination of a life estate.

remaining balance in a mortgage, the amount of principal that has not yet been repaid.

remaining term the original amortization term minus the number of payments that have been applied to it.

rent a periodic payment paid by a lessee to a landlord for the use and possession of leased property.

replacement cost the estimated current cost to replace an asset similar or equivalent to the one being appraised.

reproduction cost the cost of building an exact duplicate of a building at current prices.

rescission canceling or terminating a contract by mutual consent or by the action of one party on default by the other party.

restriction (restrict covenant) a limitation on the way a property can be used.

reversion the return of interest or title to the grantor of a life estate.

reverse annuity mortgage when a homeowner receives monthly checks or a lump sum with no repayment until property is sold; usually an agreement between mortgagor and elderly homeowners.

revision a revised or new version, as in a contract.

right of egress (or ingress) the right to enter or leave designated premises.

right of first refusal the right of a person to have the first opportunity to purchase property before it is offered to anyone else.

right of redemption the statutory right to reclaim ownership of property after a foreclosure sale.

right of survivorship in joint tenancy, the right of survivors to acquire the interest of a deceased joint tenant.

riparian rights the rights of a landowner whose property is adjacent to a flowing waterway, such as a river, to access and use the water.

► S

safety clause a contract provision that provides a time period following expiration of a listing agreement, during which the agent will be compensated if there is a transaction with a buyer who was initially introduced to the property by the agent.

sale-leaseback a transaction in which the owner sells improved property and, as part of the same transaction, signs a long-term lease to remain in possession of its premises, thus becoming the tenant of the new owner.

sales contract a contract between a buyer and a seller outlining the terms of the sale.

salesperson one who is licensed to sell real estate in a given territory.

salvage value the value of a property at the end of its economic life.

satisfaction an instrument acknowledging that a debt has been paid in full.

second mortgage a mortgage that is in less than first lien position; see *junior mortgage.*

section as used in the rectangular survey system, an area of land measuring one square mile, or 640 acres.

secured loan a loan that is backed by property or collateral.

security property that is offered as collateral for a loan.

selling broker the broker who secures a buyer for a listed property; the selling broker may be the listing agent, a subagent, or a buyer's agent.

separate property property owned individually by a spouse, as opposed to community property.

servient tenement a property on which an easement or right-of-way for an adjacent (dominant) property passes.

setback the amount of space between the lot line and the building line, usually established by a local zoning ordinance or restrictive covenants; see *deed restrictions.*

settlement statement (HUD-1) the form used to itemize all costs related to closing of a residential transaction covered by RESPA regulations.

severalty the ownership of a property by only one legal entity.

sole proprietorship a type of company that has one owner, who assumes all responsibilities.

special assessment a tax levied against only the specific properties that will benefit from a public improvement, such as a street or sewer; an assessment by a homeowners' association for a capital improvement to the common areas for which no budgeted funds are available.

special warranty deed a deed in which the grantor guarantees the title only against the defects that may have occurred during the grantor's ownership and not against any defects that occurred prior to that time.

specific lien a lien, such as a mortgage, that attaches to one defined parcel of real estate.

specific performance a legal action in which a court compels a defaulted party to a contract to perform according to the terms of the contract, rather than awarding damages.

standard payment calculation the method used to calculate the monthly payment required to repay the remaining balance of a mortgage in equal installments over the remaining term of the mortgage at the current interest rate.

statute of frauds the state law that requires certain contracts to be in writing to be enforceable.

statute of limitations the state law that requires that certain actions be brought to court within a specified period of time.

statutory lien a lien imposed on property by statute, such as a tax lien.

steering the illegal practice of directing prospective homebuyers to or away from particular areas.

straight-line depreciation a method of computing depreciation by decreasing value by an equal amount each year during the useful life of the property.

subdivision a tract of land divided into lots as defined in a publicly recorded plat that complies with state and local regulations.

sublet the act of a lessee transferring part or all of his or her lease to a third party while maintaining responsibility for all duties and obligations of the lease contract.

subordinate to accept voluntarily a lower priority lien position than that to which one would normally be entitled.

substitution the principle in appraising that a buyer will be willing to pay no more for the property being appraised than the cost of purchasing an equally desirable property.

subrogation the substitution of one party into another's legal role as the creditor for a particular debt.

suit for possession a lawsuit filed by a landlord to evict a tenant who has violated the terms of the lease or retained possession of the property after the lease expired.

suit for specific performance a lawsuit filed for the purpose of compelling a party to perform particular acts, rather than pay monetary damages to settle a dispute.

survey a map that shows the exact legal boundaries of a property, the location of easements, encroachments, improvements, rights-of-way, and other physical features.

syndicate a group formed by a syndicator to combine funds for real estate investment.

► T

tax deed in some states, an instrument given to the purchaser at the time of sale.

tax lien a charge against a property created by law or statue. Tax liens take priority over all other types of liens.

tax rate the rate applied to the assessed value of a property to determine the property taxes.

tax sale the court-ordered sale of a property after the owner fails to pay *ad valorem* taxes owed on the property.

tenancy at sufferance the tenancy of a party who unlawfully retains possession of a landlord's property after the term of the lease has expired.

tenancy at will an indefinite tenancy that can be terminated by either the landlord or the tenant at any time by giving notice to the other party one rental period in advance of the desired termination date.

tenancy by the entirety ownership by a married couple of property acquired during the marriage with right of survivorship; not recognized by community property states.

tenancy in common a form of co-ownership in which two or more persons hold an undivided interest in property without the right of survivorship.

tenant one who holds or possesses the right of occupancy title.

tenement the space that may be occupied by a tenant under the terms of a lease.

testate the state of dying after having created a valid will directing the testator's desires with regard to the disposition of the estate.

"time is of the essence" language in a contract that requires strict adherence to the dates listed in the contract as deadlines for the performance of specific acts.

time-sharing undivided ownership of real estate for only an allotted portion of a year.

title a legal document that demonstrates a person's right to, or ownership of, a property. Note: Title is *not* an instrument. The instrument, such as a deed, gives evidence of title or ownership.

title insurance an insurance policy that protects the holder from defects in a title, subject to the exceptions noted in the policy.

title search a check of public records to ensure that the seller is the legal owner of the property and that there are no liens or other outstanding claims.

Torrens System a system of registering titles to land with a public authority, who is usually called a registrar.

township a division of land, measuring 36 square miles, in the government survey system.

trade fixtures an item of personal property installed by a commercial tenant and removable upon expiration of the lease.

transfer tax a state or municipal tax payable when the conveyancing instrument is recorded.

trust an arrangement in which title to property is transferred from a grantor to a trustee, who holds title but not the right of possession for a third party, the beneficiary.

trustee a person who holds title to property for another person designated as the beneficiary.

Truth-in-Lending Law also known as Regulation Z; requires lenders to make full disclosure regarding the terms of a loan.

▶ **U**

underwriting the process of evaluating a loan application to determine the risk involved for the lender.

undivided interest the interest of co-owners to the use of an entire property despite the fractional interest owned.

unilateral contract a one-sided contract in which one party is obligated to perform a particular act completely before the other party has any obligation to perform.

unsecured loan a loan that is not backed by collateral or security.

useful life the period of time a property is expected to have economic utility.

usury the practice of charging interest at a rate higher than that allowed by law.

▶ V

VA-guaranteed loan a mortgage loan made to a qualified veteran that is guaranteed by the Department of Veterans Affairs.

valid contract an agreement that is legally enforceable and binding on all parties.

valuation estimated worth.

variance permission obtained from zoning authorities to build a structure that is not in complete compliance with current zoning laws. A variance does not permit a non-conforming use of a property.

vendee a buyer.

vendor a seller; the property owner.

village an incorporated minor municipality usually larger than a hamlet and smaller than a town.

void contract a contract that is not legally enforceable; the absence of a valid contract.

voidable contract a contract that appears to be valid but is subject to cancellation by one or both of the parties.

▶ W

waiver the surrender of a known right or claim.

warranty deed a deed in which the grantor fully warrants a good clear title to the property.

waste the improper use of a property by a party with the right to possession, such as the holder of a life estate.

will a written document that directs the distribution of a deceased person's property, real and personal.

wraparound mortgage a mortgage that includes the remaining balance on an existing first mortgage, plus an additional amount. Full payments on both mortgages are made to the wraparound mortgagee, who then forwards the payments on the first mortgage to the first mortgagee.

writ of execution a court order to the sheriff or other officer to sell the property of a debtor to satisfy a previously rendered judgment.

▶ Z

zone an area reserved by authorities for specific use that is subject to certain restrictions.

zoning ordinance the exercise of regulating and controlling the use of a property in a municipality.

10 ▶ AMP Practice Exam 2

CHAPTER SUMMARY

This is the second of the two AMP practice tests in this book. Because you have taken the first practice test already, you should feel more confident with your test-taking skills. Use this test to see how knowing what to expect can make you feel better prepared.

You are now more familiar with the format and content of the national portion of the AMP exam, and most likely you feel more confident than you did at first. However, your practice test-taking experience will help you most if you have created a situation as close as possible to the real one.

For this exam, try to simulate real testing conditions. Find a quiet place where you will not be disturbed. Make sure you have two sharpened pencils and a good eraser. Be sure to leave enough time to complete the exam in one sitting. There is a two-hour limit on the official exam, so you'll want to practice working quickly without rushing. Use a timer or a stopwatch and see if you can work through all the exam questions in the allotted time.

The answer sheet is on the next page. An answer key and explanations follow the exam. These explanations, along with the table at the end of this chapter, will help you see where you need further study. And remember, the six other practice exams in this book, although slightly different in format than the AMP exam, all test the same basic real estate principles and concepts, so you can use them to help you further solidify your knowledge and skills.

1.	ⓐ	ⓑ	ⓒ	ⓓ
2.	ⓐ	ⓑ	ⓒ	ⓓ
3.	ⓐ	ⓑ	ⓒ	ⓓ
4.	ⓐ	ⓑ	ⓒ	ⓓ
5.	ⓐ	ⓑ	ⓒ	ⓓ
6.	ⓐ	ⓑ	ⓒ	ⓓ
7.	ⓐ	ⓑ	ⓒ	ⓓ
8.	ⓐ	ⓑ	ⓒ	ⓓ
9.	ⓐ	ⓑ	ⓒ	ⓓ
10.	ⓐ	ⓑ	ⓒ	ⓓ
11.	ⓐ	ⓑ	ⓒ	ⓓ
12.	ⓐ	ⓑ	ⓒ	ⓓ
13.	ⓐ	ⓑ	ⓒ	ⓓ
14.	ⓐ	ⓑ	ⓒ	ⓓ
15.	ⓐ	ⓑ	ⓒ	ⓓ
16.	ⓐ	ⓑ	ⓒ	ⓓ
17.	ⓐ	ⓑ	ⓒ	ⓓ
18.	ⓐ	ⓑ	ⓒ	ⓓ
19.	ⓐ	ⓑ	ⓒ	ⓓ
20.	ⓐ	ⓑ	ⓒ	ⓓ
21.	ⓐ	ⓑ	ⓒ	ⓓ
22.	ⓐ	ⓑ	ⓒ	ⓓ
23.	ⓐ	ⓑ	ⓒ	ⓓ
24.	ⓐ	ⓑ	ⓒ	ⓓ
25.	ⓐ	ⓑ	ⓒ	ⓓ
26.	ⓐ	ⓑ	ⓒ	ⓓ
27.	ⓐ	ⓑ	ⓒ	ⓓ
28.	ⓐ	ⓑ	ⓒ	ⓓ
29.	ⓐ	ⓑ	ⓒ	ⓓ
30.	ⓐ	ⓑ	ⓒ	ⓓ
31.	ⓐ	ⓑ	ⓒ	ⓓ
32.	ⓐ	ⓑ	ⓒ	ⓓ
33.	ⓐ	ⓑ	ⓒ	ⓓ
34.	ⓐ	ⓑ	ⓒ	ⓓ
35.	ⓐ	ⓑ	ⓒ	ⓓ

36.	ⓐ	ⓑ	ⓒ	ⓓ
37.	ⓐ	ⓑ	ⓒ	ⓓ
38.	ⓐ	ⓑ	ⓒ	ⓓ
39.	ⓐ	ⓑ	ⓒ	ⓓ
40.	ⓐ	ⓑ	ⓒ	ⓓ
41.	ⓐ	ⓑ	ⓒ	ⓓ
42.	ⓐ	ⓑ	ⓒ	ⓓ
43.	ⓐ	ⓑ	ⓒ	ⓓ
44.	ⓐ	ⓑ	ⓒ	ⓓ
45.	ⓐ	ⓑ	ⓒ	ⓓ
46.	ⓐ	ⓑ	ⓒ	ⓓ
47.	ⓐ	ⓑ	ⓒ	ⓓ
48.	ⓐ	ⓑ	ⓒ	ⓓ
49.	ⓐ	ⓑ	ⓒ	ⓓ
50.	ⓐ	ⓑ	ⓒ	ⓓ
51.	ⓐ	ⓑ	ⓒ	ⓓ
52.	ⓐ	ⓑ	ⓒ	ⓓ
53.	ⓐ	ⓑ	ⓒ	ⓓ
54.	ⓐ	ⓑ	ⓒ	ⓓ
55.	ⓐ	ⓑ	ⓒ	ⓓ
56.	ⓐ	ⓑ	ⓒ	ⓓ
57.	ⓐ	ⓑ	ⓒ	ⓓ
58.	ⓐ	ⓑ	ⓒ	ⓓ
59.	ⓐ	ⓑ	ⓒ	ⓓ
60.	ⓐ	ⓑ	ⓒ	ⓓ
61.	ⓐ	ⓑ	ⓒ	ⓓ
62.	ⓐ	ⓑ	ⓒ	ⓓ
63.	ⓐ	ⓑ	ⓒ	ⓓ
64.	ⓐ	ⓑ	ⓒ	ⓓ
65.	ⓐ	ⓑ	ⓒ	ⓓ
66.	ⓐ	ⓑ	ⓒ	ⓓ
67.	ⓐ	ⓑ	ⓒ	ⓓ
68.	ⓐ	ⓑ	ⓒ	ⓓ
69.	ⓐ	ⓑ	ⓒ	ⓓ
70.	ⓐ	ⓑ	ⓒ	ⓓ

71.	ⓐ	ⓑ	ⓒ	ⓓ
72.	ⓐ	ⓑ	ⓒ	ⓓ
73.	ⓐ	ⓑ	ⓒ	ⓓ
74.	ⓐ	ⓑ	ⓒ	ⓓ
75.	ⓐ	ⓑ	ⓒ	ⓓ
76.	ⓐ	ⓑ	ⓒ	ⓓ
77.	ⓐ	ⓑ	ⓒ	ⓓ
78.	ⓐ	ⓑ	ⓒ	ⓓ
79.	ⓐ	ⓑ	ⓒ	ⓓ
80.	ⓐ	ⓑ	ⓒ	ⓓ
81.	ⓐ	ⓑ	ⓒ	ⓓ
82.	ⓐ	ⓑ	ⓒ	ⓓ
83.	ⓐ	ⓑ	ⓒ	ⓓ
84.	ⓐ	ⓑ	ⓒ	ⓓ
85.	ⓐ	ⓑ	ⓒ	ⓓ
86.	ⓐ	ⓑ	ⓒ	ⓓ
87.	ⓐ	ⓑ	ⓒ	ⓓ
88.	ⓐ	ⓑ	ⓒ	ⓓ
89.	ⓐ	ⓑ	ⓒ	ⓓ
90.	ⓐ	ⓑ	ⓒ	ⓓ
91.	ⓐ	ⓑ	ⓒ	ⓓ
92.	ⓐ	ⓑ	ⓒ	ⓓ
93.	ⓐ	ⓑ	ⓒ	ⓓ
94.	ⓐ	ⓑ	ⓒ	ⓓ
95.	ⓐ	ⓑ	ⓒ	ⓓ
96.	ⓐ	ⓑ	ⓒ	ⓓ
97.	ⓐ	ⓑ	ⓒ	ⓓ
98.	ⓐ	ⓑ	ⓒ	ⓓ
99.	ⓐ	ⓑ	ⓒ	ⓓ
100.	ⓐ	ⓑ	ⓒ	ⓓ

▶ AMP Practice Exam 2

1. Benjamin listed a tract of land for commercial development. It is 4.86 acres and is selling for $1.25 per square foot. What is the sale price?
   a. $241,500
   b. $26,463
   c. $264,627
   d. $2,646,273

2. The lessee pays a flat rent amount each month, and the lessor pays all the costs of ownership such as taxes, maintenance, and fire and hazard insurance. What type of lease is this?
   a. a net lease
   b. a gross lease
   c. a month-to-month lease
   d. a triple net lease

3. Harry is buying a large ranch. Which statement is true regarding the mineral rights?
   a. They are part of the subsurface rights of the land and automatically convey with the property to Harry.
   b. Mineral rights are retained by the original owner and are part of his or her estate in perpetuity.
   c. The mineral rights may convey to Harry or may remain with the seller or previous owner depending on written agreement.
   d. Mineral rights are retained by the state.

4. Agent Yolanda explained to her buyer prospect the benefits of buyer representation, and the buyer authorized Yolanda to be her agent; however, no agency agreement was signed. Which of the following is true regarding Yolanda's agency relationship with this buyer?
   a. Yolanda has an implied agency.
   b. Yolanda has an express agency.
   c. Nothing was signed, and there is no agency.
   d. Yolanda has an ostensible agency.

5. A tenant in an apartment pays monthly rent and may terminate the lease at any time with one month's notice in writing to the landlord. What type of lease is this?
   a. an estate at will
   b. a periodic estate
   c. monthly leasehold
   d. an estate for years

6. The ownership of a specific property for use at a specific period of time during the year is called
   a. a time-share.
   b. joint tenancy.
   c. share in a cooperative.
   d. a leasehold.

7. Agent Albert listed Abdul's condo, and the sale is scheduled to close in two weeks. However, the title search shows a property tax lien of $865 from the previous year. Who will be responsible for paying the taxes when Agent Albert closes?
   a. Agent Albert
   b. the condominium association
   c. the escrow
   d. the new owner

8. Fancy's Gift Shop is located in a retail center, and the owner pays a base monthly rent plus a portion of the gross sales from the business. What type of lease is this?
   a. gross lease
   b. index lease
   c. percentage lease
   d. graduated lease

9. A deed that describes the property granted and then states "together with all appurtenances" means
   a. the property is encumbered by a tax lien.
   b. the utility easement runs with the land.
   c. the oil and gas rights are leased.
   d. it is located in a brownfield.

10. Which of the following creates an agency relationship?
   a. Only a signed listing agreement or a buyer's representation agreement
   b. A leasing manager assists a person in leasing an apartment.
   c. A for-sale-by-owner offers to pay any broker who may bring him a suitable buyer.
   d. A person authorizes a broker to represent her in the purchase of a tract of land.

11. Ann Hawkins deeded a house to her sister, who will live in the house and take care of their mother. Upon the death of the mother, the house will convey to Ann's son Michael. Which of the following statements describes this arrangement?
   a. This is a life estate *pur autre vie*, and Michael owns a reversionary interest.
   b. The sister owns the property fee simple until her mother's death, when it will devise to Michael.
   c. Michael owns the property as a life estate.
   d. Ann's sister owns a life estate *pur autre vie,* and Michael owns a remainder interest.

12. Dorothy retired and bought a condominium in her church's retirement community. The condo will revert back to church ownership after her death. Dorothy owns a
   a. proprietary lease.
   b. life estate *pur autre vie.*
   c. life estate.
   d. reversionary estate.

13. How many acres are in the NE $\frac{1}{4}$ of the SE $\frac{1}{4}$ of a section of land?
   a. 160
   b. 320
   c. 80
   d. 40

14. Dave and Elise, owners of Superior Home Remodeling, Inc., purchased a small office and warehouse building in the company name. They own the property
   a. as joint tenants.
   b. in severalty.
   c. as tenants in common.
   d. in partnership.

15. Broker Clarke holds $5,000 as earnest money on the purchase made by Sara Best. When can Broker Clarke remove the earnest money from the escrow account?
   a. when the buyer gives him permission
   b. when the seller gives him permission
   c. when Broker Clarke needs the money for business expenses, as long as it is replaced within five days
   d. when the purchase closes escrow

16. To secure a loan, the borrower conveys title to the property to a disinterested third party for safekeeping. In this situation, the document required is a
   a. general warranty deed.
   b. deed of trust.
   c. involuntary conveyance.
   d. mortgage.

17. A legal description using a datum and benchmarks is
   a. metes and bounds.
   b. recorded plat.
   c. air lot.
   d. township and range.

18. An appraiser may use a gross rent multiplier to determine the estimated value of a subject residential home. The subject property rents for $1,250 per month. Three comparables are as follows: #1 sold for $126,900 and rents for $1,190 per month; #2 sold for $129,750 and rents for $1,230; and #3 sold for #133,500 and rents for $1,275. What is the estimated value of the subject using an average GRM?
   a. $130,050
   b. $131,579
   c. $131,000
   d. $132,025

19. A listing agent knows that the house has a roof leak, the water heater is not up to city code, and the seller must sell quickly because of financial difficulties. The agent is showing a potential buyer the property. What can the agent say?
   a. "The roof leaks and the water heater does not meet city code."
   b. "The seller will take less than the asking price because the house is in bad repair."
   c. "The seller is in financial difficulty and must sell quickly."
   d. "The roof leaks, the water heater does not meet city code, and the seller needs a quick sale."

20. Agent Gale advertised Jake's property for sale at a price they agreed on, but she did not have a written listing agreement with Jake. She located a buyer and assisted Jake in negotiating a sale; however, the sale was for less than the agreed asking price. At closing, Jake refused to pay the commission because he took less for the property. What recourse does Agent Gale have to collect her fee?
   a. She must sue in small claims court.
   b. none
   c. She may mediate a resolution of the commission.
   d. She must present a written demand to the escrow agent for the commission to be withheld at closing and paid to her.

21. To help the buyer qualify at a lower interest rate on a 95% loan and increase the lender's yield, 2.5 discount points will be charged. The buyer and seller have agreed on a sales price of $250,000, and the points will be divided equally between them. How much will each pay at closing in discount points?
   a. $5,937.50
   b. $6,250
   c. $2,968.75
   d. $3,125

22. Mr. McAfee, a life tenant, decided to remove a backyard deck and tear down the garage so he could park his truck behind the house. Can Ms. Yang, the remainderman, prevent Mr. McAfee from doing this?
   a. No. Mr. McAfee owns a life estate and may use the property during his lifetime as he wishes.
   b. A life tenant is permitted to remove any improvement on the property.
   c. Yes, but Mr. McAfee must pay Ms. Yang an amount equal to the value of the deck and garage.
   d. Yes. A life tenant may not commit waste of any kind.

23. Ali Hassan listed Abby's house at an asking price of $565,900. They agreed on a commission fee; however, Ali did not get a signed listing agreement. Ali advertised the property and held an open house. He wrote an offer for a buyer customer for $525,900 cash, after assuring the buyer that Abby's financial difficulties would force her to take the offer. At closing, Abby refused to pay the commission. Which of the following is true?
   a. Ali can sue Abby for the commission.
   b. Abby can sue Ali for breach of fiduciary duties.
   c. Abby cannot sue Ali for breach of fiduciary duties, because there was no listing agreement and no fee was paid.
   d. Abby cannot sue Ali, because Ali procured a ready, willing, and able buyer for Abby's house.

24. The Greene Valley Apartments advertising states that families with children are welcome. The management has allocated a certain section of the complex for residents with children, and those tenants must pay an additional security deposit for each child under twelve. Is this discriminatory?
   a. There is no discrimination because families with children are welcome to the complex.
   b. This is discrimination based on marital status.
   c. This is discrimination based on familial status.
   d. This is not discrimination because children are not a named protected class.

25. Clients may be liable for errors made by brokers or subagents by
   a. vicarious liability.
   b. casual liability.
   c. accidental negligence.
   d. estoppel.

26. An exclusive listing agreement should always include
  a. an advertising budget.
  b. a defined market area.
  c. a definite termination date.
  d. an agreed commission percentage.

27. Which of the following is NOT a termination of an agency relationship by operation of law?
  a. revocation by the principal
  b. death of the agent
  c. fulfillment of purpose
  d. expiration of the term

28. A listing agreement states that the seller will pay the broker any amount over the final sales price plus the seller's closing costs. This is
  a. illegal in the United States.
  b. a net listing.
  c. a triple net listing.
  d. a guarantee of a large commission.

29. Oscar received an inquiry from a prospective buyer regarding his listing. He showed the property to the prospect, who asked if the seller would consider an offer well under the asking price. Oscar agreed to write a low offer and told the buyer he would do his best to get the seller to accept. This is an example of
  a. an offer to cooperate.
  b. an implied agency.
  c. aggressive consumerism.
  d. an ostensible agency.

30. Ms. Mayberry advertised in the local newspaper for a renter. Her ad read, "Clean, fully furnished bedroom with private bath and kitchen privileges. Female only." The apartment complex nearby published an ad reading, "Efficiency apartment available. Easy access to public transportation. No students." Are these ads legal under the Federal Fair Housing laws?
  a. yes
  b. no
  c. Ms. Mayberry's ad is legal, but the apartment ad is not.
  d. The apartment ad is legal, but Ms. Mayberry's ad is not.

31. Broker Merle represented a buyer as a buyer's agent in the purchase of a home listed by Broker Shana. How may Merle be paid?
  a. only by his client, the buyer
  b. directly by the seller
  c. by Broker Shana
  d. by Broker Shana, but a subagency relationship is created

32. The obligation of protecting any deposits entrusted to an agent is an example of the fiduciary duty of
  a. competence.
  b. disclosure.
  c. accounting.
  d. obedience.

33. Three days after listing a property, Broker Renee brought the seller a full price offer meeting all of the terms of the listing agreement. The seller refused to accept the offer and wanted to raise the list price. Which of the following is true?
  a. The seller must accept the offer or risk being sued by the buyer for specific performance.
  b. The seller must accept the offer and pay the brokerage fee.
  c. The listing broker has not earned the fee because the commission is based on the closing of the property.
  d. The listing broker has earned the fee.

34. Kevin Washington listed his home with City Lights Real Estate, signed an exclusive right to sell listing agreement for six months, and gave the broker a 90-day protection period. The broker showed the house to Patsy Kayes one week prior to the expiration of the listing, and two months later, Ms. Kayes bought the house directly from Kevin. Which of the following statements is true?
  a. Kevin owes City Lights Real Estate the fee agreed to in the listing agreement.
  b. Kevin owes City Lights Real Estate the fee agreed to in the listing agreement only if the broker gave him written documentation of all prospects who saw the house during the listing period.
  c. Kevin owes nothing under any circumstances because the listing expired, thereby terminating the agency relationship.
  d. Kevin and Ms. Kayes both owe the broker a fee, because the broker was the listing broker and he also procured the buyer for the sale.

35. A broker representing both the buyer and the seller in a transaction
  a. is a dual agent and must maintain confidentiality of each party's position.
  b. is a transaction agent and must bring about the best possible price for the seller.
  c. must treat the buyer as a third-party customer.
  d. is a neutral third party.

36. Danny Broussard listed his property with Broker Steve Jefferson. Broker Lucille Lau sold the property to Fred Chang, a buyer customer. Which statement is true?
  a. Lucille Lau owes fiduciary duties to Fred Chang.
  b. Lucille Lau does not owe fiduciary duties to Danny Broussard.
  c. Steve Jefferson is a subagent of Danny Broussard and represents Fred Chang.
  d. Lucille Lau is a subagent of Steve Jefferson and owes fiduciary duties to Danny Broussard.

37. Title to land owned by the government is conveyed to a private party with an instrument known as a
  a. grant.
  b. sheriff's deed.
  c. patent.
  d. fee simple deed.

38. According the Fannie Mae guidelines, the most probable price that a property should bring in a competitive and open market under all conditions requisite to a fair sale is
   a. market price.
   b. appraised value.
   c. contract price.
   d. market value.

39. Mark Rogers signed a five-year office lease, and at the end of the third year, he needed to move to a much larger space. Mark made a total transfer of the lease to Mimi Valdez, who will pay the rent directly to the landlord, and Mark is still liable for the performance of the contract. Which statement describes this arrangement?
   a. Mark is the sublessor, and Mimi is the sublessee.
   b. Mark is the sublessee, and Mimi is the sublessor.
   c. Mark is the assignor, and Mimi is the assignee.
   d. Mark is the assignee, and Mimi is the assignor.

40. Edmund Tate is a single father with two sons, ages 13 and 16. When applying to rent an apartment, he is protected under fair housing laws under the classification of
   a. sex.
   b. marital status.
   c. gender.
   d. familial status.

41. Sean and Alice McAfee installed marble flooring in the entry; put in an expensive chandelier; remodeled the master bath, including gold fixtures; and added an outdoor kitchen before offering the house for sale. Homes in the neighborhood are selling from $225,000 and $280,000. The McAfees told their listing agent that they must have $320,000 to break even. The broker explained that even with the upgrades, the house would probably sell between $250,000 and $260,000 based on size, location, and age. What principle of value dictates the market value in this case?
   a. competition
   b. anticipation
   c. increasing and diminishing returns
   d. substitution and conformity

42. A landlord has notified the tenant to vacate the rental at the end of the lease contract in accordance with the terms of the lease agreement. Several days after the termination day, the tenant still occupies the premises. What type of tenancy is this?
   a. common law tenancy
   b. hostile tenancy
   c. tenancy at will
   d. tenancy at sufferance

43. Taylor has offered to buy Tran's property. The two parties have reached agreement, a contract has been signed by both, and notification has been made. What legal interest is held by Taylor at this time?
   a. He has no legal interest until the sale has closed.
   b. He has legal title pending payment of consideration.
   c. He has equitable title.
   d. He has vendee title.

44. When estimating value, an appraiser will consider the conformity of the subject property to the area and apply the principle of progression and regression. Which of the following is true when using this principle?
   a. A small house in a neighborhood of large homes will sell for much less per square foot than the other houses.
   b. A large house in a neighborhood will sell for the same price per square foot as any other house in the area.
   c. A small house will sell for the same price per square foot as a small house in any other area.
   d. A large house in a neighborhood will sell for less per square foot than the smaller houses in the area.

45. In return for a $100,000 loan, Julia Garza would give her bank both a deed of trust and a
   a. lien.
   b. lease.
   c. note.
   d. check.

46. What type of lease requires no notice by either the tenant or the landlord to terminate the lease?
   a. specific estate
   b. estate for years
   c. terminable lease
   d. defeasible estate

47. Jen and Roland have a contractual real estate agreement in which Jen will continue to hold legal title to the property. Roland will take possession and pay Jen $790 per month for 15 years, pay the taxes and insurance on the property, and maintain the premises. This kind of contract is a
   a. lease option.
   b. mortgage contract.
   c. contract for deed.
   d. contract of sale.

48. A broker's competitive market analysis is similar to, but not the same as,
   a. an appraiser's sales comparison approach to value.
   b. an appraiser's market price approach to value.
   c. a cost, value, or income approach to value.
   d. a cap rate approach to value.

49. If a forced sale fails to bring in enough money to pay off a lien on a 16-unit apartment building, the lender may seek a
   a. release deed.
   b. promissory note.
   c. deficiency judgment.
   d. right of redemption.

50. In each monthly payment of an amortized loan,
   a. the amount of principal and interest in each payment remains the same.
   b. the interest and principal payments each increase.
   c. the interest portion decreases and the principal portion increases.
   d. the interest portion increases and the principal portion decreases.

51. A seller is offering owner financing to the buyer. In order for the monthly payment to be affordable, the loan is structured with a five-year term and amortized for 30 years. The final payment of this loan will be
   a. a fully amortized payment.
   b. a prepayment.
   c. an adjustable payment.
   d. a balloon payment.

52. What is the difference between MIP and PMI?
   a. PMI insures conventional mortgages, and MIP insures FHA loans.
   b. PMI is the older form of mortgage insurance.
   c. MIP is required only on VA mortgage loans.
   d. There is no difference; the two terms mean the same thing.

53. Which of the following will be a seller debit at closing of escrow?
   a. accrued items the seller owes but has not paid
   b. items paid in advance
   c. homeowners insurance premium
   d. amounts remaining in an impound account

54. The buyers and sellers have reached mutual agreement on the terms of a contract, all parties have initialed and signed, and the contract has been dated. This contract
   a. is unilateral.
   b. is fully executed.
   c. is executory.
   d. is implied.

55. The term *PITI* refers to
   a. the designation of a graduate of the Property Insurance Training Institute.
   b. a participation mortgage.
   c. a broker's proof of procuring cause.
   d. the various sums that make up a monthly mortgage payment.

56. The words *to have and to hold* in a deed are known as the
   a. granting clause.
   b. fee simple clause.
   c. *habendum* clause.
   d. grantor's clause.

57. What must a mortgage loan applicant receive from the loan officer at loan application or have mailed to him or her within three days after application?
   a. a completed HUD 1 statement
   b. a GFE and the Special Information Booklet
   c. an escrow statement and receipt
   d. an AfBA disclosure statement

58. The homeowners association fee of $1,275 for the calendar year was paid in advance by the seller. How will this proration be shown on the settlement statement for a closing on April 18? Prorate through the day of closing.
  a. Debit seller $373.77 and credit buyer.
  b. Credit seller $377.26 and debit buyer.
  c. Debit seller $377.26 and credit buyer.
  d. Dredit seller $373.77 and debit buyer.

59. After Mamie Wilson's husband died, she listed her home for sale. The home sold, and at the request of the title insurance company, her stepson agreed to release any inheritance claim he may have had on the property. Which document did he sign?
  a. trust deed
  b. executor's deed
  c. quitclaim deed
  d. probate deed

60. What are "trigger terms" under Regulation Z?
  a. terms that trigger an increase in the interest rate on an ARM
  b. terms that trigger the borrower's right of rescission on a HOEPA loan
  c. terms used in advertising that require full loan information disclosure
  d. terms used in a promissory note accelerating the payment of the balance

61. Florence is buying her first home for $100,000 and will pay a 1% loan origination fee, $367 in legal fees, $1,218 for a one-year insurance policy, $582 prorated interest, $187 for two months of taxes, and $127 in other costs. She has a 1.5% UF MIP that is being financed with her loan of $97,750. What is the total of Florence's move-in costs?
  a. $5,730.50
  b. $7,174.75
  c. $5,709.50
  d. $3,458.50

62. The buyer defaulted on the sale just prior to the closing on a parcel of real estate. The $6,000 earnest money deposit was claimed by the seller and, by mutual agreement of all parties, was paid to the seller. The listing broker
  a. is not entitled to be paid anything, because the sale did not close.
  b. may be entitled to half of the $6,000 if it is so stated in the listing agreement.
  c. is entitled to half of the $6,000, but it will be deducted from any future commission paid on the sale of this property.
  d. will collect half of the earnest money.

63. Alphonse is selling his house, and the buyer is assuming the current mortgage loan. If the lender will not release Alphonse from liability, he should stipulate in the contract that he requires
  a. a release of liability from the buyer.
  b. a deed of trust security amendment.
  c. a release deed from the buyer.
  d. a deed of trust to secure assumption.

64. The right of a lessee to take possession of leased premises and not be evicted by anyone who claims superior rights to the lease is called the
a. covenant of possession.
b. occupancy guarantee.
c. covenant of protection.
d. covenant of quiet enjoyment.

65. Which of the following would not have the legal capacity to enter into a valid and enforceable contract?
a. an illiterate person
b. a minor
c. a person in a nursing home
d. an authorized officer of a corporation

66. The law provides for the distribution of an intestate person's property by
a. escheat.
b. intestate alienation.
c. intestate succession.
d. involuntary alienation.

67. Jing Le is making a 5% down payment on a $345,000 house and will be paying UF PMI of 1.25%, which he is financing with the loan. There will be no additional annual PMI premium. The loan is a 30-year amortization at 6.25% interest paid at $6.1572 per $1,000. What will be Jing's monthly PI payment?
a. $2,150.79
b. $2,015.80
c. $2,043.25
d. $2,018.02

68. An appraiser uses all of the following approaches in determining an opinion of value for real estate EXCEPT
a. cost approach.
b. replacement approach.
c. income approach.
d. sales comparison approach.

69. A rental house has been sold, and the closing is February 14. The landlord is holding a security deposit of $1,400. How will this be shown on the settlement statement?
a. Debit seller $1,400 and credit buyer.
b. Debit seller $700 and credit buyer.
c. Debit seller $650 and credit buyer.
d. Debit buyer $700 and credit seller.

70. Agent Kemp has been asked by his seller not to advertise in a Spanish-language newspaper. Agent Kemp and his office would not violate the law if
a. his seller directed him in writing.
b. his office has never used the paper because of the high rates charged by the paper.
c. the paper does not serve the market area of his office.
d. he doesn't like the paper's editorial positions on many issues.

71. To determine the appraised value of an income producing property, the appraiser will
a. divide the NOI by the cap rate.
b. divide the cap rate by the NOI.
c. multiply the NOI by the cap rate.
d. select recent sales of comparable properties and estimate the value.

72. Broker Hector Santos has an agreement with his agent, Marie, to pay her 65% of anything she produces and an agreement with new agent Lucinda for 55%. Lucinda sold Marie's listing for $439,250. The total commission fee was 5% with half paid to the listing side and half to the selling side of the transaction. How much did Broker Santos receive?
a. $10,981
b. $9,542
c. $8,785
d. $10,813

73. Mike and Jeanne opened a gourmet kitchen shop in a shopping mall and agreed to pay a minimum base rent of $1,450 per month plus 4.5% of gross sales over $325,000 per year. If their gross sales for the year are $437,600, what is the average rent per month?
a. $2,246.70
b. $6,517
c. $4,222.50
d. $1,872.25

74. A real estate listing is usually an example of
a. a universal agency.
b. a special agency.
c. a general agency.
d. an ostensible agency.

75. Broker Mel Mertz sponsors salesperson Ruby LaClare, who will be performing property management services for client Harvey Meyer. A trust account will be opened at a bank for operation of the properties. The account should be in the name(s) of
a. Mertz and LaClare.
b. LaClare and Meyer.
c. Mertz and Meyer.
d. LaClare.

76. Broker Kwan sponsors Salesperson Wang, who has several listings. Who is the agent representing the sellers of these listings, and what is the agency relationship between Kwan and Wang?
a. Salesperson Wang is the general agent of Broker Kwan, who is the agent of the sellers.
b. Salesperson Wang is the agent of the sellers and is an independent agent under Kwan.
c. Salesperson Wang is the agent of the sellers and has no agency relationship to Kwan.
d. Salesperson Wang is the general agent of both the sellers and Broker Kwan.

77. The subject property of an appraisal has a one-car garage and no fireplace. Two similar nearby properties sold in the last month, and each one has a two-car garage and a fireplace. In making adjustments to use the sold properties as comparables, the appraiser will
a. add value to the comparables.
b. use the recorded sales prices of each property.
c. subtract value from the comparables.
d. use two properties with one-car garages and no fireplace that sold last year.

78. Juan and Estella Villareal agreed to sign a buyer's representation agreement with a real estate agent who showed them homes in predominantly Hispanic areas only. This is an example of
a. boycotting certain neighborhoods.
b. customer service.
c. cultural sensitivity.
d. channeling.

79. A seller owes $147,894 on his mortgage loan. If he makes a principal and interest payment of $899 before closing and his interest rate is 6%, what will be the loan balance at closing?
   a. $146,995
   b. $147,154.53
   c. $147,840.06
   d. $147,734.47

80. David and Lily Li agreed to pay $275,000 for a house, make a 5% down payment, and finance the balance. They have deposited $5,000 in escrow as earnest money. They will pay a 1% loan origination fee, 2 discount points, and other closing costs of $1,045. How much will they owe at closing?
   a. $17,632.50
   b. $22,632.50
   c. $23,045
   d. $21,587.50

81. The broker who is sued for an unintentional mistake can expect court costs to be paid by the
   a. seller in the transaction involved.
   b. local association of REALTORS®.
   c. company underwriting the broker's errors and omissions policy.
   d. broker's company funds.

82. A land developer recorded a map in the office of the county clerk where the development is located. What is this map called?
   a. a recorded rectangular survey
   b. a planned unit survey
   c. a township plat
   d. a recorded subdivision plat

83. An apartment complex is leased at 97% occupancy. This may indicate that
   a. the property is well managed and profitable.
   b. the property is poorly managed.
   c. the complex is in an excellent location.
   d. the rents are too low.

84. Which of the following is NOT a criterion for independent contractor status?
   a. The salesperson possesses a valid sales license.
   b. A written agreement states that the individual is not an employee.
   c. The salesperson is given specific duties and procedures.
   d. Most of the salesperson's income in the relationship comes from personal sales production.

85. All of the salespersons in Al's brokerage firm work as independent contractors. Their office most likely provides them with which of the following?
   a. access to the MLS
   b. health insurance
   c. income tax withholding
   d. paid vacations

86. An electric utility company owns an easement across the back of a row of residential lots; the company has the right to install power lines and to enter the property to service the lines when necessary. What kind of easement is this?
   a. an easement by necessity
   b. a dedication easement
   c. an easement appurtenant
   d. an easement in gross

87. The agency relationship created by the agreement between a broker and a sponsored salesperson means that
   a. it is a special agency relationship and the broker owes fiduciary duties to the salesperson.
   b. it is a general agency relationship and the salesperson owes fiduciary duties to the broker.
   c. it is a universal agency relationship and both the salesperson and the broker owe fiduciary duties to all customers.
   d. it is a general agency relationship and fiduciary duties do not apply.

88. Paul Thorsen's oak tree shades the west side of his house, and the tree limbs extend past his property line over his neighbor's driveway. The neighbor's house is for sale, and several prospective buyers have complained about the tree limbs. The tree limbs are
   a. an encumbrance.
   b. an encroachment.
   c. an aerial easement.
   d. Paul's personal property.

89. Superior Home Remodeling, Inc., buys and sells houses. Who is competent to sign contracts and deeds in these transactions?
   a. any officer of the corporation
   b. the officer or officers of the corporation so authorized by the board of directors
   c. the president and secretary of the corporation
   d. the chairman of the board and the secretary of the corporation

90. Sunlin Chen is closing on her new house on June 27. Her loan will be $350,000 at 6.5% interest with payments to be due on the first of each month. How much interest will Sunlin owe in prepaid interest at closing, and when will her first full payment be due? Use a banker's year.
   a. $252.78, with the first payment due August 1
   b. $249.32, with the first payment due August 1
   c. $189.58, with the first payment due July 1
   d. $250.78, with the first payment due August 1

91. A broker has a general agency property management agreement with the owner of a building. Which of the following is NOT true?
   a. The broker may sign leases on behalf of the landlord.
   b. The broker may collect rents and pay all operating expenses from a joint trust account.
   c. The broker may negotiate the sale of the property and sign a deed of conveyance.
   d. The broker may contract for maintenance services and repairs of the building.

92. Clayton is handicapped and must use a wheelchair. He is renting an apartment and requesting that certain modifications be made to the unit to accommodate his needs. Under the Fair Housing Act, how will this be handled?
   a. The landlord, at her expense, must make reasonable modifications for Clayton.
   b. The landlord is not required to make any adjustments to the rental.
   c. Clayton must be allowed to make the modifications as his expense and return the unit to its original condition upon vacating.
   d. Clayton must be allowed to make the modifications with no further obligation.

93. Hubert and Tonia leased a home from Eduardo. They told him that they may want to purchase the home, and they want to know if he gets a valid offer so that they have the opportunity to match that offer. What is this type of agreement called?
   a. lease purchase
   b. right of lease rescission
   c. lease with option to purchase
   d. right of first refusal

94. Aaron closed on his new house, received and accepted the deed from the seller, and recorded the deed at the courthouse where the property is located. Why did he record the deed?
   a. The deed is not valid unless it is recorded.
   b. He recorded the deed for safekeeping.
   c. The recording of the deed gives actual notice of his interest in the property.
   d. The recording of the deed gives constructive notice of his interest in the property.

95. A broker listed a property and is confident that should the property sell during the term of the listing, she will be paid the agreed commission fee. What type of listing does the broker have?
   a. exclusive agency
   b. exclusive right to sell
   c. exclusive authority to purchase
   d. exclusive multiple listing

96. A seller wants to receive $352,300 net at closing. If the broker's commission is 5.5% and all the seller's settlement costs are $5,382.50, how much must the property sell for?
   a. $377,355
   b. $378,500
   c. $377,058
   d. $379,000

97. Broker Cornelius showed buyer client Stella two properties, one for $378,000 and one for $355,900. The lower priced property was in the best location and in good condition. The higher priced property was larger, but in poor condition, and in an area of declining values. What advice should Cornelius give Stella?
   a. Offer $370,000 for the $378,000 property.
   b. Offer full price for the $355,900 property.
   c. Offer full price for the $378,000 property.
   d. Offer $350,000 for the $355,900 property.

98. RESPA applies to all the following EXCEPT
   a. a condo unit.
   b. a duplex purchased for investment.
   c. an apartment in a cooperative.
   d. a 200-acre tract of land.

99. The maximum listing commission to be charged by a broker is determined
   a. by the state licensing regulators.
   b. by negotiation and stated in the listing agreement.
   c. by the seller.
   d. when a buyer makes an offer.

100. An investor wants to buy an income property that produces an annual net operating income of $33,250. What is the maximum price she can pay to achieve a 9.5% rate of return?
   a. $350,000
   b. $332,500
   c. $315,875
   d. $351,875

► Answers

1. **c.** 4.86 acres × 43,560 sq. ft. per acres =
   211,701.6 sq. ft. total
   211,701.6 sq. ft. × $1.25 per ft. = $264,627
   sales price

2. **b.** In a net lease, the lessee pays some or all of
   the operating expenses of the property.

3. **c.** Mineral rights may be reserved by a seller if
   the buyer agrees or conveyed to the buyer if
   the seller agrees or split between them.

4. **b.** This is an express agreement, and Yolanda
   owes full fiduciary duties to the buyer. An
   agency relationship may be established orally,
   but it is always better to have it in writing.

5. **b.** A periodic estate is a leasehold that renews
   itself as long as the tenant or the landlord
   wishes. It may be month to month, year to
   year, or another time frame, and may be terminated by either party with proper notice.

6. **a.** A time-share can include fee simple ownership of a specific property for the same
   period of time each year.

7. **a.** Condominiums are taxed as individual units,
   and each owner is responsible for payment.

8. **c.** A percentage of the gross sales is added to
   the base rent. The concept is that the tenant
   and the landlord both benefit from the location and amenities of the center.

9. **b.** Appurtenances to real property are privileges
   and improvements that belong to, and pass
   with the transfer of, the land.

10. **d.** Agency arises when someone authorizes the
    broker to represent him or her and has control
    over the agent in dealing with third parties.

11. **d.** A life estate *pur autre vie* ("for the life of
    another") is owned by the sister and will go
    to Michael at the mother's death. It does not

devise by a will. A reversionary interest
would mean that the property would revert
back to Ann.

12. **c.** A life estate is for the lifetime of the owner,
    and the church has a reversionary interest in
    the property.

13. **c.** 640 acres per section $\times \frac{1}{4}$ = 160 acres in the
    SE $\frac{1}{4}$ of the section
    160 acres in one quarter $\times \frac{1}{4}$ = 40 acres in the
    NE $\frac{1}{4}$ of the SE $\frac{1}{4}$ of the section

14. **b.** A corporation is an individual entity and
    owns property in severalty.

15. **d.** The broker cannot remove earnest money
    until the purchase closes escrow or the par-
    ties involved in the transaction declare the
    contract null and void, and direct the return
    of the earnest monies by mutual agreement.

16. **b.** A trust deed, or deed of trust, involves three
    persons: the borrower (trustor), the lender
    (beneficiary), and a trustee who holds title
    for the benefit of the lender. The trustee will
    reconvey ownership after the borrower has
    satisfied the debt.

17. **c.** A position above or below ground is
    described by reference to a datum that is
    established at a certain benchmark, such as
    sea level, at a certain place.

18. **d.** Divide each comparable sale price by the rent
    to get the multiplier.
    $126,900 ÷ $1,190 = 106.67 GRM
    $129,750 ÷ $1,230 = 105.49 GRM
    $133,500 ÷ $1,275 = 104.71 GRM
    (106.67 + 105.49 + 104.71) ÷ 3 = 105.62
    average GRM

19. **a.** The agent represents the seller and owes him
    or her the fiduciary duty of confidentiality.
    The agent must disclose material facts
    regarding the condition of the property, but

may not reveal any personal or confidential information to any party that the seller did not authorize the broker to reveal.

20. c. If there is no written listing agreement signed by the seller, the broker cannot sue the seller for a fee.

21. c. $250,000 sales price × 95% LTV = $237,500 loan amount
$237,500 × 2.5% discount points = $5,937.50 total points
$5,937.50 ÷ 2 = $2,968.75 to be paid by each party

22. d. A life tenant may not do anything that would damage the property or the interest of the remainderman. The remainderman has the right to bring court action against a current possessor who commits waste.

23. b. Even though there was no written agency agreement, an oral agency relationship was expressed when they agreed to the price and the commission fee and Ali marketed the property. Payment of a fee does not create agency. Ali created implied agency with the buyer.

24. c. Familial status refers to persons under the age of 18 living with a parent or legal guardian. Discrimination includes allowing tenants to rent only in limited areas or charging additional security deposits or additional rent.

25. a. The principal bears responsibility for acts of his or her representing agent or subagents. Vicarious liability is created because of the relationship between the liable party and the other party or parties.

26. c. The exclusive listing must include an expiration date because the seller is not free to work with any other broker during the term of the listing. A commission may be a flat fee as opposed to a percent of the sales price.

27. a. Termination by acts of the parties may include the principal revoking the agency relationship; the agent renouncing the agency; or both parties agreeing to mutually terminate the agency relationship.

28. b. A listing agreement in which the broker receives all monies above the sales price and seller costs is a net listing. Because of the possibilities of unethical practices, it is illegal in some states.

29. b. Oscar has led the buyer to believe he is working on her behalf by implied agency. Because he already represents the seller, he has breached his fiduciary duties and created an undisclosed dual agency, which is illegal.

30. a. While it is discriminatory to refuse to rent based on gender, a person in his or her own home may limit the accommodations to his or her own sex. However, it is important to note that this federal exemption, often referred to as "Mrs. Murphy's Exemption," is not recognized by all states. Students are not a protected class under Fair Housing laws, but may be protected by some local ordinances.

31. c. The listing broker may pay the selling broker an agreed portion of his or her commission without creating an agency relationship between the selling broker, Merle, and the seller.

32. c. Agents must be able to account for and produce anything of value entrusted to their care. This includes advances of marketing fees, earnest money deposits, and escrows.

33. d. The broker brought a ready, willing, and able buyer meeting the seller's terms. However, the seller does not have to accept the offer.

34. b. The protection period with an override clause protects the broker in case a buyer whom the broker negotiated prior to the expiration of the listing later purchases the property.

35. a. A broker must have written consent of both parties to act as a dual agent and must maintain a neutral position between them while assisting with the transaction. Common law dual agency is not permitted in some states.

36. d. A subagent is the agent of an agent. The buyer is a customer and is not Lucille Lau's client.

37. c. A patent conveys real property from the state or federal government to an individual.

38. d. Market price is the actual selling price. Appraised value is the appraiser's estimate of value.

39. c. An assignment of a lease is total transfer of the tenant's rights to another person. A sublease transfers a portion of the rights to another and the sublessee pays the rent to the sublessor, who pays the landlord.

40. d. Familial status protects families with children under the age of 18.

41. c. The cost of added amenities will not increase the value of improvements above the comparable values of a particular location. The house is overimproved.

42. d. The tenant is wrongfully holding over, without the consent of the landlord, after the landlord has given notice to vacate.

43. c. The interest held by a buyer or vendee under a purchase agreement gives the buyer the equitable right to acquire legal title to the property by deed.

44. d. The principle of regression means that a larger or more costly house will sell for less in an area of less expensive homes, and conversely, the smaller, less costly house will sell for more in an area of larger homes.

45. c. The deed of trust serves as security for the debt, which the borrower promises to repay by signing a promissory note.

46. b. An estate for years has a specific beginning date and a specific ending date with no automatic renewal provision.

47. c. A contract for deed may also be called a land contract or an installment contract. The seller retains legal title, and the buyer has equitable title until all required payments are made, at which time the seller is required to pass title to the buyer.

48. a. A broker's CMA is not an appraisal but is similar in characteristic to the appraiser's sales comparison approach.

49. c. The lender who does not receive full payment after foreclosure of a loan may seek a deficiency judgment against the borrower.

50. c. As the debt is paid down, the amount of interest due each month becomes smaller, and more of the payment is available to be applied to the principal.

51. d. This is a partially amortized loan with a large payment due at the end of five years.

52. a. MIP (mortgage insurance premium) is charged on government insured FHA loans. PMI (private mortgage insurance) applies to most conventional loans over 80% LTV.

53. a. Property taxes and other items that are due or will be due in the future are prorated and charged to the seller. These amounts are then credited to the buyer, who will be responsible for paying the charges when they are due.

54. c. An executory contract is one in which all parties have reached full agreement but something remains to be done by one or both parties. It is partially performed. When all parties have fully performed and the transaction is closed, it will be fully executed.

55. d. PITI stands for the principal, interest, taxes, and insurance. The total is used to determine the financial qualification of a loan applicant in the debt-to-income ratio.

56. c. This clause describes the interest being conveyed from the grantor to the grantee.

57. b. It is mandated by the Real Estate Settlement Procedures Act that the Good Faith Estimate of closing costs and the booklet explaining the settlement costs as listed on the HUD 1 Settlement statement be provided to all applicants for a home mortgage loan.

58. b. Use calendar days. January has 31 days, February has 28 days, March has 31 days, and April has 18 days. The total number of days is 108. ($1,275 annual fee ÷ 365 days) × 108 days = $377.26

59. c. By releasing the any claim to the fee simple owner, a quitclaim deed removes any possible cloud on the title.

60. c. Regulation Z of the Truth-in-Lending Act requires full disclosure if any of the following are stated in any advertising: amount of down payment, percentage of down payment, amount of a payment, number of payments, amount of finance charge, or term of loan.

61. c. The UF MIP is not included in actual move-in costs because it is being financed.
$100,000 sales price − $97,750 loan = $2,250 down payment
$97,750 × 1% loan origination fee = $977.50 LO fee
$2,250 + $977.50 + $367 legal fee + $1,218 insurance + $582 interest + $187 taxes + $127 other costs = $5,708.50 total

62. b. The broker may collect a portion of the money according to the listing agreement and may still collect a full fee from any future sale made during the listing term.

63. d. A deed of trust to secure assumption is a security instrument giving the seller (beneficiary) the right to appoint a trustee to foreclose in case of buyer (trustor) default on the assumed debt.

64. d. After a valid lease is signed by the parties, the landlord is usually bound by the implied covenant of quiet enjoyment or quiet possession.

65. b. Persons unable to read or write may make their mark, and a person must be declared incompetent by a court to have legal capacity to contract removed.

66. c. A person who dies intestate does not have a valid will. States have varying rules regarding how property is distributed, but usually it begins with a surviving spouse, then children and other next of kin.

67. c. $345,000 sales price × 95% LTV = $327,750 base loan amount
$327,750 × 1.25% up front PMI premium = $4,096.88 UF PMI
$327,750 base loan + $4,096.88 UF PMI = $331,846.88 total loan amount
$331,846.88 ÷ 1,000 × 6.1572 = $2,043.25 principal and interest

68. b. Cost approach is used for determining the actual cost to replace or reproduce an improvement. Income approach is used in appraising investment property, and the sales approach is used primarily in residential appraisal.

69. a. The entire amount of the deposit is credited from the seller to the buyer, who is the new landlord and who will hold the deposit until the termination of the lease and then distribute the money according to the lease agreement.

70. b. The broker must make all advertising decisions based on accepted business practices, not by the race or color of the intended reader. He would be in violation of Fair Housing laws if he refrained from advertising in the paper with the intent to keep Hispanic buyers from seeing the property.

71. **a.** Value of income producing properties is determined by using capitalization rates of comparable properties and the net operating income (NOI) of the subject property. This transfers the income stream into an estimate of value.

72. **c.** ($439,250 sales price × 5% commission) ÷ 2 = $10,981.25
$10,981.25 × 35% from listing side = $3,843.44 to broker
$10,981.25 × 45% from selling side = $4,941.56 to broker
$3,843.44 + $4,941.56 = $8,785 total commission paid to Hector Santos

73. **d.** $437,600 gross sales − $325,000 = $112,600 gross sales over $325,000
$112,600 × 4.5% rent rate = $5,067 additional annual rent
$5,067 ÷ 12 months = $422.25 average due over base rent
$1,450 base rent + $422.25 over base rent = $1,872.25 total average monthly rent

74. **b.** A special agent is authorized to perform one particular act, as in finding a ready, willing, and able buyer for a piece of property.

75. **c.** The broker, Mel Mertz, is the agent for the client, Harvey Meyer, and the account should be in the name of the broker and the client.

76. **a.** All business is done in the name of the sponsoring broker, and that broker is the agent of the client. All sponsored salespersons are general agents of the sponsoring broker.

77. **c.** The appraiser will subtract for the difference in the garage and fireplace, giving the comparables a value as if they were exactly like the subject property.

78. **d.** Steering, or channeling, is the practice of taking people to or away from certain areas because of race, national origin, ethnicity, religion, or any of the protected classes under Fair Housing laws.

79. **d.** $147,894.00 loan balance × 6% annual interest rate = $8,873.64 one year interest
$8,873.64 ÷ 12 months = $739.47 one month's interest
$899.00 payment − $739.47 interest = $159.53 principal paid
$147,894 principal balance − $159.53 principal paid = $147,734.47 loan balance at closing

80. **a.** $275,000 sales price × 5% down = $13,750 down payment
$275,000 sales price × 95% LTV = $261,250 loan amount
$261,250 loan × (1% origination + 2% discount) = $7,837.50 loan origination plus points
$13,750 down + $7,837.50 origination plus points + $1,045 closing costs = $22,632.50
$22,632.50 − $5,000 earnest money deposit = $17,632.50 owed at closing

81. **c.** An E & O insurance underwriter will defend the broker and pay legal costs, as well as judgments if the mistake was not deliberate.

82. **d.** A recorded subdivision plat creates legal descriptions using lots, blocks, and sections.

83. **d.** The property manager has a duty to show a good cash flow for the owner, and when occupancy reaches very high levels, higher rents are justified.

84. **c.** A broker may give objectives to a salesperson, but he or she may not tell the salesperson how to meet those objectives.

85. **a.** Federal income tax regulations state that an independent contractor may not receive anything that resembles an employee benefit.

86. **d.** An easement in gross belongs to an individual or commercial entity, and the sale of the land does not affect the ownership of the easement. There is no dominant or servient estate, and the easement benefits the user only.

87. b. Fiduciary duties are owed from the agent to the principal in all agency relationships. The salesperson is the agent, and the broker is the principal.

88. b. An encroachment occurs when a physical object, man-made or natural, intrudes into someone's property. This can be subsurface, surface, or aerial.

89. b. Legal instrument such as contracts, deeds, or promissory notes must be authorized by the corporation's board of directors, and only those officers authorized by the board may sign such documents.

90. a. The buyer will pay prepaid interest for June 27 through June 30, four days. Interest is paid in arrears except for prepaid interest paid at the closing of a loan. June interest will be fully paid at closing and no interest will be due until August 1, when a payment will be due and will pay the interest on the loan for July.
$350,000 loan amount × 6.5% interest = $22,750 one year's interest
$22,750 ÷ 360 days in a banker's year = $63.1944 per day interest
$63.1944 × 4 days = $252.78 due in prepaid interest

91. c. The general agency agreement may give the property manager authority to operate the property in all aspects, but he or she cannot sell and convey it.

92. c. A landlord may not refuse to permit a person to make reasonable alterations to a dwelling at his or her expense, but may require the tenant to restore the dwelling to its previous condition if it is reasonable to do so.

93. d. A right of first refusal protects a tenant from having the property sold before he or she has the opportunity to match or better the offer from another prospective buyer.

94. d. Actual notice is from what one has seen, heard, or read. Constructive notice to the world is given by filing a document in a public record.

95. b. An exclusive right to sell protects the broker during the listing period because, no matter who sells the property, the broker is entitled to a fee.

96. b. $352,300 net to seller + $5,382.50 costs = $357,682.50 before commission
$357,682.50 ÷ 94.5% = $378,500 required sales price

97. d. The buyer is the broker's client, and the broker owes her fiduciary duties. While he could make a larger commission fee on the more expensive property, he must give his best advice. Because the buyer is his client, he may advise a price lower than the asking price. If the buyer is a customer and not a client, the broker cannot advise any price less than the list price.

98. d. The Real Estate Settlement Procedures Act applies to all federally related loans secured by all one- to four-family residential properties.

99. b. A broker may have a predetermined commission policy, or the commission may be negotiated between the broker/agent and the seller client.

100. a. $33,250 NOI ÷ 9.5% rate of return = $350,000
The maximum price for a certain rate of return is determined by dividing the net operating income by the desired rate of return or capitalization rate.

► Scoring

Again, evaluate how you did on this practice exam by finding the number of questions you got right, disregarding for the moment the ones you got wrong or skipped. On the official exam, you need to answer 75% correctly to pass.

If you didn't score as well as you would like, ask yourself the following: Did I run out of time before I could answer all the questions? Did I go back and change my answers from right to wrong? Did I get flustered and sit staring at a difficult question for what seemed like hours? If you had any of these problems, be sure to go over the LearningExpress Test Preparation System in Chapter 2 to review how best to avoid them.

You probably have seen improvement between your first practice exam score and this one, but if you didn't improve as much as you'd like, here are some options:

If you scored well below your personal goal, you should seriously consider whether you're ready for the exam at this time. A good idea would be to take some brush-up courses in the areas in which you feel less confident. If you don't have time for a course, you might try private tutoring.

If you scored close to your personal goal, you need to work as hard as you can to improve your skills. Go back to your real estate license course textbooks to review the knowledge you need to do well on the exam. If math is your problem area, check out the Learning-Express book *Practical Math Success in 20 Minutes a Day*. Also, reread and pay close attention to the information in Chapter 7, Real Estate Broker Refresher Course; Chapter 8, Real Estate Broker Math Review; and Chapter 9, Real Estate Glossary. Take the other practice exams in this book. It might also be helpful to ask friends and family to make up mock test questions and quiz you on them.

If you scored well above your personal goal, that's great! You are well on the road to passing your broker's license exam. Don't lose your edge, though; keep studying right up to the day before the exam.

Now, revise your study schedule according to the time you have left, emphasizing those parts that gave you the most trouble this time. Use the following table to see where you need more work, so that you can concentrate your preparation efforts.

AMP Practice Exam 2 for Review

Topic	Question Numbers
Financing	16, 21, 45, 49, 50, 51, 52, 55, 60, 67
Listing Property	1, 3, 9, 13, 17, 20, 23, 26, 28, 33, 35, 38, 41, 44, 48, 53, 59, 62, 63, 68, 71, 72, 74, 76, 77, 79, 82, 86, 88, 95, 99
Property Management	2, 5, 8, 18, 24, 30, 39, 42, 46, 64, 69, 75, 83, 91
Professional Responsibilities/ Fair Practice/Administration	15, 25, 29, 32, 34, 70, 81, 84, 85, 87
Selling Property	4, 10, 19, 27, 31, 36, 40, 43, 47, 54, 57, 61, 65, 73, 78, 80, 90, 92, 93, 97, 100
Settlement/Transfer of Ownership	6, 7, 11, 12, 14, 22, 37, 56, 58, 66, 89, 94, 96, 98

11 ▶ Promissor Practice Exam 2

CHAPTER SUMMARY

This is the second of the two Promissor practice tests in this book. Because you have taken the first Promissor practice test already, you should feel more confident with your test-taking skills. Use this test to see how knowing what to expect can make you feel better prepared.

You are now more familiar with the format and content of the national portion of the Promissor exam, and most likely, you feel more confident than you did at first. However, your practice test-taking experience will be most helpful if you have created a situation as close as possible to the real one.

For this exam, try to simulate real testing conditions. Find a quiet place where you will not be disturbed. Make sure you have two sharpened pencils and a good eraser. Be sure to leave enough time to complete the exam in one sitting. There is a four-hour limit on the official exam, so you'll want to practice working quickly without rushing. Use a timer or a stopwatch and see if you can work through all the exam questions in the allotted time.

The answer sheet is on the next page. An answer key and explanations follow the exam. These explanations, along with the table at the end of this chapter, will help you see where you need further study. Remember, the six other practice exams in this book, although slightly different in format than the Promissor exam, all test the same basic real estate principles and concepts, so you can use them to help you further solidify your knowledge and skills.

1.	(a)	(b)	(c)	(d)	31.	(a)	(b)	(c)	(d)	61.	(a)	(b)	(c)	(d)
2.	(a)	(b)	(c)	(d)	32.	(a)	(b)	(c)	(d)	62.	(a)	(b)	(c)	(d)
3.	(a)	(b)	(c)	(d)	33.	(a)	(b)	(c)	(d)	63.	(a)	(b)	(c)	(d)
4.	(a)	(b)	(c)	(d)	34.	(a)	(b)	(c)	(d)	64.	(a)	(b)	(c)	(d)
5.	(a)	(b)	(c)	(d)	35.	(a)	(b)	(c)	(d)	65.	(a)	(b)	(c)	(d)
6.	(a)	(b)	(c)	(d)	36.	(a)	(b)	(c)	(d)	66.	(a)	(b)	(c)	(d)
7.	(a)	(b)	(c)	(d)	37.	(a)	(b)	(c)	(d)	67.	(a)	(b)	(c)	(d)
8.	(a)	(b)	(c)	(d)	38.	(a)	(b)	(c)	(d)	68.	(a)	(b)	(c)	(d)
9.	(a)	(b)	(c)	(d)	39.	(a)	(b)	(c)	(d)	69.	(a)	(b)	(c)	(d)
10.	(a)	(b)	(c)	(d)	40.	(a)	(b)	(c)	(d)	70.	(a)	(b)	(c)	(d)
11.	(a)	(b)	(c)	(d)	41.	(a)	(b)	(c)	(d)	71.	(a)	(b)	(c)	(d)
12.	(a)	(b)	(c)	(d)	42.	(a)	(b)	(c)	(d)	72.	(a)	(b)	(c)	(d)
13.	(a)	(b)	(c)	(d)	43.	(a)	(b)	(c)	(d)	73.	(a)	(b)	(c)	(d)
14.	(a)	(b)	(c)	(d)	44.	(a)	(b)	(c)	(d)	74.	(a)	(b)	(c)	(d)
15.	(a)	(b)	(c)	(d)	45.	(a)	(b)	(c)	(d)	75.	(a)	(b)	(c)	(d)
16.	(a)	(b)	(c)	(d)	46.	(a)	(b)	(c)	(d)	76.	(a)	(b)	(c)	(d)
17.	(a)	(b)	(c)	(d)	47.	(a)	(b)	(c)	(d)	77.	(a)	(b)	(c)	(d)
18.	(a)	(b)	(c)	(d)	48.	(a)	(b)	(c)	(d)	78.	(a)	(b)	(c)	(d)
19.	(a)	(b)	(c)	(d)	49.	(a)	(b)	(c)	(d)	79.	(a)	(b)	(c)	(d)
20.	(a)	(b)	(c)	(d)	50.	(a)	(b)	(c)	(d)	80.	(a)	(b)	(c)	(d)
21.	(a)	(b)	(c)	(d)	51.	(a)	(b)	(c)	(d)					
22.	(a)	(b)	(c)	(d)	52.	(a)	(b)	(c)	(d)					
23.	(a)	(b)	(c)	(d)	53.	(a)	(b)	(c)	(d)					
24.	(a)	(b)	(c)	(d)	54.	(a)	(b)	(c)	(d)					
25.	(a)	(b)	(c)	(d)	55.	(a)	(b)	(c)	(d)					
26.	(a)	(b)	(c)	(d)	56.	(a)	(b)	(c)	(d)					
27.	(a)	(b)	(c)	(d)	57.	(a)	(b)	(c)	(d)					
28.	(a)	(b)	(c)	(d)	58.	(a)	(b)	(c)	(d)					
29.	(a)	(b)	(c)	(d)	59.	(a)	(b)	(c)	(d)					
30.	(a)	(b)	(c)	(d)	60.	(a)	(b)	(c)	(d)					

► Promissor Practice Exam 2

1. Which of the following is a private restriction on the use of land?
   a. zoning
   b. building codes
   c. deed restrictions
   d. subdivision regulations

2. Mary White and Elizabeth Brown, widowed sisters, are buying a home together. To ensure that if one dies her share will go to her children, they should purchase the property as
   a. tenants in severalty.
   b. tenants by the entirety.
   c. tenants in common.
   d. joint tenants with right of survivorship.

3. When tenant Heather Grayson opened her ice cream shop in the mall, she installed counters and special freezers. When Heather closes the shop, can she remove them?
   a. It depends on whether her lease specifically states that she can.
   b. No, because as a tenant she gives up the right of possession.
   c. Yes, if she repairs any damage caused by their removal.
   d. No, because, as fixtures, they have become part of the real estate.

4. The Simons have defaulted on their loan payments and are behind in paying the rest of their bills, so their home is being sold in a foreclosure auction. Of the many liens against the house, which will have first claim on the proceeds of the sale?
   a. the first mortgage recorded
   b. unpaid real estate taxes
   c. mechanic's lien
   d. home equity loan

5. The furnace at 39 State Street doesn't work properly. However, because the prospective buyers inspect the house in July, there is no indication of this. The condition of the furnace is known as
   a. an encumbrance.
   b. a cloud on title.
   c. a latent defect.
   d. an economic obsolescence.

6. The unlawful practice of commingling is to
   a. mix your clients' funds together.
   b. mix your client's funds with your own.
   c. mix your funds with your broker's funds.
   d. mix earnest money funds with rent money.

7. The highest form of real property ownership wherein the owner controls who inherits the property and has the fewest limitations on the property rights is known as
   a. a freehold estate.
   b. fee simple absolute.
   c. a defeasible fee estate.
   d. *pur autre vie.*

8. Fred Darcy, a single man, sells his longtime home. How much capital gain can he realize without owing any federal income tax?
  a. $125,000
  b. $250,000
  c. $500,000
  d. an unlimited amount

9. Which of the following factors would a listing agent NOT be required to disclose to a prospective buyer?
  a. The property has been on the market for more than a year.
  b. The land was once used as a gas station.
  c. An addition to the building was not built in accordance with local building codes.
  d. Radon gas has been found in the building.

10. If a client purchases a self-storage facility and, after closing, discovers that a former tenant caused an oil spill that resulted in contamination of the property, who is responsible for the cleanup?
  a. the tenant
  b. the tenant and seller
  c. the seller and buyer
  d. the tenant, seller, and buyer

11. A property owner is in violation of the Fair Housing Act of 1968 if the owner
  a. refuses to rent a room in a single-family home occupied by the owner.
  b. discriminates in the rental of a building of four or fewer units, one of which is occupied by the owner.
  c. denies housing on the basis of race.
  d. denies nonmembers of a private club sleeping quarters when occupancy is limited to club members.

12. Which of the following may NOT be disclosed to a prospective buyer or tenant?
  a. the presence of lead-based paint if the property was built after 1978
  b. the property owner's motivation for selling
  c. that there is a tax lien on the property
  d. that a current or previous occupant has HIV or AIDS

13. A salesperson with Beacon Hill Realty knowingly misrepresents the condition of a property listed with the firm. Who is responsible for this misrepresentation?
  a. the salesperson who made the misrepresentation
  b. the salesperson's broker if he or she knew of the misrepresentation
  c. the salesperson's broker even if he or she did not know of the misrepresentation
  d. all of the above

14. Zoning regulations establish the permitted uses of land as well as
  a. building heights, setbacks, and density.
  b. the price of improvements, appurtenances, and amenities.
  c. restrictions on ownership.
  d. property rights.

15. A planned development consists of
  a. structures such as factories or hotels that have been converted to residential use.
  b. residential apartment units that share common elements, such as hallways and recreational areas, within a larger building.
  c. a high-rise building that includes apartments as well as commercial units, such as movie theaters and stores.
  d. parcels owned separately and areas owned in common for use by parcel owners.

16. A farmers' market had been in operation continuously for 50 years at the intersection of Routes 50 and 29. A new master plan, approved by the local jurisdiction, placed that tract of land in a residential zone. In order to stay in business, the owner of the farmers' market should
- **a.** apply for a new zoning category.
- **b.** modernize and expand the facility.
- **c.** raze and reconstruct a new market.
- **d.** keep the business going without modification.

17. Which of the following must be included in every advertisement placed by a real estate broker?
- **a.** the fact that the broker holds a real estate license
- **b.** the Fair Housing symbol
- **c.** the contact information of the state authority that issued the license
- **d.** none of the above

18. The government has the power to do all of the following EXCEPT
- **a.** tax real estate.
- **b.** enact reasonable land use laws.
- **c.** take land if necessary for the public welfare.
- **d.** enter upon private property at any time.

19. If a jurisdiction requires private property for public use, the first step begins with
- **a.** an amicable negotiation.
- **b.** seeking an injunction against transfer of the property to a third party.
- **c.** obtaining a writ of attachment.
- **d.** beginning condemnation proceedings.

20. The most important requirement of the federal lead-based paint law is that the
- **a.** owner is required to remove lead-based materials prior to the sale or lease of property.
- **b.** agent must arrange for an inspection by a certified remediator.
- **c.** buyer has ten days in which to arrange for an inspection to evaluate the extent of the hazardous materials.
- **d.** lender must warrant that the property is free from lead problems.

21. In a situation in which the law and ethics conflict, which must take priority in the operation of a brokerage firm?
- **a.** whichever is stated in the firm's policy and procedures manual
- **b.** The law must take priority.
- **c.** Ethical standards must take priority.
- **d.** Neither one takes priority.

22. An agent who is empowered to act for a principal in a broad range of matters with the ability to bind the principal is known as a(n)
- **a.** special agent.
- **b.** general agent.
- **c.** brokerage agent.
- **d.** universal agent.

23. All of the following are depreciable for investment property EXCEPT
- **a.** the physical structure.
- **b.** mechanical components.
- **c.** the land.
- **d.** furniture and fixtures.

24. An expressed agency relationship is created by
   a. words, whether written or oral.
   b. the actions of the parties.
   c. written contract only.
   d. payment of a commission.

25. When an owner sells a principal residence, the capital gain is calculated by
   a. subtracting selling expenses from the sales price.
   b. subtracting the sales price from the original purchase price.
   c. reducing the realized selling price by the property's adjusted basis.
   d. subtracting the selling expenses from the original purchase price.

26. Which of the following programs would probably be of the most benefit to owners of property located in the lowlands along a river?
   a. the Superfund and Reauthorization Act
   b. the National Flood Insurance Act
   c. the Resources Conservation and Recovery Act
   d. the Interstate Land Sales Full Disclosure Act

27. A broker with a listing agreement with a seller is normally considered to be what kind of an agent?
   a. general
   b. special
   c. universal
   d. realty

28. At a general meeting of a brokers' trade association, several members begin talking about fees and business practices. This sort of activity could be considered
   a. a violation of the Sherman Anti-Trust Act.
   b. activity prohibited by the Better Business Bureau.
   c. an appropriate activity within the association.
   d. a good way for brokers to learn about the different practices nationwide.

29. Which of the following statements is true regarding an agent's duty of obedience to his or her principal?
   a. The agent must obey all instructions of the principal.
   b. The agent must obey only written instructions of the principal.
   c. The agent may ignore instructions that the broker's greater knowledge tells him or her would not be in the principal's best interest.
   d. The agent must obey all lawful instructions of the principal.

30. A rectangular tract of land measures 860 feet by 560 feet. How many acres is this?
   a. 11 acres
   b. 10.5 acres
   c. 8.6 acres
   d. 12.8 acres

31. A mini-ranch is being established on a newly acquired 25-acre parcel of land. The new owner plans to enclose the property with a split-rail fence. The rectangular lot has 1,000 feet of frontage on the state road. How many feet of fencing will be needed?

    a. 2,090 feet
    b. 4,178 feet
    c. 4,270 feet
    d. 4,595 feet

32. Which of the following would NOT be required to be disclosed to a prospective buyer by the listing agent?

    a. a material defect in the property
    b. a title defect known to the seller and broker
    c. the fact that the seller is in financial trouble
    d. the presence of toxic substances on the property

33. A purchaser contracts a new home for $250,000 and, after making a 20% down payment, applies for a 30-year fixed-rate loan at the rate of 7.5%. At the settlement on April 10, the lender collects interest up to May 1. What is the interest charge to the buyer shown on the settlement statement?

    a. $1,250
    b. $416.60
    c. $833.33
    d. $875

34. Jeff and Alexandra Clancey have paid a total of $10,500 in mortgage interest and $1,500 in property taxes in this tax year. If they are in the 28% tax bracket, their tax savings are

    a. $12,000
    b. $1,000
    c. $294
    d. $3,360

35. James Kingsley has just settled on his new home. He obtained a new loan of $151,000 at 8% that requires a monthly payment of $7.34 per thousand. He also has an estimated annual property tax of $2,900 and an insurance premium of $560 per year, which he will pay in monthly deposits into escrow. What is the monthly payment for James?

    a. $1,108.34
    b. $1,396.67
    c. $1,350
    d. $1,156

36. A legal relationship between an agent and a principal that entails trust and confidence is known as a

    a. formalized relationship.
    b. fiduciary relationship.
    c. trust relationship.
    d. principal relationship.

37. An agency relationship created after the fact is known as

    a. agency by ratification.
    b. agency by post action.
    c. implied agency.
    d. resultant agency.

38. A salesperson has earned $120,000 in gross commissions this year. If the average commission is 2.6% per transaction, and the salesperson receives 60% of the commission from each transaction, approximately how much sales volume has that salesperson settled this year?

    a. $7,200,000
    b. $4,615,380
    c. $7,692,300
    d. $8,000,000

39. A seller states that the minimum proceeds from the sale must be $108,000 after paying 18% in selling fees and other charges. For a transaction to occur, the sales price must be at least
a. $127,445.50
b. $88,560
c. $131,707.31
d. $125,000

40. A heating and cooling engineer is drawing up the specifications for the HVAC system in a new building. The floor space measures 200' × 150', and the ceiling is 12' high. How much air space does the engineer have to heat and cool?
a. 33,333 square yards
b. 300,000 square feet
c. 13,333 cubic yards
d. 36,000 cubic feet

41. In using direct capitalization, an appraiser would determine value by
a. dividing the NOI by the capitalization rate.
b. dividing the mortgage by the constant.
c. dividing the income by the rent multiplier.
d. dividing the equity by the dividend rate.

42. A buyer obtained a loan of $135,000 with a 9.25% interest rate for the purchase of a home. After paying the first monthly payment of $1,111.05, the remaining balance will be
a. $134,929.57
b. $133,888.95
c. $135,070.43
d. $135,000

43. The seller accepts an offer to purchase in the amount of $395,000. After paying a brokerage fee of 5.5%, paying off a loan of $300,000, and paying various settlement fees totaling 4% of the sale price, what are the seller's net proceeds?
a. $57,475
b. $73,275
c. $58,344
d. $373,275

44. A listing agreement wherein a broker is paid the commission no matter who procures the buyer is known as an
a. exclusive agency listing.
b. exclusive right to sell listing.
c. open listing.
d. none of the above

45. The duties of the property manager include all of the following EXCEPT
a. maintaining the property while preserving finances.
b. marketing for a constant tenant base.
c. seeking interested buyers.
d. preparing budgets.

46. The relationship of a property manager with the owner is a
a. special agency.
b. general agency.
c. limited partnership.
d. dual agency.

47. The management agreement does all of the following EXCEPT
   a. identify the parties.
   b. authorize the manager to make personal deals resulting in outside compensation by suppliers.
   c. describe the manager's responsibilities and authorities.
   d. state the owner's overall goals for the property.

48. Which of the following kinds of listing agreements would allow a property owner to employ multiple brokers with the obligation to pay a broker only if he or she procures a ready, willing and able buyer?
   a. a net listing
   b. a reward listing
   c. a nonagency listing
   d. an open listing

49. Economic or external obsolescence refers to loss of value because of
   a. wear and tear.
   b. outdated design.
   c. factors outside the property lines.
   d. incurable defects in the subject property.

50. A cap rate is used in what type of appraisal?
   a. reproduction
   b. income approach
   c. tax assessment
   d. competitive market analysis

51. The type of depreciation always classified as incurable is
   a. physical deterioration.
   b. fictional IRS depreciation.
   c. functional obsolescence.
   d. economic or external obsolescence.

52. The provisions of RESPA are applicable to all of the following EXCEPT
   a. loans on commercial property.
   b. loans insured by the Federal Housing Administration.
   c. mortgages guaranteed by the Department of Veterans Affairs.
   d. loans sold to FNMA.

53. RESPA requires all of the following EXCEPT that the
   a. buyer receives the HUD information booklet from the lender.
   b. lender makes a good-faith estimate of closing costs for the buyer.
   c. buyer is offered a loan that is 2% below market rate.
   d. closing will be conducted using the HUD 1 Uniform Settlement Statement.

54. Which of the following statements most accurately describes a contract?
   a. a written agreement between two parties
   b. a written or oral agreement between two parties
   c. a legally enforceable agreement
   d. a legal document signed by both parties

55. Which of the following effects, if any, does zoning have on property values?
   a. Values are unchanged because owners have the freedom to develop land as they wish.
   b. Value is enhanced because of the principle of conformity.
   c. Value is diminished because of the lack of creative use of land.
   d. Value is not related to zoning; it is a product of supply and demand.

56. When available units outnumber potential tenants, there is a(n)
   a. interaction of supply and demand.
   b. technical oversupply.
   c. economic oversupply.
   d. lower rent.

57. Which of the following changes in zoning should result in compensation to the owner?
   a. spot zoning
   b. down-zoning
   c. buffer zoning
   d. taking

58. A contract that may be terminated by one of the parties (rescinded) is said to be
   a. valid.
   b. voidable.
   c. void.
   d. unenforceable.

59. The federal ban on discrimination based on familial status is intended to provide equal access to rental properties for
   a. unmarried couples.
   b. people with children.
   c. single tenants.
   d. the elderly.

60. No federal Fair Housing laws are violated if a landlord refuses to rent to
   a. families with children.
   b. tenants of Vietnamese descent.
   c. deaf persons.
   d. students.

61. The penalty for a first violation of Federal Fair Housing laws can be as much as
   a. $1,000
   b. $5,000
   c. $10,000
   d. $100,000

62. A landlord is NOT allowed to charge a tenant extra rent because the tenant has a
   a. dog.
   b. second car.
   c. child.
   d. recreational vehicle.

63. Which of the following is true about discount points?
   a. They allow for cut-rate lending.
   b. They are based on the purchase price of the property.
   c. They are charged when a mortgage is resold.
   d. They increase the effective yield to the lender.

64. The alienation clause found in most security instruments states that the full amount will be immediately due and payable if the
   a. borrower is late with three monthly payments.
   b. property is sold to a new owner.
   c. hazard insurance policy is allowed to lapse.
   d. homeowner borrows more money on the property.

65. What kind of contract may be formed by the actions of the parties?
   a. express
   b. indirect
   c. actionable
   d. implied

66. Which of the following gives an example of a bilateral contract first and a unilateral contract second?
   a. option to buy vs. purchase contract
   b. purchase contract vs. option to buy
   c. option to buy vs. lease
   d. lease vs. purchase contract

67. What is a contract called that has been signed by all the parties but the promises contained therein have yet to be performed?
   a. executory
   b. executed
   c. performable
   d. none of the above

68. The Federal Reserve affects the real estate market by its influence of
   a. interest rates.
   b. FHA mortgages.
   c. discount points.
   d. secondary markets.

69. The law that requires that contracts for the sale of real estate must be in writing to be enforceable in a court of law is called the
   a. Written Agreement Statute.
   b. Law of Contracts.
   c. Statute of Frauds.
   d. Statute of Enforceability.

70. Lenders across the country are likely to offer a certain type of mortgage plan after an announcement that mortgages with certain specifications will be purchased by
   a. the Office of Thrift Supervision.
   b. the Federal Deposit Insurance Corporation.
   c. Fannie Mae.
   d. HUD.

71. With an amortized loan, each month,
   a. the amount of principal and interest in each payment remain the same.
   b. the interest and principal payments each increase.
   c. the interest portion decreases and the principal portion increases.
   d. the interest portion increases and the principal portion decreases.

72. The manager who sets rental rates should take into consideration the
   a. price the owner paid for the property.
   b. income the property must produce.
   c. going rates elsewhere in the neighborhood.
   d. owner's total expenses, including debt service.

73. So that the buyers could afford to make their mortgage payments, the seller arranged for them to pay him on a 30-year payment schedule. At the end of five years, though, all of the remaining debt must be paid off in one large
   a. amortized payment.
   b. prepayment.
   c. adjustable payment.
   d. balloon payment.

74. If the parties to a purchase agreement wish to substitute a new contract that would completely replace the previous contract, they would want a(n)
   a. assignment.
   b. transfer.
   c. realignment.
   d. novation.

75. A buyer decides to back out of a deal. The seller wishes to force the buyer to close as promised. The seller would sue the buyer for
a. damages.
b. default.
c. specific performance.
d. general performance.

76. A real estate appraiser reports a dollar amount that
a. analyzes value.
b. determines value.
c. estimates value.
d. assesses value.

77. Which of the following is NOT an essential element of a real estate sales contract?
a. competent parties
b. offer and acceptance
c. legality of object
d. address

78. The function of the Federal Housing Administration (FHA) is to
a. make loans.
b. insure loans.
c. guarantee loans.
d. buy loans.

79. The veteran who receives a guaranteed VA loan is borrowing the money from
a. the state veterans' agency.
b. the Department of Veterans Affairs.
c. Fannie Mae.
d. a local lending institution.

80. Once a contract is fully signed by both the seller and buyer, the buyer is said to have
a. no title in the property.
b. equitable title in the property.
c. statutory title in the property.
d. bare title in the property.

▶ Answers

1. c. Deed restrictions are generally private covenants, whereas zoning, building codes, and subdivision regulations are all imposed by government.

2. c. Tenants in common have the right to devise their shares to any chosen heirs. Severalty applies to single ownership, and the other two answers involve automatic inheritance by one owner if the other dies.

3. c. Trade fixtures, installed for use in a trade or business, may be removed by the tenant prior to the expiration of the lease if the premises are returned to their original condition.

4. b. Whether or not they are entered in the public records, real property taxes automatically take priority over all other liens.

5. c. Latent or hidden defects are those that cannot be seen by a normal prudent inspection.

6. b. To commingle funds is for an agent to mix his or her own funds with a client's funds.

7. b. Fee simple absolute, also known as fee simple, is the highest form of ownership with the greatest bundle of rights held by the property owner.

8. b. The Taxpayer Relief Act of 1997 set $250,000 as the exclusion for a single-filer taxpayer and $500,000 as the exclusion for a couple filing jointly.

9. a. Although buyers often want to know how long a property has been on the market, it is not considered material to the transaction. Environmental factors and building issues must be disclosed.

10. d. Under the CERCLA, a potentially responsible person is anyone who has owned, operated, or provided a service on the property.

11. c. Discrimination on the basis of race is a violation of the Civil Rights Act of 1866. The other possible answers would be exemptions under the Fair Housing Act of 1968.

12. d. The presence of an occupant with HIV or AIDS may not be disclosed under the handicap status of federal Fair Housing law.

13. d. The salesperson and his or her broker are both responsible for the misrepresentation, whether or not the broker knew of the misrepresentation.

14. a. Under the police powers given by the state, local jurisdictions regulate and control the use of the land by enacting and enforcing zoning laws. These laws also address issues such as building heights and setbacks.

15. d. A planned development includes individually owned lots and other lots or areas owned in common.

16. d. This is an example of a non-conforming use, which will be grandfathered so long as the owner does not expand, modernize, or do anything more than make necessary repairs.

17. a. The Fair Housing symbol, although recommended, is not required in all ads, nor is the contact information of the state licensing authority. The public must be informed that the ad they are looking at has been placed by a person or entity that holds a real estate license.

18. d. The Constitution establishes certain protections against the violation of civil rights, such as the Fourth Amendment protection against unreasonable search and seizure.

19. a. The jurisdiction attempts to purchase the property in a friendly manner.

20. c. In the purchase of target housing—residential property constructed prior to 1978—the buyer is to receive an informational pamphlet describing the hazards of lead in a home. The buyer has ten days in which to have the property inspected.

21. b. When there is a conflict between law and ethics, the law must take priority.

22. b. A general agent may bind the principal in a broad range of acts. A special agent may not bind the principal, and a universal agent may bind the principal in all matters.

23. c. Under normal circumstances, land is not depreciated.

24. a. An express agency is created by words. Although a written agreement is preferred, express agency may also be created orally.

25. c. Taxable capital gain from the sale of a principal residence is calculated by subtracting the adjusted basis from the realized selling price.

26. b. The NFIA makes flood insurance available at reasonable rates to property owners in flood-prone areas.

27. b. A broker with a listing is considered a special agent. Although the agent may act for the principal, he or she may not bind the principal.

28. a. Any discussion of fees between competitors could be viewed as an attempt to conspire to set the cost of real estate brokerage services, a violation of anti-trust law.

29. **d.** The agent must obey any lawful instruction of the principal. The instruction may be written or oral. The instruction does not have to be in what the agent believes is in the principal's best interest.

30. **a.** (860 feet × 560 feet) ÷ 43,560 square feet per acre = 11.06 acres

31. **b.** (25 acres × 43,560 square feet per acre) ÷ 1,000 front-feet = 1,089 feet deep (1,000 feet × 2 sides) + (1,089 feet × 2 sides) = 4,178 feet

32. **c.** The fact that the seller is in financial trouble is not material to the property and cannot be disclosed by the seller's agent without the permission of the seller.

33. **d.** At closing, interest on new loans is collected in advance from the day of closing until the first of the next month. No payment is due until the following month, and that payment includes the 30 days just earned. ([$250,000 × 0.8 × 0.075] ÷ 360) × 21 days = $875

34. **d.** The taxpayer is permitted to deduct $12,000 from earned income. At the 28% tax rate, the savings would be $3,360. ($10,500 + $1,500) × 0.28 = $3,360

35. **b.** 151 × 7.34 = $1,108.34 (principal and interest) ($2,900 + $560) divided by 12 = $288.33 (taxes and insurance) $1,108.34 + $288.33 = $1,396.67 (payment)

36. **b.** Fiduciary relationships are formal, legal relationships between an agent and a principal. Relationships between lawyers and their clients or CPAs and their clients are both examples of fiduciary relationships.

37. **a.** An agency relationship created after the fact is called an agency by ratification. It is created when a principal accepts a previously unauthorized act to the benefit of the principal.

38. **c.** $120,000 divided by 0.60 is $200,000. $200,000 divided by 0.026 is approximately $7,692,300.

39. **c.** The seller's minimum represents 82% of the contract: $108,000 divided by 0.82 is $131,707.31.

40. **c.** Air space is three dimensional and is measured length × width × height = cubic feet. The number of cubic feet is divided by 27 to arrive at cubic yards.

41. **a.** Value is equal to the income (NOI) divided by the rate (CAP).

42. **a.** ($135,000 × 0.0925) divided by 12 = $1,040.63 interest $1,111.05 − $1,040.62 = $70.43 principal $135,000 − $70.43 = $134,929.57

43. **a.** $395,000 × 0.055 = $21,725 commission $395,000 × 0.04 = $15,800 settlement fees $395,000 − $21,725 − $15,800 − $300,000 = $57,475 net proceeds

44. **b.** This agreement is known as the exclusive right to sell. The exclusive agency allows the sellers to sell to buyers they procure themselves without paying a commission.

45. **c.** The property manager typically is not involved in selling the property.

46. **b.** Because the property manager makes decisions on behalf of the owner, such as tenant selection, budget preparation, and employee relations, the property manager is a general agent.

47. **b.** The manager must avoid conflicts of interest by refusing to accept gratuities from suppliers.

48. **d.** An open listing agreement may be signed by a property owner with as many brokers as the seller pleases. A commission is paid to the broker who first procures a ready, willing, and able buyer. No commission is paid if the seller finds a buyer without a broker.

49. **c.** External obsolescence refers to outside factors (a nearby landfill, unemployment in the community) that affect the value of the subject property.

50. **b.** The capitalization rate is an analysis of how much investors are willing to spend in a certain neighborhood in return for a certain amount of income.

51. **d.** Economic obsolescence is caused by factors outside the property and is considered incurable.

52. **a.** Federally related loans for first mortgages on residences fall under the provisions of RESPA.

53. **c.** The RESPA regulations have nothing to do with rates.

54. **c.** A contract is a legally enforceable agreement. Some contracts do not have to be in writing. Many agreements are not contracts because they cannot be legally enforced. Some legal documents, such as some notices, are legal documents but are not contracts.

55. **b.** Careful zoning will increase property value.

56. **b.** When the rents are priced too high, it is called economic oversupply; an oversupply of units is called a technical oversupply.

57. **d.** When property is rezoned so that it severely limits land use, it may be considered the same as being condemned or taken. This is a legal issue.

58. **b.** A contract that may be terminated or disaffirmed by one of the parties is said to be voidable.

59. **b.** Familial status refers to a parent or guardian who lives with one or more children under the age of 18.

60. **d.** Student status is not a protected class under federal Fair Housing laws.

61. **c.** HUD's penalty for a first offense can be $10,000. The Justice Department may fine for a pattern of repeat violations up to $100,000.

62. **c.** The Fair Housing Amendments Act of 1988 added the presence of children in a family as a protected class.

63. **d.** Each point is 1% of the amount being borrowed and serves as extra interest income to the lender.

64. **b.** The term *alienation* means transfer of title. The lender reserves the right to call in the loan if the property is sold.

65. **d.** A contract formed by the actions on the parties is an implied contract. An example would be a person ordering food in a restaurant. The restaurant implies it will serve food if ordered, and the customer implies that he or she will pay for the meal afterward.

66. **b.** A purchase contract is a promise of the seller to sell exchanged for a buyer's promise to buy, whereas an option to buy contains only a seller's promise to sell.

67. **a.** Although *executed* is sometimes used to simply mean *signed*, it would not be correct in this instance. Because the promises are waiting to be performed (executed), the contract is said to be executory.

68. **a.** When the Fed raises the discount rate at which banks borrow from district reserve banks, the change is often reflected in mortgage rates across the country, making it harder for borrowers to afford to buy real estate.

69. **c.** The Statute of Frauds requires contracts for the sale of real estate to be in writing to be enforceable in a court of law.

70. **c.** Fannie Mae buys large packages of mortgages that meet its particular specifications and has great influence on the primary mortgage market.

71. **c.** As the debt is paid down, the amount of interest due each month becomes smaller, and more of the payment is available to be applied to the principal.

72. **c.** Rental rates are set by supply and demand.

73. **d.** The buyers should start looking for a new loan as much as a year before their final large balloon payment comes due.

74. **d.** The complete substitution of one party or contract for another is called novation.

75. **c.** A suit for specific performance is a lawsuit to compel action called for in a contract.

76. **c.** Even the most skilled appraisal is only an estimate of value.

77. **d.** An address is not required for a real estate sales contract. The legal description is used to identify the property.

78. **b.** The FHA does not lend any money; it administers an insurance program that allows homebuyers to borrow almost the full purchase price with a low down payment.

79. **d.** The VA guarantees the loan, which is obtained from a regular lending institution.

80. **b.** While a property is under contract, the buyer is said to have equitable title, meaning title in fairness.

► Scoring

Again, evaluate how you did on this practice exam by finding the number of questions you got right, disregarding for the moment the ones you got wrong or skipped. On the official exam, you need to answer 75% correctly to pass.

If you didn't score as well as you would like, ask yourself the following: Did I run out of time before I could answer all the questions? Did I go back and change my answers from right to wrong? Did I get flustered and sit staring at a difficult question for what seemed like hours? If you had any of these problems, be sure to go over the LearningExpress Test Preparation System in Chapter 2 to review how best to avoid them.

You probably have seen improvement between your first practice exam score and this one; but if you didn't improve as much as you'd like, here are some options:

If you scored well below your personal goal, you should seriously consider whether you're ready for the exam at this time. A good idea would be to take some brush-up courses in the areas in which you need the most improvement. If you don't have time for a course, you might try private tutoring.

If you scored close to your personal goal, you need to work as hard as you can to improve your skills. Go back to your real estate license course textbooks to review the knowledge you need to do well on the exam. If math is your problem area, check out the Learning-Express book *Practical Math Success in 20 Minutes a Day*. Also, reread and pay close attention to the information in Chapter 7, Real Estate Broker Refresher Course; Chapter 8, Real Estate Broker Math Review; and Chapter 9, Real Estate Glossary. Take the other practice exams in this book. It might also be helpful to ask friends and family to make up mock test questions and quiz you on them.

If you scored well above your personal goal, that's great! You are well on the road to passing your broker's license exam. Don't lose your edge, though; keep studying right up to the day before the exam.

Now, revise your study schedule according to the time you have left, emphasizing those parts that gave you the most trouble this time. Use the following table to see where you need more work, so that you can concentrate your preparation efforts.

Promissor Practice Exam 2 for Review

Topic	Question Numbers
Real Property Characteristics Definitions, Ownerships, Relations, and Transfer	1, 2, 3, 4, 7, 14, 15, 16, 18, 19, 30, 31, 40, 55, 57
Property Valuations and the Appraisal Process	23, 41, 49, 50, 51, 76
Contracts and Agency Relationships with Buyers and Sellers	22, 24, 27, 29, 32, 36, 37, 38, 39, 44, 48, 54, 58, 65, 66, 67, 69, 74, 75, 77, 80
Property Conditions and Disclosures	5, 9, 10, 12, 20, 26
Federal Laws Governing Real Estate Activities	8, 11, 25, 28, 34, 59, 60, 61
Financing the Transaction and Settlement	33, 35, 42, 43, 52, 53, 63, 64, 68, 70, 71, 73, 78, 79
Leases, Rents, and Property Management	45, 46, 47, 56, 62, 72
Brokerage Operations	6, 13, 17, 21

12 ▶ Thomson Prometric (Experior) Practice Exam 2

CHAPTER SUMMARY

This is the second of the two Thomson Prometric (formerly Experior) practice tests in this book. Because you have taken the first practice test already, you probably feel more confident with your test-taking skills. Use this test to see how knowing what to expect can make you feel better prepared.

You are now more familiar with the format and content of the national portion of the Thomson Prometric exam, and most likely you feel more confident than you did at first. However, your practice test-taking experience will help you most if you have created a situation as close as possible to the one you will encounter on exam day.

For this exam, try to simulate real testing conditions. Find a quiet place where you will not be disturbed. Make sure you have two sharpened pencils and a good eraser. Be sure to leave enough time to complete the exam in one sitting. There is a two-hour limit on the official exam, so you'll want to practice working quickly without rushing. Use a timer or a stopwatch and see if you can work through all the exam questions in the allotted time.

The answer sheet is on the next page. An answer key and explanations follow the exam. These explanations, along with the table at the end of this chapter, will help you see where you need further study. Remember, the six other practice exams in this book, although slightly different in format than the Thomson Prometric exam, all test the same basic real estate principles and concepts, so you can use them to help you even further solidify your knowledge and skills.

1.	(a)	(b)	(c)	(d)
2.	(a)	(b)	(c)	(d)
3.	(a)	(b)	(c)	(d)
4.	(a)	(b)	(c)	(d)
5.	(a)	(b)	(c)	(d)
6.	(a)	(b)	(c)	(d)
7.	(a)	(b)	(c)	(d)
8.	(a)	(b)	(c)	(d)
9.	(a)	(b)	(c)	(d)
10.	(a)	(b)	(c)	(d)
11.	(a)	(b)	(c)	(d)
12.	(a)	(b)	(c)	(d)
13.	(a)	(b)	(c)	(d)
14.	(a)	(b)	(c)	(d)
15.	(a)	(b)	(c)	(d)
16.	(a)	(b)	(c)	(d)
17.	(a)	(b)	(c)	(d)
18.	(a)	(b)	(c)	(d)
19.	(a)	(b)	(c)	(d)
20.	(a)	(b)	(c)	(d)
21.	(a)	(b)	(c)	(d)
22.	(a)	(b)	(c)	(d)
23.	(a)	(b)	(c)	(d)
24.	(a)	(b)	(c)	(d)
25.	(a)	(b)	(c)	(d)
26.	(a)	(b)	(c)	(d)
27.	(a)	(b)	(c)	(d)
28.	(a)	(b)	(c)	(d)
29.	(a)	(b)	(c)	(d)
30.	(a)	(b)	(c)	(d)

31.	(a)	(b)	(c)	(d)
32.	(a)	(b)	(c)	(d)
33.	(a)	(b)	(c)	(d)
34.	(a)	(b)	(c)	(d)
35.	(a)	(b)	(c)	(d)
36.	(a)	(b)	(c)	(d)
37.	(a)	(b)	(c)	(d)
38.	(a)	(b)	(c)	(d)
39.	(a)	(b)	(c)	(d)
40.	(a)	(b)	(c)	(d)
41.	(a)	(b)	(c)	(d)
42.	(a)	(b)	(c)	(d)
43.	(a)	(b)	(c)	(d)
44.	(a)	(b)	(c)	(d)
45.	(a)	(b)	(c)	(d)
46.	(a)	(b)	(c)	(d)
47.	(a)	(b)	(c)	(d)
48.	(a)	(b)	(c)	(d)
49.	(a)	(b)	(c)	(d)
50.	(a)	(b)	(c)	(d)
51.	(a)	(b)	(c)	(d)
52.	(a)	(b)	(c)	(d)
53.	(a)	(b)	(c)	(d)
54.	(a)	(b)	(c)	(d)
55.	(a)	(b)	(c)	(d)
56.	(a)	(b)	(c)	(d)
57.	(a)	(b)	(c)	(d)
58.	(a)	(b)	(c)	(d)
59.	(a)	(b)	(c)	(d)
60.	(a)	(b)	(c)	(d)

61.	(a)	(b)	(c)	(d)
62.	(a)	(b)	(c)	(d)
63.	(a)	(b)	(c)	(d)
64.	(a)	(b)	(c)	(d)
65.	(a)	(b)	(c)	(d)
66.	(a)	(b)	(c)	(d)
67.	(a)	(b)	(c)	(d)
68.	(a)	(b)	(c)	(d)
69.	(a)	(b)	(c)	(d)
70.	(a)	(b)	(c)	(d)
71.	(a)	(b)	(c)	(d)
72.	(a)	(b)	(c)	(d)
73.	(a)	(b)	(c)	(d)
74.	(a)	(b)	(c)	(d)
75.	(a)	(b)	(c)	(d)
76.	(a)	(b)	(c)	(d)
77.	(a)	(b)	(c)	(d)
78.	(a)	(b)	(c)	(d)
79.	(a)	(b)	(c)	(d)
80.	(a)	(b)	(c)	(d)

►Thomson Prometric (Experior) Practice Exam 2

1. The purpose of the TILA, Regulation Z, is to
   a. regulate creditors' advertising and marketing.
   b. require the use of the HUD settlement statement in residential transactions.
   c. promote the informed use of credit by requiring disclosure of the true cost of credit.
   d. give consumers the right to inspect and correct their credit reports.

2. A legal instrument that is used to pledge real property and provides security for a loan is a
   a. general warranty deed.
   b. promissory note.
   c. mortgage.
   d. certificate of indefeasible title.

3. All the following are true in an open listing EXCEPT
   a. the seller retains the right to sell independently without obligation.
   b. a broker sets the list price.
   c. only the agent who is procuring cause is compensated.
   d. there are multiple agents.

4. Which of the following is true regarding the federal Truth-in-Lending Act?
   a. TILA is implemented by the Federal Reserve Board's Regulation Z.
   b. TILA is implemented by HUD's Regulation Z.
   c. TILA is a 1974 amendment to the Home Mortgage Disclosure Act.
   d. TILA applies only to loans on one- to four-family residential transactions.

5. Broker Mike McBride agreed to represent Harvey Meyer in the purchase of a property but did not have a written buyer's representation agreement. Which of the following is true?
   a. This is a violation of the law of agency.
   b. Agency relationships may be created orally by a spoken agreement that is never put in writing.
   c. All state real estate licensing laws require agency agreements to be in writing to be legal.
   d. The broker will not owe fiduciary duties to Mr. Meyer in this case.

6. Emil Dusek is buying a home and applying for a mortgage loan. Under RESPA, what must his lender provide at the time or application or mail to him within three business days?
   a. statement explaining the APR
   b. good faith estimate of the settlement costs
   c. notice of his three-day right of rescission
   d. list of approved settlement service providers

7. All of the following are examples of buyer agency agreements EXCEPT an
   a. exclusive buyer agency.
   b. open buyer agency.
   c. exclusive agency.
   d. exclusive right to buy agency.

8. Which of the following is an example of special agency?
   a. A broker has a written listing agreement with an owner.
   b. A broker has a written property management agreement with an owner.
   c. A salesperson has a written independent contractor agreement with a broker.
   d. A tenant has a written long-term retail lease agreement with an owner.

9. What type of legal description uses a point of beginning and monuments as reference marks?
   a. recorded subdivision plat
   b. government survey
   c. metes and bounds
   d. rectangular survey

10. What is the clause in both the promissory note and the mortgage that allows the mortgagee to call the total balance of the loan due and payable upon default?
   a. due-on-sale clause
   b. acceleration clause
   c. release clause
   d. power of sale clause

11. Omar called Janice Evans Realty and spoke to Janice about listing his house for sale. She told Omar that the fee would be 6% of the sales price at closing. When he asks if 6% is standard for the area, Janice should say,
   a. "Yes, members of the local MLS all charge the same fee for services."
   b. "Most of the brokers in this area charge 6%."
   c. "I don't know what other brokers charge; our company's fee is 6%."
   d. "Except for discounters, every other broker charges the same fee."

12. Once an abstract of title is obtained, who may give an opinion regarding the validity of the title?
   a. real estate broker
   b. attorney
   c. real estate broker or attorney
   d. appraiser or attorney

13. Lionel Johnson was hired by the property manager of an apartment complex to maintain the property. He regularly replaces air conditioner filters. This is an example of
   a. preventive maintenance.
   b. corrective maintenance.
   c. housekeeping.
   d. improvement.

14. Who can give advice to a prospective buyer on how much to offer for a property?
   a. the seller's broker
   b. the buyer's broker
   c. the facilitator only
   d. either the seller's broker or the buyer's broker

15. What does an abstract of title contain?
   a. the summary of a title search
   b. an attorney's opinion of title
   c. a registrar's certificate of title
   d. a quiet title lawsuit

16. The legal rights of real property ownership known as the bundle of rights include the rights of
   a. exclusion, consideration, and disposition.
   b. exclusion, enjoyment, and disposition.
   c. possession, control, and consideration.
   d. possession, disposition, and appreciation.

17. What type of loan is purchased by Fannie Mae or Freddie Mac on the secondary market?
   a. conforming FHA
   b. FHA and any conventional
   c. conforming conventional
   d. any type of conventional

18. The concept that no two parcels of real estate are exactly the same and that all parcels differ geographically with one legal description is known as
    a. novation.
    b. nuncupative.
    c. nonhomogeneity.
    d. non-conforming.

19. What is meant by judicial foreclosure?
    a. The mortgage document gives the lender the right to foreclose without a court decree.
    b. Foreclosure must be carried out through the court system.
    c. The foreclosure did not result in sufficient funds to pay the debt and required a deficiency judgment to be filed.
    d. The mortgagor was judged to be in default.

20. Which of the following ads requires full financing disclosure under TILA?
    a. "Lovely country home with owner financing available"
    b. "Move-in ready and only 3% down required"
    c. "Great starter home with assumable loan"
    d. "Special financing for first-time homebuyers"

21. Some of the essential elements of a valid real estate contract are
    a. consideration, earnest money, mutual agreement, and in writing and signed.
    b. competent parties, a definite closing date, and mutual agreement.
    c. lawful objective, earnest money, competent parties, and mutual agreement.
    d. legal description, consideration, competent parties, and in writing and signed.

22. The subject house of an appraisal has a pool and 2.5 baths. A comparable house with three full baths and no pool sold for $475,000. If the appraiser makes a $15,000 adjustment for the pool and a $4,500 adjustment for the third full bath, what value will this comparable have in the appraisal?
    a. $464,500
    b. $485,500
    c. $494,500
    d. $455,500

23. The federal law that prohibits discrimination against people with disabilities in commercial properties is the
    a. Fair Housing Act of 1968.
    b. Civil Rights Act of 1964.
    c. ADA of 1992.
    d. HMDA of 1975.

24. Edgar D'Amato is the top listing agent in his company and regularly contacts for sale by owners by phone. Under federal Do Not Call laws, this practice is
    a. permissible because the owner has advertised his or her phone number.
    b. permissible only if Edgar has a bona fide buyer for the property.
    c. not permissible under any circumstances.
    d. permissible only for persons in Edgar's past client database.

25. Lili Chang, a broker, operates a brokerage firm and sponsors more than 50 agents. For continued success and legal operation of her business, Lili should
  a. offer two or more generous compensation plans to her agents and carry E & O insurance.
  b. adopt a policy manual outlining transaction procedures, record keeping, and advertising for all associates of the firm.
  c. hire an attorney on a retainer to handle every complaint.
  d. use only state-promulgated forms for all transactions.

26. Hugh and Bridget Fitzpatrick, a married couple, inherited a ten-acre tract of land from her uncle Cedric and were granted the right to use the land forever. Which of the following do they hold?
  a. an estate for years
  b. a joint tenancy
  c. a life estate
  d. a fee simple estate

27. What type of loan allows Raul and Stella to draw against the equity in their home on an as-needed basis?
  a. equity ARM
  b. equity debit
  c. HELOC
  d. HOEPA

28. Walter listed Ruth's property for six months. It was agreed that should Walter procure a buyer, she would pay a full commission fee, but if Ruth procured a buyer without Walter's assistance, she would owe him no fee. This is an example of
  a. an open listing.
  b. a for-sale-by-owner.
  c. an exclusive agency listing.
  d. an exclusive right to sell listing.

29. An owner of property who builds a room addition without a building permit may
  a. post a bond assuring the jurisdiction that the work is completed as though a permit had been issued.
  b. render the title unmarketable.
  c. pay a substantial cash penalty to continue the use.
  d. sell the property "as is" to avoid notifying the buyer of the lack of a permit.

30. The government has the power to do all of the following EXCEPT
  a. tax real estate.
  b. enact reasonable land use laws.
  c. take land if necessary for the public welfare.
  d. enter upon private property at any time.

31. Louise Jacobson and Jose Mareno have reached a mutual agreement, and a purchase agreement has been signed by both with full notification from offeree to offeror. The closing will take place within 21 days. This is now
  a. an executory contract.
  b. an executed contract.
  c. a fully executed contract.
  d. a discharged contract.

32. After entering into contract to purchase a tract of land, Helen discovered that the seller had deliberately misrepresented the availability of utilities from the city. Which of the following statements is true?

a. Helen is bound by the contract but may renegotiate the price to compensate for the cost to extend utility access from the city.

b. This is a voidable contract because of fraud.

c. The seller must provide the promised utilities to execute the agreement fully.

d. The parties must attach an addendum to the contract reconciling the cost of the utility access.

33. A general warranty deed warrants that

a. title to the property is clear of encumbrances and duly filed of record.

b. the grantor has ownership of the property and has the legal right to convey title.

c. the appraised value at the time of conveyance is true and correct.

d. there are no encumbrances, encroachments, or easements of record on the described property.

34. What does the appraisal term *highest and best use* mean?

a. the best use for the land with no restrictions

b. the best use of the land regarding health, safety, and the environment

c. the use of the land that will generate the greatest net economic return over a given period of time

d. the use of the land most desired by the purchaser

35. Ruth Jacob is getting an FHA loan and adding the 1.5% up front MIP to the loan of $126,000. What is her principal and interest payment on the 6.5%, 30-year loan with P&I paid at $6.32 per $1,000?

a. $808.26

b. $818.62

c. $796.32

d. $953.82

36. The agreed sale price in a contract is $550,000, but the lender's appraiser estimated the value at $536,400 for loan purposes. The parties agreed to change the sale price to $540,000, and the buyer is to pay $3,600 in additional down payment. What was attached to the original contract to make this change?

a. an addendum

b. an assignment

c. an amendment

d. a novation

37. Marty Gould manages a small retail center valued at $2,200,000. The owner has instructed Marty that she wants to see a capitalization rate of no less than 9%. The gross income per month is $35,000 with an annual estimated 8% vacancy rate. The expected annual expenses are $181,610 and monthly debt service is $14,532. Can Marty show a capitalization rate (cap rate) that will satisfy the owner?

a. No, the cap rate is 1.38%.

b. Yes, the cap rate is 9.3%.

c. Yes, the cap rate is 13.8%.

d. No, the cap rate is 7.93%.

38. What is a three-party legal document that transfers equitable title to a trustee and serves as security for a home loan?

 a. deed in trust

 b. mortgage trust

 c. land trust

 d. deed of trust

39. Which of the following will terminate an agency representation agreement?

 a. A written offer to purchase is accepted by the seller.

 b. The listed price of a property is adjusted after a predetermined period of time.

 c. The listed property is sold, and the transaction is closed.

 d. The owner refuses to accept an offer presented by the listing broker.

40. A broker can protect and indemnify himself or herself against legal actions brought by consumers by purchasing

 a. contingency insurance.

 b. errors and omissions insurance.

 c. errors and compensation insurance.

 d. loss and casualty insurance.

41. Ali sold his house to Zachary, who defaulted on the purchase agreement. If Ali keeps the earnest money, which of the following remedies under the law has he chosen?

 a. rescission

 b. suit for partial performance

 c. liquidated damages

 d. money damages

42. In applying to lease a house, Alice Rivera was told that because she had three children under 12 years old, she would have to pay $200 per child in addition to the $750 standard security deposit. This is a violation of federal Fair Housing laws covering which protected class?

 a. national origin

 b. marital status and age

 c. ethnicity

 d. familial status

43. Agent Larry Kryder receives an offer for $369,000 on his $379,000 listing. He holds the offer for two days, waiting for a better offer, before communicating with his client seller. Larry has

 a. fulfilled his fiduciary duties by seeking a full price offer.

 b. breached his fiduciary duties by not presenting the offer immediately.

 c. followed good business practices by seeking two offers for the seller.

 d. been faithful to his client by verifying the prospective buyer's financial ability to purchase before presenting the offer.

44. Maria, Monica, and Marcella purchased an investment property as tenants in common. None of them may

 a. transfer her interest to someone by will.

 b. claim a certain portion of the property for personal use.

 c. convey ownership to another without the consent of the others.

 d. use her interest in the property as collateral for a mortgage loan.

45. Mount Vernon Estate, Inc., owns an office building in the center of town. It is owned
   a. in severalty.
   b. by joint tenancy.
   c. as tenants in common.
   d. by joint venture.

46. An agent owes third parties and customers the duty of
   a. disclosure of material facts about the property.
   b. loyalty and obedience.
   c. accounting.
   d. confidentiality.

47. Brian received an offer from Catherine to purchase his house. Brian sent a letter to her indicating that he would accept an offer for $10,000 more than she offered, and with closing to be within 30 days instead of 40 days. What is this?
   a. a rejection of offer with a counteroffer
   b. an acceptance with changes
   c. a novation
   d. a binder

48. A buyer has paid a fee for the right to purchase a property within a set time frame and at a set price. What is this, and is it bilateral or unilateral?
   a. a bilateral option
   b. a unilateral option
   c. a bilateral lease purchase
   d. a unilateral offer

49. Tony Marcella sold his house to Wen Huang for $157,000 and financed $141,000. Tony is to receive P&I payments of $938 per month for five years, at which time the balance of $132,735 will be due. This loan is
   a. not amortized.
   b. partially amortized.
   c. a term loan.
   d. a subprime loan.

50. A title company provided marketing brochures for real estate agent Dana King's listings, and Dana channeled her title business to them. Which of the following statements is true?
   a. Dana's clients receive priority services because of this relationship.
   b. This is legal under RESPA because no money was paid to Dana.
   c. This is illegal under HUD's business relationship laws.
   d. This is a violation of Section 8 of RESPA regarding kickbacks and referral fees.

51. The relationship of a property manager with the owner is generally a
   a. special agency.
   b. general agency.
   c. limited partnership.
   d. dual agency.

52. What type of deed may be given by an owner to a lender conveying mortgaged property in which the owner is in default?
   a. deed in lieu of judicial action
   b. release deed
   c. deed of reconveyance
   d. deed in lieu of foreclosure

53. Flossie's Florist Shop was in an area recently rezoned as single family residential. She obtained the right to continue operating the business as a non-conforming use in the area. The shop burned to the ground a year later. Flossie will now
   a. rebuild the shop exactly as it was prior to the fire.
   b. sell the land and use her insurance proceeds to relocate the shop in a retail zone.
   c. rebuild a shop that looks like a single family home.
   d. obtain a variance and rebuild.

54. The minimum requirements of a listing agreement include
   a. an automatic date for renewal if the expiration date is reached.
   b. the legal description of the property and all chattels to be retained by the seller.
   c. authority granted to the broker and lowest price acceptable to the seller.
   d. the legal description of the property and an expiration date of the agreement.

55. What is the broker's responsibility at the closing?
   a. interpret the terms and conditions contained in the loan documents
   b. explain the clauses found in the deed
   c. review the title report for clouds or other problems
   d. verify the settlement statement and receive the brokerage fee

56. The provisions of RESPA are applicable to all of the following EXCEPT
   a. loans on commercial property.
   b. loans insured by the Federal Housing Administration.
   c. mortgages guaranteed by the Department of Veterans Affairs.
   d. loans sold to FNMA.

57. Gus and Gracie are taking out a home equity line of credit to remodel their home. Which of the following is true?
   a. The consumer has a right of rescission up to three days after signing his or her closing or loan documents.
   b. The loan is a type of mortgage loan and, therefore, has no right of rescission.
   c. HELOCs are high-interest subprime loans and, therefore, have rescission rights.
   d. Because funds are disbursed on the day of closing, there is no right of rescission.

58. Title to real property that is transferred by a last will and testament is
   a. involuntary alienation.
   b. voluntary alienation.
   c. an intestate devise.
   d. a bequest or legacy after proper probate.

59. Leland and Rhonda are in contract to purchase a lot to build a new home, but have found another lot they like better and are refusing to close on the first lot. What is this action?
   a. rescission of agreement
   b. forfeiture of contract
   c. breach of contract
   d. default of earnest money

60. Which of the following is a specific lien?
   a. judgment for unpaid student loan
   b. federal income tax lien
   c. ad valorem school tax lien
   d. lien for unpaid state business tax

61. Bill Milford, Josephine Bazan, and Heidi Padilla are brokers. Over lunch, they discuss the business practices of a local home builder, Green Homes. Josephine Bazan thinks the builder uses poor materials and does shoddy workmanship. The others agree and plan to avoid showing and selling Green's houses. What is this?
   a. a real estate broker's consumer protection agreement
   b. a fair agreement to do business with whomever one chooses
   c. a conspiracy to boycott under federal anti-trust laws
   d. a competition avoidance conspiracy under state licensing laws

62. Agent Joe listed Bill's farm and began marketing and advertising. Jeanette contacted Joe about the farm, and he showed her the property. She wanted to make an offer lower than the list price of $850,000, and Joe told her that he thought Bill would probably take about $800,000. Which of the following is true?
   a. Joe is exercising his agency authority to negotiate and obtain a sale for Bill.
   b. Joe has created an undisclosed dual agency by implication.
   c. Jeanette is Joe's client.
   d. Bill and Jeanette will both receive full fiduciary duties from Joe.

63. Prohibited acts under federal Fair Housing laws include all of the following EXCEPT
   a. changing the terms of sale or lease for different prospective buyers or tenants.
   b. the rental of a single-family home by its owner only to a couple with no children.
   c. refusing to rent an apartment after receiving a bona fide offer from a member of a minority group.
   d. saying that a property is not available when it is, in fact, available.

64. The instructions for the final transfer of title is found in the
   a. listing contract.
   b. buyer broker agreement.
   c. sales contract.
   d. multiple listing.

65. Anthony has a mortgage lien on his property, and Annabelle has an *ad valorem* tax lien on her property. Which of the following statements is true?
   a. Anthony has a specific, involuntary lien, and Annabelle has a specific, voluntary lien.
   b. Anthony has a specific, voluntary lien, and Annabelle has a specific, involuntary lien.
   c. Anthony has a general, voluntary lien, and Annabelle has a general, involuntary lien.
   d. Anthony has a specific, voluntary lien, and Annabelle has a general, involuntary lien.

66. Malik owns an easement appurtenant as the dominant tenement. Which statement is true?
   a. His property is encumbered by the easement.
   b. The easement is valid as long as he owns the land.
   c. This type of easement is for ingress and egress only.
   d. He receives the benefit of the easement.

67. Claude is in contract to buy a condo but will not be obligated to close the sale if he cannot get financing approval. What is the name of the clause in the contract that gives Claude this right?
   a. escalation clause
   b. contingency clause
   c. reversion clause
   d. rescission clause

68. What is the purpose of owner's title insurance?
   a. to provide the property owner a guarantee of clear title
   b. to give an attorney's opinion of the validity of title to property at the time of closing
   c. to insure the policyholder against losses should the value of the property fall below the appraised value
   d. to insure the policyholder against losses because of undiscovered title defects or encumbrances

69. David Epstein sold his rental house to Marvella Howard, closing on June 14. On July 1, the tenant paid Epstein the rent of $1,350 for the month. The rent will be prorated through the day of closing. Which of the following is correct?
   a. Debit seller and credit buyer $630.
   b. Credit seller and debit buyer $720.
   c. Credit seller and debit buyer $630.
   d. Debit seller and credit buyer $720.

70. A listing agent must disclose to a seller
   a. the termination date of the broker's license.
   b. the true value of the seller's property.
   c. the names of all buyers and other brokers who inquire about the property.
   d. the location and prices of all the broker's other listings.

71. Which of the following approaches would an appraiser most likely use to appraise a church?
   a. market data approach
   b. cost approach
   c. income approach
   d. gross rent multiplier approach

72. Economic or external obsolescence refers to loss of value because of
   a. wear and tear.
   b. outdated design.
   c. factors outside the property lines.
   d. incurable defects in the subject property.

73. Conveyance of title to real property is complete when
   a. the deed, signed by the grantor, is filed in the deed records.
   b. the deed, signed by the grantor, is delivered to and accepted by the grantee.
   c. both the grantor and the grantee have signed the deed and it is notarized.
   d. the deed, signed by the grantor, is notarized and filed in the deed records.

74. Associates with PR Realty are encouraged to show Asian buyers properties in predominately Asian areas only. Non-Asian buyers are usually not shown properties in these neighborhoods. This is an example of
   a. steering to or away from certain areas based on a protected class.
   b. making buyers more comfortable in their surroundings.
   c. blockbusting a subdivision.
   d. a violation of ECOA.

75. The purpose of state licensing laws is primarily to
   a. regulate brokerage fees.
   b. regulate brokers and salespersons and promulgate purchase agreements.
   c. protect the public from unscrupulous real estate practitioners.
   d. protect the public from unscrupulous builders and home sellers.

76. In determining the market value of the subject property, which of the following factors would be of most importance?
   a. market value less depreciation
   b. market price of comparable properties
   c. market value of recently sold properties
   d. adjustment between market value and market price

77. Bud Lucas wanted to lease a building and include a right of first refusal should the seller decide to sell the property. His broker, Larry Barton, wrote an addendum to the lease agreement detailing the right of first refusal. Which of the following statements is true?
   a. Barton, not being an attorney, was practicing law without a license.
   b. Barton, a duly licensed real estate broker, performed his fiduciary duty of obedience.
   c. If the seller agrees to the addendum, it is acceptable and legal.
   d. Barton should discourage Lucas from such an arrangement.

78. In the market or sales data approach to appraisal, the sales prices of similar, recently sold properties are
   a. assessed.
   b. analyzed.
   c. adjusted.
   d. added.

79. May Wu showed Devin Jackson her listing, and he wants to make an offer to buy the house. Devin asked May for her advice as to the price he should offer. What is May's best answer?
   a. "The seller is asking $375,000 but needs a quick sale."
   b. "The list price is $375,000, but it probably will not appraise for that much."
   c. "The seller is asking $375,000, but you should offer $365,000."
   d. "The list price is $375,000, and you may make any offer you want."

80. A land contract for the purchase of real estate is also known as
 a. an installment sales contract.
 b. a lease with option to buy.
 c. an executed contract.
 d. a voidable contract.

▶ Answers

1. c. The Truth-in-Lending Act is a consumer protection law requiring disclosures of the cost of credit at the time of loan application and at the time of settlement.

2. c. A promissory note is evidence of the loan, and the mortgage or a deed of trust is the legal instrument securing the collateral for the loan.

3. b. The seller, not the broker, decides the list price.

4. a. The Federal Consumer Protection Act of 1969 is known as the Truth-in-Lending Act, and Congress gave the Federal Reserve Board oversight of the law. It is implemented under Regulation Z.

5. b. An agency relationship may be legally created by oral agreement, and the agent owes fiduciary duties to the principal. A written agreement will be required to sue for a commission if the principal refuses to pay, and some state laws also require written agency representation contracts.

6. b. The lender must give the settlement cost information booklet and a good faith estimate including loan origination fees.

7. d. There are three basic buyer agency agreements: exclusive buyer agency, open buyer agency, and exclusive agency.

8. a. Special agency creates a short term, specific relationship with limited authority such as listing agreements and buyer representation agreements.

9. c. A metes and bounds legal description begins at a specified point; follows the boundaries of the land by measures, distances, compass directions, and landmarks; and returns to the point of beginning.

10. b. Due on sale refers to sale of the property, release occurs when the entire principal is fully paid, and power of sale refers to foreclosure. The acceleration clause gives the lender to right to call the note due upon default.

11. c. Price fixing is a violation of the federal Sherman Anti-Trust Act to conspire with other businesses to set fees or prices for services or goods.

12. b. The legal validity of title to real estate as determined by the chain of title and history of all liens, encumbrances, or easements must be rendered by a licensed attorney.

13. a. Preventive maintenance preserves the property and corrective maintenance repairs an item that is not functioning.

14. b. The buyer's own broker, if one is involved, should advise on the proper offering price. The seller's broker can advise the buyer to offer the list price only because he or she must work in the seller's best interests, not the buyer's. However, the seller's broker should tell the buyer he will present any offer.

15. a. An abstract reports the entire results of a title search of the public records back to the sovereignty of the soil.

16. b. The right of exclusion means to keep others from entering or occupying the property. Enjoyment means to use the property in any legal manner, and disposition means to be able to dispose of the property by sale, gift, or will. Two other rights are possession and control.

17. c. The only loans purchased by Fannie Mae and Freddie Mac conform specifically to their guidelines regarding income ratios, loan maximums, documentation, and other criteria.

18. c. Immobility, indestructibility, and nonhomogeneity are the basic physical characteristics of land. Novation is the substitution of a new legal agreement for an old one. Nuncupative means not written, as in a nuncupative will. Non-conforming in real estate finance terms means a conventional loan that does not conform to Fannie Mae guidelines.

19. b. Liens such as second mortgages or junior liens may be foreclosed only by judicial decree.

20. b. Stating the amount of down payment is a trigger term under TILA and requires full financing disclosure, including the cash price of the property; cash down required; number, amount, and frequency of payments; and the APR.

21. d. A valid real estate contract must have competent parties, mutual agreement, lawful objective, legal description, and consideration, and must be in writing and signed by the parties.

22. b. Add the adjustment value when the comparable is inferior to the subject and subtract the adjustment value when the comparable is superior to the subject.
$475,000 comparable value + $15,000 for pool − $4,500 for third bath = $485,500 adjusted value

23. c. The Americans with Disabilities Act requires that existing public buildings make reasonable modifications to provide access to peo-

ple with disabilities and that new construction and remodeling meet even higher standards of access.

24. b. Edgar may call phone numbers not in the national Do Not Call database or in his firm's in-house Do Not Call database to pursue listing appointments. If he has a legitimate, qualified buyer, he may call to show the property, but he may not discuss listing unless the seller inquires about listing services.

25. b. A broker is legally responsible for all the actions of his or her associates while they are acting on behalf of the broker.

26. d. An estate for years is a lease with a specific termination date. Joint tenancy includes rights of survivorship, and a life estate is for the duration of the life of a person.

27. c. A home equity line of credit allows owners to borrow up to specified amounts against the equity in their home. The Homeowner's Equity Protection Act (HOEPA) requires additional disclosures on such loans.

28. c. In an exclusive agency listing, the owner hires one broker who may advertise and sell the property, but the owner retains the right to sell without the broker and owe no fee.

29. b. The improvement of a property without a building permit typically renders the title unmarketable. It is required that the seller convey this information to prospective buyers.

30. d. The U.S. Constitution establishes certain protections against the violation of civil rights, such as the Fourth Amendment protection against unreasonable search and seizure.

31. a. The contract was executed when they signed and dated the contract, making it an executory contract from that time until closing. When all parties have performed, it is fully executed.

32. b. A voidable contract is one that can be disaffirmed by one party without liability. Provable fraud makes a contract voidable by the defrauded party.

33. b. The covenant of seisin warrants that the grantor owns the property. The warranty deed also includes the covenant against encumbrances, which warrants that the property is not encumbered by undisclosed encroachments, easements, liens, or other rights of third parties.

34. c. The greatest return over time considering zoning, restrictions, location, and demand is a property's highest and best use.

35. a. $126,000$ loan $\times 1.5\%$ UFMIP $= \$1,890$
$126,000$ loan $+ \$1,890$ financed MIP $=$
$\$127,890$ total amount financed
$\$127,890 \div 1,000 \times 6.32 = \$808.26$ P&I payment

36. c. An addendum is additional material attached and made part of the original contract. An amendment is used for changes made while the contract is still executory.

37. b. Monthly rent $\$35,000 \times 12 = \$420,000$
annual gross income
$\$420,000 - 8\%$ vacancy rate $= \$386,400$
annual effective income
$\$386,400 - \$181,610$ annual expenses $=$
$\$204,790$ net operating income
$\$204,790$ NOI $\div \$2,200,000$ value $= 9.3\%$
capitalization rate
The debt service is not considered in calculating the capitalization rate.

38. d. A deed of trust is a mortgage instrument that allows for nonjudicial foreclosure by a trustee named by the lender who is beneficiary under the trust. A deed in trust transfers title to a trustee, usually in a land trust, to manage the property for the owner.

39. c. Agency is terminated by accomplishment of the purpose, expiration of the term, mutual agreement, death or incapacity of a party, bankruptcy, property destroyed, or the loss or revocation of a broker's license.

40. b. A broker may purchase E & O insurance for legal protection from consumer lawsuits resulting from mistakes or negligence, but it does not cover fraudulent behavior, punitive damages, or claims on personal transaction of the broker or agents.

41. c. Earnest money serves to show serious intent by the purchaser and may be used to liquidate damages in the event of default.

42. d. It is illegal to discriminate in any way against a person because he or she has a child under 18 years of age living with him or her. Charging more rent or security deposit for families with children is a form of discrimination.

43. b. Fiduciary duties require that all offers be presented objectively and as quickly as possible, unless instructed otherwise by the principal in writing.

44. b. Each owns an undivided interest in the whole property and may will it, sell it, or pledge it as collateral for a mortgage loan.

45. a. A corporation is a legal entity and owns property in severalty or sole ownership. Severalty is ownership by one person or entity, meaning that it is a severed or separated ownership.

46. a. The agent owes the fiduciary duties of loyalty, obedience, accounting, confidentiality, full disclosure, and reasonable care and diligence to clients.

47. a. Brian, the offeree, changed the terms of the offer proposed by the offeror, thereby rejecting the offer. He then became the offeror by making a counteroffer, and Catherine is now the offeree and may accept or reject his offer.

48. b. The buyer is an optionee, and the owner is the optionor, giving the option to the buyer. An option is unilateral because the optionor has agreed to sell on the terms of the offer but the optionee has not yet made the commitment to purchase.

49. b. The payments are insufficient to repay the entire debt in five years, resulting in a balloon payment at the end of the term.

50. d. The Real Estate Settlement Procedures Act (RESPA) prohibits giving anything of value in exchange for business referrals among settlement service providers.

51. b. Because the property manager makes decisions on behalf of the owner, such as tenant selection, budget preparation, and employee relations, the property manager is a general agent.

52. d. This is an alternative to foreclosure action and transfers title to the mortgagee.

53. b. A non-conforming use is usually allowed when it existed prior to the zoning ordinance, but the use cannot be expanded, changed, or rebuilt and continued after destruction or abandonment.

54. d. An agency agreement, such as a listing, may not include an automatic renewal, and chattels are personal property.

55. d. The settlement or escrow officer is responsible for all of the details of the closing. The broker is responsible for providing professional real estate advice to his or her client.

56. a. Federally related loans for mortgage loans on residences fall under the provisions of RESPA.

57. a. Under Truth-in-Lending laws, consumers have a three day right to rescind open-end credit loans in which a security interest is retained by the lender on their principal dwelling.

58. b. Voluntary alienation, or transfer of ownership, includes patent from a sovereign government, deed signed by a legal grantor, and a valid will.

59. c. Failure to perform according to the terms of a contract without legal excuse is breach of contract.

60. c. A general lien is directed against the debtor and may attach to all of his or her property. A specific lien is against certain property such as *ad valorem* property tax line, mortgage lien, home equity lien, or mechanic's lien.

61. c. Under federal anti-trust laws, a group boycott is an agreement or conspiracy between two or more people to exclude another from fair participation in the marketplace with the purpose to hurt or destroy the other's business.

62. b. Bill is Joe's client through the listing agreement. Joe implied to Jeanette that he was working for her as her agent, thus creating an undisclosed dual agency. An agent cannot represent both clients and provide full fiduciary duties to each. Dual agency presents a conflict of interest and, in those states in which it is legal, must be disclosed and consented to by both parties. Dual agency reduces the level of service to that of a facilitator between the parties.

63. b. Provided that the owner does not own more than three such homes, no licensed real estate broker is involved in the transaction, and no discriminatory advertising is used, this owner is exempt from these laws. Please note, however, that some states do not recognize the "Mrs. Murphy" exemption. In all states, the more restrictive law prevails.

64. c. The sales contract should anticipate and settle all questions about each party's rights and duties at closing.

65. b. Anthony's lien was created by his own free will and is specific to his property. Annabelle's lien is specific to her property but was created statutorily by a taxing entity such as a city or county.

66. d. The servient tenement is encumbered by the easement that runs with the land. An easement appurtenant may be for ingress and egress but may also be a party wall or joint driveway for use by two or more parties. The dominant tenement is served by the servient tenement.

67. b. A contingency provision in a contract requires the completion of a certain act or happening. If this does not occur, such as when the buyer cannot get financing, the buyer may terminate the contract and usually receives a refund of any earnest money paid.

68. d. There is no guarantee that an abstract or title opinion is without error.

69. d. Epstein collected the full month's rent of $1,350 on the first of the month. He owes the buyer the remainder of the month, or 16 days of rent.
$1,350 ÷ 30 days in June = $45 rent per day
$45 × 16 days remaining in June = $720 rent due to the buyer from the seller

70. b. An agent must disclose all material facts that could influence the seller's decision to accept or reject any offers.

71. b. Unique property that does not produce income is appraised by estimating reproduction or replacement cost.

72. c. External obsolescence refers to outside factors (a nearby landfill, unemployment in the community) that affect the value of the subject property.

73. b. Only the grantor, the seller, signs the deed. Delivery and acceptance are required for title to pass from seller to buyer.

74. a. Steering or channeling based on race, religion, national origin, or any protected class under Fair Housing laws is a violation of the law.

75. c. Licensing laws are consumer protection laws requiring real estate professionals to meet certain minimum education, competency, and ethical standards.

76. b. The market price of the comparable (recently sold) properties is used to determine market value for the subject property.

77. a. Drafting contracts, addenda, or other legal documents requires the services of an attorney.

78. c. Sale prices of comparable properties are adjusted to match the specifications of the subject property.

79. d. As the listing agent, May owes fiduciary duties to the seller and must work on behalf of the seller. She may write an offer for Devin, but she cannot encourage an offer less that the asking price unless she has written authority from the seller to do so.

80. a. A land contract is known in some areas as an installment contract or a contract for deed.

► Scoring

Evaluate how you did on this practice exam by finding the number of questions you got right, disregarding for the moment the ones you got wrong or skipped. On the official exam, you need to answer 75% correctly to pass.

If you didn't score as well as you would like, ask yourself the following: Did I run out of time before I could answer all the questions? Did I go back and change my answers from right to wrong? Did I get flustered and sit staring at a difficult question for what seemed like hours? If you had any of these problems, be sure to go over the LearningExpress Test Preparation System in Chapter 2 to review how best to avoid them.

You probably have seen improvement between your first practice exam score and this one, but if you didn't improve as much as you'd like, you still have some options:

If you scored well below your personal goal, you should seriously consider whether you're ready for the exam at this time. A good idea would be to take some brush-up courses in the areas in which you feel less confident. If you don't have time for a course, you might try private tutoring.

If you scored close to your personal goal, you need to work as hard as you can to improve your skills. Go back to your real estate license course textbooks to review the knowledge you need to do well on the exam. If math is your problem area, check out the Learning-Express book *Practical Math Success in 20 Minutes a Day*. Also, reread and pay close attention to the information in Chapter 7, Real Estate Broker Refresher Course; Chapter 8, Real Estate Broker Math Review; and Chapter 9, Real Estate Glossary. Take the other practice exams in this book. It might also be helpful to ask friends and family to make up mock test questions and quiz you on them.

If you scored well above your personal goal, that's great! You are well on your way to passing your broker's license exam. Don't lose your edge, though; keep studying right up to the day before the exam.

Now, revise your study schedule according to the time you have left, emphasizing those parts that gave you the most trouble this time. Use the following table to see where you need more work, so that you can concentrate your preparation efforts.

Thomson Prometric Practice Exam 2 for Review

Topic	Question Numbers
Agency and Listing	3, 5, 7, 8, 14, 28, 39, 46, 54, 62, 70, 79
Business Practices and Ethics	1, 4, 6, 11, 12, 20, 24, 25, 40, 42, 50, 61, 63, 74, 75, 77
Closing/Settlement and Transferring of Title	15, 33, 55, 56, 58, 68, 69, 73
Financing Sources	2, 10, 17, 19, 27, 35, 38, 49, 52, 57
Property Characteristics, Descriptions, Ownership Interests, and Restrictions	9, 16, 18, 26, 29, 30, 44, 45, 53, 60, 65, 66
Property Management	13, 23, 37, 51
Property Valuation and the Appraisal Process	22, 34, 71, 72, 76, 78
Real Estate Sales Contracts	21, 31, 32, 36, 41, 43, 47, 48, 59, 64, 67, 80

CHAPTER

13 ▶ PSI Practice Exam 2

CHAPTER SUMMARY

This is the second of the two PSI practice tests in this book. Because you have taken the first PSI practice test already, you should feel more confident with your test-taking skills. Use this test to see how knowing what to expect can make you feel better prepared.

You are now more familiar with the format and content of the national portion of the PSI exam, and you probably feel more confident than you did at first. However, your practice test-taking experience will help you most if you have created a situation as close as possible to the real one.

For this exam, try to simulate real testing conditions. Find a quiet place where you will not be disturbed. Make sure you have two sharpened pencils and a good eraser. Be sure to leave enough time to complete the exam in one sitting. There is a two-hour limit on the official exam, so you'll want to practice working quickly without rushing. Use a timer or a stopwatch and see if you can work through all the exam questions in the allotted time.

The answer sheet is on the next page. An answer key and explanations follow the test. These explanations, along with the table at the end of this chapter, will help you see where you need further study. Remember, the six other practice exams in this book, although slightly different in format than the PSI exam, all test the same basic real estate principles and concepts, so you can use them to help you even further solidify your knowledge and skills.

1.	ⓐ	ⓑ	ⓒ	ⓓ
2.	ⓐ	ⓑ	ⓒ	ⓓ
3.	ⓐ	ⓑ	ⓒ	ⓓ
4.	ⓐ	ⓑ	ⓒ	ⓓ
5.	ⓐ	ⓑ	ⓒ	ⓓ
6.	ⓐ	ⓑ	ⓒ	ⓓ
7.	ⓐ	ⓑ	ⓒ	ⓓ
8.	ⓐ	ⓑ	ⓒ	ⓓ
9.	ⓐ	ⓑ	ⓒ	ⓓ
10.	ⓐ	ⓑ	ⓒ	ⓓ
11.	ⓐ	ⓑ	ⓒ	ⓓ
12.	ⓐ	ⓑ	ⓒ	ⓓ
13.	ⓐ	ⓑ	ⓒ	ⓓ
14.	ⓐ	ⓑ	ⓒ	ⓓ
15.	ⓐ	ⓑ	ⓒ	ⓓ
16.	ⓐ	ⓑ	ⓒ	ⓓ
17.	ⓐ	ⓑ	ⓒ	ⓓ
18.	ⓐ	ⓑ	ⓒ	ⓓ
19.	ⓐ	ⓑ	ⓒ	ⓓ
20.	ⓐ	ⓑ	ⓒ	ⓓ
21.	ⓐ	ⓑ	ⓒ	ⓓ
22.	ⓐ	ⓑ	ⓒ	ⓓ
23.	ⓐ	ⓑ	ⓒ	ⓓ
24.	ⓐ	ⓑ	ⓒ	ⓓ
25.	ⓐ	ⓑ	ⓒ	ⓓ
26.	ⓐ	ⓑ	ⓒ	ⓓ
27.	ⓐ	ⓑ	ⓒ	ⓓ
28.	ⓐ	ⓑ	ⓒ	ⓓ
29.	ⓐ	ⓑ	ⓒ	ⓓ
30.	ⓐ	ⓑ	ⓒ	ⓓ
31.	ⓐ	ⓑ	ⓒ	ⓓ
32.	ⓐ	ⓑ	ⓒ	ⓓ
33.	ⓐ	ⓑ	ⓒ	ⓓ
34.	ⓐ	ⓑ	ⓒ	ⓓ
35.	ⓐ	ⓑ	ⓒ	ⓓ
36.	ⓐ	ⓑ	ⓒ	ⓓ
37.	ⓐ	ⓑ	ⓒ	ⓓ
38.	ⓐ	ⓑ	ⓒ	ⓓ
39.	ⓐ	ⓑ	ⓒ	ⓓ
40.	ⓐ	ⓑ	ⓒ	ⓓ
41.	ⓐ	ⓑ	ⓒ	ⓓ
42.	ⓐ	ⓑ	ⓒ	ⓓ
43.	ⓐ	ⓑ	ⓒ	ⓓ
44.	ⓐ	ⓑ	ⓒ	ⓓ
45.	ⓐ	ⓑ	ⓒ	ⓓ
46.	ⓐ	ⓑ	ⓒ	ⓓ
47.	ⓐ	ⓑ	ⓒ	ⓓ
48.	ⓐ	ⓑ	ⓒ	ⓓ
49.	ⓐ	ⓑ	ⓒ	ⓓ
50.	ⓐ	ⓑ	ⓒ	ⓓ
51.	ⓐ	ⓑ	ⓒ	ⓓ
52.	ⓐ	ⓑ	ⓒ	ⓓ
53.	ⓐ	ⓑ	ⓒ	ⓓ
54.	ⓐ	ⓑ	ⓒ	ⓓ
55.	ⓐ	ⓑ	ⓒ	ⓓ
56.	ⓐ	ⓑ	ⓒ	ⓓ
57.	ⓐ	ⓑ	ⓒ	ⓓ
58.	ⓐ	ⓑ	ⓒ	ⓓ
59.	ⓐ	ⓑ	ⓒ	ⓓ
60.	ⓐ	ⓑ	ⓒ	ⓓ
61.	ⓐ	ⓑ	ⓒ	ⓓ
62.	ⓐ	ⓑ	ⓒ	ⓓ
63.	ⓐ	ⓑ	ⓒ	ⓓ
64.	ⓐ	ⓑ	ⓒ	ⓓ
65.	ⓐ	ⓑ	ⓒ	ⓓ
66.	ⓐ	ⓑ	ⓒ	ⓓ
67.	ⓐ	ⓑ	ⓒ	ⓓ
68.	ⓐ	ⓑ	ⓒ	ⓓ
69.	ⓐ	ⓑ	ⓒ	ⓓ
70.	ⓐ	ⓑ	ⓒ	ⓓ
71.	ⓐ	ⓑ	ⓒ	ⓓ
72.	ⓐ	ⓑ	ⓒ	ⓓ
73.	ⓐ	ⓑ	ⓒ	ⓓ
74.	ⓐ	ⓑ	ⓒ	ⓓ
75.	ⓐ	ⓑ	ⓒ	ⓓ
76.	ⓐ	ⓑ	ⓒ	ⓓ
77.	ⓐ	ⓑ	ⓒ	ⓓ
78.	ⓐ	ⓑ	ⓒ	ⓓ
79.	ⓐ	ⓑ	ⓒ	ⓓ
80.	ⓐ	ⓑ	ⓒ	ⓓ

▶ PSI Practice Exam 2

1. Which of the following is an example of a non-inheritable estate?
   a. a year-to-year tenancy
   b. a conventional life estate
   c. a fee simple absolute
   d. a fee simple defeasible

2. An agency agreement with a single listing broker that requires the broker to be paid unless the seller finds a buyer without the assistance of the broker is called
   a. an exclusive agency.
   b. an exclusive right to sell.
   c. an open listing.
   d. a net listing.

3. A tremendous storm causes a river to flood and, in the process, about 15 feet of shoreline on Peter Haley's property is washed downstream. After the flood subsides, his neighbor's beach is widened by 15 feet. Which of the following is NOT true in this situation?
   a. Peter has a claim against his homeowners insurance company.
   b. The land was lost because of avulsion.
   c. New land has been created by the addition of alluvion.
   d. The adjacent owner is not required to compensate Peter in any way for the lost waterfront.

4. The right to occupy a property without interference for a specified period of time is known as a
   a. trespass.
   b. prescriptive easement.
   c. leasehold.
   d. suit for possession.

5. A tenant with a commercial lease pays, on a monthly basis, $1,000 base rental plus the $18,000 annual tax bill and 3% of his gross receipts. If the tenant takes in $75,000 in the month of May, what is the rental payment for June?
   a. $4,750
   b. $3,750
   c. $3,250
   d. $7,400

6. Tenancy by the entirety differs from other forms of co-ownership in that
   a. neither owner can force a sale.
   b. each owner is free to devise his or her share to chosen heirs.
   c. shares may be acquired at different times.
   d. the property must be a principal residence.

7. A lease would NOT be terminated in which of the following situations?
   a. The tenant becomes the owner.
   b. The property is destroyed by fire.
   c. The landlord has the tenant evicted from the property.
   d. The tenant defaults in lease payments.

8. Jane McGraw and Richard Kim, who are not married, want to buy a house together. In order to ensure that if one dies, the other automatically becomes full owner, their deed must state that they are
   a. joint tenants with rights of survivorship.
   b. tenants in common.
   c. tenants in severalty.
   d. tenants by the entirety.

9. Riparian and littoral rights belong to owners of
  a. a homestead.
  b. subsurface minerals.
  c. land bordering bodies of water.
  d. remainder and reversionary interests.

10. Which of the following is used to assure good title?
  a. a quitclaim deed
  b. a title insurance policy
  c. a rectangular survey
  d. a datum

11. In a title theory state, which of the following statements is true when the owner places a mortgage lien on the property?
  a. The owner has legal title.
  b. The owner has equitable title.
  c. The lender has equitable title.
  d. The lender has no title rights.

12. A commercial property is estimated to generate $5,500 in monthly net income. Using a capitalization rate of 11%, the appraiser's opinion of value would be
  a. $50,000
  b. $726,000
  c. $60,500
  d. $600,000

13. A certain subdivision has a deed restriction requiring houses to be at least 2,000 square feet. The town, however, has no such restriction and gives the Long-Watsons a building permit for a little bungalow in the subdivision. If the neighbors object, their best course of action would be to
  a. attempt to negotiate with the building inspector's office.
  b. wait until a clear violation has occurred before taking any legal action.
  c. request a change of the local zoning ordinance.
  d. ask a court to prevent the construction or to order that the bungalow be expanded.

14. Of the following liens, which has highest priority?
  a. an unrecorded judgment
  b. the loan with the highest balance
  c. the mortgage recorded earliest
  d. a mortgage that has been subordinated to another

15. The lender's underwriting criteria would accept a housing expense to income ratio of 33% and a ratio of total debt service of up to a maximum of 38% of monthly gross income. The applicant has an outstanding college loan payable at the rate of $250 per month and a car payment of $450 monthly. Gross annual income is established at $100,000 per annum. What is the maximum PITI the lender will approve?
  a. $2,750
  b. $2,566.67
  c. $2,666.67
  d. $2,716.54

16. Title insurance protects the owner or lender against unexpected claims arising from past
  a. forged documents.
  b. zoning ordinances.
  c. unpaid general creditors.
  d. recorded easements.

17. Federal lead-based paint regulations apply to most residential properties built before
  a. 1965
  b. 1978
  c. 1981
  d. 1884

18. Sellers of real property must disclose any known property defects
  a. before the property is shown to a prospective buyer.
  b. before listing the property with a broker.
  c. before placing any advertisement for the property.
  d. before any purchase contract is signed with a buyer.

19. A buyer offers, in writing, to pay $295,000 for a property. The buyer makes a down payment of 30% and finances the balance by obtaining a 30-year conventional loan. The factor for the PI payment is $7.34 per thousand. The lender opens an escrow account for payment of the annual property taxes of $3,000 and the property insurance premium of $600, collecting of those amounts with the monthly payment. What is the monthly PITI payment for this borrower?
  a. $1,515.71
  b. $1,815.71
  c. $2,798
  d. $2,498

20. When a written agreement spells out the responsibilities of the principal and the agent, the relationship created is called
  a. a limited partnership.
  b. an express agency.
  c. an ostensible agency.
  d. an implied agency.

21. The fiduciary duty of obedience followed in some states would include
  a. following instructions as long as they are legal.
  b. delegating tasks to other agents when possible.
  c. avoiding overburdening the principal with all the details about the sale.
  d. giving legal interpretations of documents.

22. Once an agency relationship is ended, any confidential information learned by the agent during the relationship is
  a. shared with future clients.
  b. still confidential.
  c. considered immaterial.
  d. a part of the MLS historical database.

23. A licensee appearing to represent both parties in the transaction, while actually being agent to only one, is at risk of being
  a. an agent coupled with an interest.
  b. an undisclosed dual agent.
  c. a middleman.
  d. a buyer's broker.

24. To be legally entitled to a commission related to a real estate transaction, the agent must be all of the following EXCEPT
   a. licensed.
   b. authorized to be involved in the marketing effort.
   c. the procuring cause of the transaction.
   d. under contract to either the buyer or the seller.

25. Gratuities for referring prospects to a broker are legal if paid to a
   a. salesperson affiliated with another firm.
   b. relative of the buyer.
   c. licensed broker.
   d. federal employee.

26. A broker may enter a listing into a multiple-listing service. The data provided may include all of the following EXCEPT
   a. the chattels and amenities being offered as a part of the real estate.
   b. an offer to share compensation.
   c. the legal description.
   d. the reason for sale.

27. A buyer prepares two offers on a property. One is at full listing price, and the other is at 85% of listing price. The cooperating agent, who is a subagent of the seller, is instructed to present the low offer first. If the owner rejects it, only then may the full price offer be introduced. Which of the following is true in this situation?
   a. The agent may follow those instructions.
   b. Both offers must be presented simultaneously.
   c. The buyer must be encouraged to increase the low offer to 90% of the listing price.
   d. The low offer is to be torn up prior to the presentation meeting.

28. Brokers typically choose to work with salespersons as independent contractors so that the broker
   a. has greater control of the level of production.
   b. benefits in terms of taxes.
   c. can develop a more cohesive organization.
   d. can increase mass marketing programs.

29. Mark Thomas has a signed buyer agency agreement with the Boghosians. The Boghosians have decided to make an offer on a property that is listed with Mark's brokerage firm. In this case, which of the following statements is true?
   a. Mark is responsible only to his clients, the Boghosians, and is no longer under the supervision of his broker.
   b. Mark is still responsible to the sellers, because they are clients of his firm.
   c. Mark's broker will represent only the sellers, and Mark will represent the Boghosians.
   d. Mark's broker is in a dual agency position, with responsibility to both the buyer clients, the Boghosians, and also to the sellers who have listed with his firm.

30. Which of the following people is generally entitled to the selling commission?
   a. the subagent
   b. the agent determined to be the procuring cause
   c. the agent who first showed the property
   d. the agent who wrote the contract

31. A broker lists a property for sale. As time goes by, it is evident that the property is not very desirable. The broker and a partner observe that with a zoning variance and some modest remodeling, the character of the property could be changed to make it more valuable and saleable. The partner purchases the property without revealing the plan to the seller or identifying his relationship with the broker. Which of the following is true of this transaction?
   a. The broker has acted appropriately, because the property was ultimately sold.
   b. The seller received all of the benefits of having an agent.
   c. The business relationship between the broker and the buyer should have been disclosed.
   d. The buyer should have offered the seller the opportunity to participate in the venture.

32. Which of the following pieces of information relating to a property requires disclosure to interested buyers or tenants?
   a. The property is rumored to possess spirits.
   b. The seller is forced to sell to avoid foreclosure.
   c. The property is located in a flood zone.
   d. The occupants of an adjacent property are members of a minority group.

33. A seller, anxious to sell, tells a cooperating salesperson during a showing that the salesperson will be given a riding lawnmower if he brings an acceptable offer by the end of the week. All of the following are true in this situation EXCEPT that the
   a. salesperson may accept the lawnmower because it is not cash.
   b. salesperson should report the incident to the listing broker.
   c. salesperson would be in violation of the law if he took the lawnmower.
   d. cooperating salesperson could legally receive the lawnmower from his broker.

34. Which of the following acts or laws established requirements for access to places of public accommodation?
   a. the Fair Housing Act of 1968
   b. the National Model Zoning Law
   c. the Americans with Disabilities Act
   d. the Civil Rights Act of 1964

35. A new office building has been constructed on a parcel of land. All of the following are necessary considerations before tenants are allowed to move in EXCEPT
   a. compliance with building codes.
   b. payment of property taxes.
   c. proper building permits.
   d. certificate of occupancy.

36. Which of the following would NOT have to be disclosed to a prospective buyer?
   a. environmental issues
   b. agency relationships
   c. seller's motivation for moving
   d. defects in the property

37. Real estate salesperson Amelia Morris is associated with Midtown Realty. When selling property she has an ownership interest in, Amelia must disclose
   a. her ownership interest.
   b. the fact that she holds a real estate license.
   c. any material defects she is aware of.
   d. all of the above

38. The Webers own three pieces of real estate: their house, a lakeside cottage, and a tract of woodland. Which of the following expenses may be deducted for all three properties on the Webers' income tax return?
   a. mortgage interest
   b. insurance premiums
   c. property taxes
   d. both mortgage interest and property taxes

39. The buyer under a land contract has an interest in the property legally known as
   a. equitable title.
   b. a leasehold.
   c. a remainder interest.
   d. a reverter.

40. The Civil Rights Act of 1866 prohibits discrimination in real estate based on
   a. color.
   b. race and gender.
   c. handicap and country of origin.
   d. gender and religion.

41. Before a mortgage loan is made, lending institutions often require a(n)
   a. survey.
   b. walk-through.
   c. inspection.
   d. assessment.

42. At closing, the lending institution may ask the buyer to
   a. pay the state transfer tax.
   b. sign a disclosure of property condition.
   c. deposit money in an escrow account.
   d. reimburse the seller for prepaid property taxes.

43. Zoning ordinances typically regulate the
   a. number of occupants allowed for each building.
   b. permitted uses of each parcel of land.
   c. maximum rent that may be charged.
   d. adherence to Fair Housing laws.

44. Governments have the ability to regulate the construction and use of buildings through their right of
   a. police power.
   b. escheat.
   c. eminent domain.
   d. condemnation.

45. A building permit may be issued without question even if the proposed structure violates existing
   a. zoning laws.
   b. deed restrictions.
   c. building codes.
   d. setback requirements.

46. The land between a large factory and a residential neighborhood has been zoned for use as a park or playground. This is an example of a
   a. buffer zone.
   b. spot zone.
   c. variance.
   d. non-conforming use.

47. Any federally related loan may require the borrower to carry special insurance if the property is located in
a. an earthquake area.
b. a flood zone.
c. an ocean hazard district.
d. a desert.

48. The Flynns have lost their jobs, have fallen behind on loan payments, and are about to lose their home to judicial foreclosure proceedings, which have already started. At the last minute, Hugo Flynn's father agrees to give them all the money they owe plus legal costs. The Flynns can stop the foreclosure using their
a. right of redemption.
b. deed in lieu of foreclosure.
c. defeasance clause.
d. deficiency judgment.

49. The provisions of the Real Estate Settlement Procedures Act (RESPA) apply to
a. one- to four-family residential mortgage loans.
b. all residential mortgage loans.
c. all mortgages except home equity loans.
d. installment contracts.

50. Anna Jamison rents a small building for her boutique. In addition to rent, she also pays property taxes, utility bills, and insurance on the property. She has a
a. net lease.
b. percentage lease.
c. variable lease.
d. ground lease.

51. All of the following statements with regard to the purchase or sale of agricultural property are true EXCEPT
a. a mortgage loan on agricultural property will have different conditions from those found in mortgage lending for a single-family house.
b. a detailed survey of the property is very important in agricultural sales.
c. any agent with a real estate license is totally knowledgeable about agricultural purchases.
d. agricultural lending must allow for the cyclical nature of agriculture.

52. Office space is usually rented by the
a. cubic foot.
b. square foot.
c. percentage of business done.
d. cost of living index.

53. Nancy Tomsic's tenants all had several months remaining on their leases when she sold her six-unit apartment building to Chuck Dwight. Tenants in this situation typically
a. must renegotiate their leases with the new landlord.
b. can be required to leave with one month's notice.
c. lose their leases when the new owner takes possession.
d. need do nothing and may remain until the end of their leases.

54. Under federal Fair Housing law, a handicap is defined as
a. any impairment.
b. a physical or mental impairment.
c. a physical or mental impairment that substantially limits one or more major life activities.
d. a physical or mental impairment that substantially limits one or more general life activities.

55. An assessment is a special type of appraisal used for
a. property tax purposes.
b. income tax returns.
c. estate tax returns.
d. divorce settlements.

56. The veteran who receives a guaranteed VA loan is borrowing the money from
a. the state veterans' agency.
b. the Department of Veterans Affairs.
c. Fannie Mae.
d. a local lending institution.

57. Newly constructed buildings are best appraised by giving most weight to the
a. cost approach.
b. sales comparison approach.
c. income approach.
d. gross rent multiplier.

58. Which of the following is the most accurate definition of familial status under Fair Housing law?
a. having persons under the age of 18 living in a unit
b. having persons with too many children living in a unit too small to handle that number of occupants
c. having multiple families living in a unit
d. having persons under the age of 18 living with a parent or legal guardian

59. A large organization that influences the amount of money available for lending by purchasing mortgages in the secondary market is
a. HUD.
b. FIRREA.
c. FHLMC.
d. RESPA.

60. Tom Dupre asks Sarah Shah, a real estate salesperson, to help him set the right asking price for his home. Sarah's broker will help her prepare
a. a reconciliation of value.
b. an assessment analysis.
c. a competitive market analysis.
d. a limited appraisal.

61. The appraisal principle of substitution states that
a. the buyer is paying for expected benefits in the future.
b. some improvements have a larger payoff in increased value than others.
c. maximum value is reached where there is reasonable uniformity in the neighborhood.
d. no one will pay more if something equally desirable is available for less.

62. Dennis Sorensen is buying land on which he plans to build a cabin. He wants 200 feet in road frontage and a lot 500 feet deep. If the asking price is $9,000 an acre for the land, how much will Dennis pay for his lot?
a. $10,000
b. $20,700
c. $22,956
d. $24,104

63. The unlawful practice of guiding prospective buyers to or away from an area because of a protected classification under Fair Housing laws is known as
a. steering.
b. unlawful guiding.
c. less favorable treatment.
d. redlining.

64. In order to determine an appropriate price to pay for a single-family home to be used as a rental property, the prospective investor-buyers would most likely use which of the following ways to determine value of a property?
a. market approach
b. cost approach
c. income approach
d. gross rent multiplier

65. Prices are likely to rise when there is a
a. buyer's market.
b. seller's market.
c. thin market.
d. broad market.

66. If a comparable property has a $15,000 garage and the subject property has no garage, the appraiser would
a. subtract $15,000 from the sale price of the comparable property.
b. add $15,000 to the appraised price of the subject.
c. add $15,000 to the sale price of the comparable property.
d. subtract $7,500 from the estimated price of the subject.

67. The purchase contract is the most important document in the sales process because
a. the agent is not guaranteed payment without it.
b. it provides the road map for the closing.
c. preparing sales agreements is good for the legal business.
d. unless a real estate transaction is in writing, state law dictates how the money is spent and distributed.

68. A buyer and seller have each signed a written purchase agreement. The Uniform Vendor and Purchaser Risk Act states that until the buyer has either possession of or title to a property, responsibility for the physical condition of the property
a. remains with the seller.
b. is delegated to the buyer, who has equitable title to the property.
c. is insured under errors and omissions insurance.
d. is assumed by the seller's homeowners insurance company.

69. The buyer wishes to be relieved of her obligations under a contract and locates a qualified
person to enter into a new agreement with the
seller. The existing contract can be ended by
   a. rescission.
   b. flipping.
   c. transference.
   d. default.

70. The amount of commission a salesperson
receives is set by
   a. state law.
   b. negotiation between lister and seller.
   c. agreement between broker and associate.
   d. the Department of Commerce.

71. During contract negotiations, the broker,
despite knowledge to the contrary, assures the
buyer that the property is suitable for multifamily use. Prior to closing, the buyer learns
that zoning regulations prohibit this use of the
property. By law, this contract is
   a. valid and binding on all parties.
   b. voidable at the option of the buyer.
   c. voidable by either party.
   d. assigned to the broker.

72. A passenger enters a taxi and gives the driver
instructions to her destination. The driver and
passenger have entered into a
   a. contract by implication.
   b. designated representation.
   c. special assignment.
   d. limited agency.

73. Under what circumstances, if any, might a broker collect a commission from both buyer and
seller?
   a. under no circumstances
   b. only with approval from the state licensing
   authorities
   c. if both parties give informed consent
   d. if doing so does not violate company policy

74. A deed is the instrument used to convey ownership of
   a. personal property.
   b. short-term use of real estate.
   c. real property.
   d. crops and other produce.

75. One example of an easement in gross is the
right of
   a. owners to cut across their neighbors' property in order to reach their lot.
   b. a roofing company working on repairs to
   store some of their equipment in the neighbor's yard.
   c. owners to use the neighbor's backyard for
   their summer office party.
   d. utility companies to access a property in
   order to maintain wires or pipes.

76. The Statute of Frauds requires that
   a. real estate brokers answer buyers' and sellers'
   questions honestly.
   b. the seller of real estate provide a written disclosure about the condition of the property.
   c. certain contracts, including those for the
   sale of real estate, be in writing to be
   enforceable.
   d. a mortgage borrower has three days in
   which to cancel the loan.

77. Under federal Fair Housing law, blockbusting is the unlawful practice of
  a. buying blocks at below market prices for the purpose of building group homes for the mentally impaired.
  b. having a city condemn property to turn it over to a private developer.
  c. convincing prospective buyers that a specific block of property will drop in value more than others in the area.
  d. inducing panic selling because of to the entry, or prospective entry, of persons belonging to a protected class under federal Fair Housing laws.

78. A tax bill computed by a cost per front-foot is a
  a. personal property tax.
  b. special assessment.
  c. license.
  d. use permit.

79. Dave Gates, a widower, died without leaving a will or other instruction. His surviving children received ownership of his real estate holdings by
  a. adverse possession.
  b. eminent domain.
  c. escheat.
  d. law of intestate succession.

80. Consideration to bind a contract may be in the form of
  a. cash or cash equivalent only.
  b. anything that the parties agree upon, as long as it has monetary value.
  c. money, promises, or services.
  d. thoughtful treatment of the other party's feelings.

▶ Answers

1. b. The legal life estate (one based on the holder's life) terminates at the death of the holder and thus cannot be passed on by a will.

2. a. The exclusive agency agreement allows the seller to sell to a buyer without paying a commission if the buyer was found without the broker's assistance.

3. a. Insurance companies do not generally insure against loss of land. This is an example of land being relocated as an act of nature, in which case property is lost or increased.

4. c. A lease defines the period of time during which the tenant has the right to occupy and enjoy a property. At the end of that period, the right reverts to the owner.

5. a. $1,000 + $1,500 + $2,250 = $4,750

6. a. When a married couple buys any real estate as tenants by the entirety, neither can obtain a court order for partition.

7. d. A default would not terminate a lease; all other listed options would.

8. a. Joint tenants are often known as joint tenants with right of survivorship. If Jane dies, Richard will automatically receive Jane's share, no matter what her will might say.

9. c. Riparian rights apply to owners of land bordering rivers and streams, while littoral rights apply to those owning land on lakes and oceans.

10. b. A quitclaim deed does not assure title; a rectangular survey is used for legal description; and a datum is a specific point used for surveying.

11. b. In a title theory state, the lender retains legal title and the owner has equitable title. In a lien theory state, the owner would have legal title and the lender would have equitable title. The lender could obtain legal title only if the purchaser defaulted and the property was foreclosed on.

12. **d.** NOI divided by cap rate equals value.
($5,500 × 12) ÷ 0.11 = $600,000

13. **d.** If a deed restriction is more restrictive than a local zoning ordinance, it takes precedence and can be enforced in court. The neighbors would have a good case.

14. **c.** Priority of liens is established by date of recording. The earliest recorded lien against a property has the highest priority, unless it has been subordinated to another or is a property tax lien.

15. **b.** ($100,000 ÷ 12) × 0.38 = $3,166.67 − ($150 + $450) = $2,566.67

16. **a.** Of the items listed, only forged documents are covered by title insurance.

17. **b.** The lead-based paint regulations apply to most residential property built before 1978. Known lead-based paint hazards must always be disclosed, but the federal regulations are specific to units built before 1978.

18. **d.** Although the disclosures should be made before any of the first three, the only really mandated time frame is before contract.

19. **b.** $295,000 × 0.7 = $206,500 loan
206.5 × 7.34 = $1,515.71 principal and interest
($3,000 + $600) ÷ 12 = $300 taxes and insurance
$1,515.71 + $300 = $1,815.71 PITI

20. **b.** When the terms of the agency relationship are formalized in writing, it is known as an express agency.

21. **a.** The duty of obedience includes the obligation to follow the instructions of the principal as long as they are legal, ethical, moral, and possible. This would also be true under the statutory duties of protecting and promoting the best interests of the client.

22. **b.** Confidential information remains confidential forever, with few exceptions.

23. **b.** A licensee attempting to represent both sides of the transaction without the informed consent of the parties is an undisclosed dual agent, illegal in most states.

24. **d.** The agent could be acting as a cooperating subagent to the listing broker, in which case the agent would not have a specific contract with either buyer or seller. However, in the case of buyer agency, the agent would have a contract with the buyer. The listing broker would always have a contract with the seller.

25. **c.** Referral fees may be paid only to licensed brokers.

26. **d.** The reason for sale is confidential. All other responses are necessary to prepare an offer to purchase or to encourage the cooperation of other brokers.

27. **b.** The cooperating agent's duty of disclosure to the seller requires that the seller client be made aware of both offers simultaneously. To follow the buyer's instructions might cast the agent into the role of being an undisclosed dual agent.

28. **b.** Independent contractor status is primarily for tax purposes because the broker is excluded from the obligation to withhold taxes and Social Security payments.

29. **d.** The broker is always responsible for the supervision of all agents affiliated with his or her firm. The broker also has an agency responsibility to all clients, whether they are buyers or sellers.

30. **b.** The agent who is deemed to have set into motion an unbroken series of events leading to a transaction is the procuring cause, and is generally entitled to the commission.

31. c. The agent is required to disclose relationships when family, friends, or business partners are involved in a transaction. The agent must also disclose any situation in which he has a personal interest.

32. c. Disclosure of all material adverse facts about the property itself is required. In some states, it is also required to disclose facts about adjacent properties that might affect the property value, such as an adjacent property being rezoned for an office park.

33. a. Salespersons may receive compensation only from their principal broker. Gifts of merchandise, use of luxury cars, trips, and outings are also compensation and may only be given to a broker who disposes of them in accord with the company policy.

34. c. The ADA was enacted in 1990 to address employment and accessibility rights of individuals with disabilities.

35. b. While unpaid property taxes are a lien on the property, they will not prevent tenants from occupying the premises.

36. c. A seller's reasons for moving are generally considered confidential unless they materially relate to the condition of the property.

37. d. Law requires Amelia to disclose all of the items listed.

38. c. All property taxes paid are income tax deductible. Interest deductions are available only for one's first and second homes. Insurance premiums are not deductible.

39. a. The buyer on a land contract has an equitable title to the property, meaning that the buyer will gain legal title at some point in time when certain actions have been completed, usually upon completion of payment as prescribed in the contract.

40. a. The law that followed the close of the Civil War extended equal rights in real property to members of all colors.

41. a. Whether the survey is paid for by buyer or seller is specified in the contract; local custom varies in this matter, but most lenders will require a survey.

42. c. If the lender is to handle the homeowner's insurance premiums and property tax bills, the escrow account is established at closing.

43. b. Typical zones permit residential, multifamily, or commercial buildings within a given zone.

44. a. Many people are surprised to learn that the term *police power* covers all of the government's authority to protect the public's health, safety, and welfare.

45. b. Deed restrictions are private and nongovernmental, set by previous owners of the property. They are enforced through neighbors' lawsuits, not by local building authorities.

46. a. A buffer zone is often used to soften the transition between residential and other uses.

47. b. The government issues flood hazard maps, and for mortgage loans within those areas, borrowers must carry flood insurance, which is available from the federal government.

48. a. The right of redemption allows the borrower to avoid foreclosure by coming up with all the money due, plus costs.

49. a. RESPA covers federally related one- to four-family mortgage loans, including equity loans.

50. a. Anna's is actually a quadruple net lease because she pays all the expenses on the building.

51. c. Agricultural sales is a specialty that requires extra study and experience working with an expert in that field. Agricultural lending must be based on the cyclical nature of agriculture.

52. **b.** It's common to quote rent for office space on the basis of square footage per annum.

53. **d.** A lease survives the sale, and the new landlord is in exactly the same position with tenants as the old one was.

54. **c.** A handicap may be physical or mental but must limit a major life activity.

55. **a.** Assessors set the value at which real estate will be taxed.

56. **d.** The VA guarantees the loan, which is obtained from a regular lending institution.

57. **a.** The cost approach is usually the most accurate for unique buildings and those newly constructed.

58. **d.** Having persons under the age of 18 living with a parent or legal guardian is the definition under the Fair Housing Amendment Act of 1988.

59. **c.** The Federal Home Loan Mortgage Corporation buys packages of mortgages. The other initials stand for the Department of Housing and Urban Development; the Financial Institutions Reform, Recovery and Enforcement Act; and the Real Estate Settlement Procedures Act.

60. **c.** The CMA, competitive market analysis, is a simple analysis intended to assist a seller in determining an asking price for the property.

61. **d.** Choice **a** defines the appraisal principle of anticipation, choice **b** the principle of contribution, choice **c** the principle of conformity.

62. **b.** The lot will measure 200" by 500", or 100,000 square feet in all (200" × 500"). An acre contains 43,560 square feet, so the lot contains approximately 2.3 acres (100,000 divided by 43,560). At $9,000 per acre, the total cost is $20,700 (2.3 × $9,000).

63. **a.** Steering, also known as channeling, is the illegal practice of guiding prospective buyers to or away from an area because of their color, race, religion, sex, national origin, handicap, or familial status.

64. **d.** The gross rent multiplier is a way to determine value based on market rents for the area. Other properties are researched, and by dividing the sales price by the rent, a GRM can be obtained. The GRM is then multiplied by average market rent to obtain an appropriate value for the property.

65. **b.** In a seller's market, buyers are competing for the few homes on the market and are likely to offer more for them.

66. **a.** When the comparable property has a better feature, the value of that feature is subtracted from its sale price to bring the comparable property equal to the subject property.

67. **b.** The purchase contract outlines the rights, duties, and responsibilities of the parties and gives guidance to the closing officer about allocation of fees.

68. **a.** When a contract for sale is ratified, by virtue of equitable and insurable title being conveyed to the buyer, responsibility for any hazard damage to the property rests with the seller if the state has adopted the Uniform Vendor and Purchaser Risk Act.

69. **a.** The seller is free to enter into a new agreement with a different party after the existing agreement is rescinded.

70. **c.** Each real estate company has its own policy on how commissions are split between the office and the salesperson.

71. **b.** Contracts brought about by fraud or misrepresentation are voidable at the option of the injured party.

72. a. When a customer such as a taxi passenger, restaurant diner, or client in a hair salon requests a specific service, there is the implication that the provider will deliver the service and that the customer will pay the agreed compensation.

73. c. Particularly in commercial transactions, payment by both parties does occur; each must agree to the arrangement.

74. c. A deed conveys ownership of real property; personal property is conveyed by lease, bill of sale, or title.

75. d. Public utility companies are given access over properties for the purpose of maintenance and repair of necessary lines, pipes, and other equipment.

76. c. Every state has adopted the statute of frauds, which requires offers, acceptances, land contracts, and other real estate documents to be in writing in order to be enforceable.

77. d. Blockbusting is also known as *panic peddling*. It is the unlawful act of inducing property owners to sell because of the entry of members of a protected class into the area.

78. b. Special assessments are generally for repayment to the government for the cost of installing utilities, or curbs and gutters. Each owner is billed for their share of the expense calculated by their proportion of the benefit to their property.

79. d. Each state has a set of laws that define the distribution of real estate owned by someone who dies without leaving written instruction. If no heirs are located, the property reverts to the state.

80. c. If the parties agree, consideration need not be valuable in order to be considered good enough.

► Scoring

Evaluate how you did on this practice exam by finding the number of questions you got right, disregarding for the moment the ones you got wrong or skipped. On the official exam, you need to answer 60 of the 80 questions (75%) correctly to pass.

If you didn't score as well as you would like, ask yourself the following: Did I run out of time before I could answer all the questions? Did I go back and change my answers from right to wrong? Did I get flustered and sit staring at a difficult question for what seemed like hours? If you had any of these problems, be sure to go over the LearningExpress Test Preparation System in Chapter 2 to review how best to avoid them.

You probably have seen improvement between your first practice exam score and this one, but if you didn't improve as much as you'd like, here are some options:

If you scored well below your personal goal, you should seriously consider whether you're ready for the exam at this time. A good idea would be to take some brush-up courses in the areas in which you feel less confident. If you don't have time for a course, you might try private tutoring.

If you scored close to your personal goal, you need to work as hard as you can to improve your skills. Go back to your real estate license course textbooks to review the knowledge you need to do well on the exam. If math is your problem area, check out the Learning-Express book *Practical Math Success in 20 Minutes a Day*. Also, reread and pay close attention to the information in Chapter 7, Real Estate Broker Refresher Course; Chapter 8, Real Estate Broker Math Review; and Chapter 9, Real Estate Glossary. Take the other practice exams in this book. It might also be helpful to ask friends and family to make up mock test questions and quiz you on them.

If you scored well above your personal goal, that's great! You are well on your way to passing your broker's license exam. Don't lose your edge, though; keep studying right up to the day before the exam.

Now, revise your study schedule according to the time you have left, emphasizing those parts that gave you the most trouble this time. Use the following table to see where you need more work, so that you can concentrate your preparation efforts.

PSI Practice Exam 2 for Review

Topic	Question Numbers
Property Ownership	1, 3, 4, 6, 8, 9, 75
Land Use Controls and Regulations	13, 35, 43, 44, 45, 46, 47
Valuation and Market Analysis	55, 57, 60, 61, 65, 66
Financing	14, 38, 48, 49, 56, 59, 78
Laws of Agency	2, 20, 21, 22, 24, 25, 26, 27, 28, 73
Mandated Disclosures	17, 18, 23, 31, 32, 36, 37
Contracts	39, 41, 50, 67, 68, 69, 71, 72, 76, 80
Transfer of Property	10, 11, 16, 42, 74, 79
Practice of Real Estate	29, 30, 33, 34, 40, 54, 58, 63, 70, 77
Real Estate Calculations	5, 12, 15, 19, 62, 64
Specialty Areas	7, 51, 52, 53

14▶ Brokerage Office Operations

CHAPTER SUMMARY

You may be seeking your broker license because you want the additional knowledge you will obtain in preparing for the exam. You may also desire the prestige that accompanies the advanced license. But the majority of those who will pursue the broker license do so in order to take on the additional responsibilities it allows and the financial rewards that accompany them.

▶ Office Operations Tracks

There are three paths for a broker who wishes to manage other real estate agents.

1. Many states require that each office of a multi-office real estate company have a supervising broker. That person has responsibility for managing the independent contractors who operate from the location. He or she is particularly responsible for overseeing compliance with federal, state, and local regulations. The supervising broker may be made a salaried employee or be given a percentage of the commissions of the agents who are located in the office.

2. By purchasing an existing real estate company, a broker receives the assets of that company, without investing a significant period time in acquiring them. These may include current listings, lists of past clients and customers, a group of experienced sales agents, and the company's reputation within the industry and the community.

3. A broker also has the option to start a new real estate company. There is a great deal of excitement in opening a new firm. In addition to the financial rewards, there is a feeling of accomplishment when the new entity is successful.

The Legal Environment

The most important obligation of the supervising broker or broker/owner is monitoring compliance with the laws and regulations that govern the industry. In many cases, they are liable for the actions of their employees and the independent contractors who represent the company.

Federal Laws and Regulations

ADA

The Federal Fair Housing Act Amendment was discussed in Chapter 4. The Americans with Disabilities Act (ADA) has many similar requirements but extends them. The ADA was passed in 1990 and has four sections. Real estate brokers are affected by Titles I and III.

Title I: Employment

Title I requires employers with 15 or more employees to provide equal employment opportunities to qualified individuals with disabilities. It bans discrimination in recruiting, hiring, promotions, pay, training, and social activities.

ADA limits the questions that can be asked about an applicant's disability before a job offer is extended. It requires that employers make reasonable accommodations for known physical or mental impairments of otherwise qualified individuals, unless it results in undue hardship.

Title I governs how potential and present employees and independent contractors are treated. Candidates with disabilities must be treated the same as those without. Recruiters may not ask questions about a candidate's disability. Preemployment medical examinations are prohibited. Post-employment examinations may be required if they are also administered to all other employees. Drug screening is permitted to ensure that employees who are enrolled in or have completed rehabilitation remain drug free.

Brokers must make accommodations, such as wheelchair accessibility, for workers with disabilities. The idea of creating these accommodations may seem daunting at first. However, the Equal Employment Opportunity Commission has found that in 69% of cases, these adjustments will cost less than $500, and in only 1% of cases will they cost more than $5,000.

After they have been hired, persons with disabilities must be provided with all the opportunities that their coworkers receive. But that only makes sense: Their success is your success.

An important point to remember is that persons with disabilities are just as likely to excel at their jobs as any other individuals. They are also no more likely to miss work because of illness than other personnel. A disability is a condition, not a disease.

Title III: Public Accommodations

The act states:

"No individual shall be discriminated against on the basis of disability in the full and equal enjoyment of the goods, services, facilities, privileges, advantages, or accommodations of any place of public accommodation."

Title III governs businesses and nonprofit service providers that are public accommodations and commercial facilities. Public accommodations are private entities who own, lease, lease to, or operate facilities such as restaurants, retail stores, hotels, movie theaters, or private schools.

For real estate companies, Title III impacts their office facilities, schools, other real estate that they own or lease, and the facilities or potential facilities owned, leased or managed by clients, or which the firm manages for them.

Public accommodations must not exclude, segregate, or treat unequally persons with disabilities. They must also "comply with specific requirements related to architectural standards for new and altered buildings; reasonable modifications to policies, practices, and procedures; effective communication with people with hearing, vision, or speech disabilities; and other access requirements."[1]

In addition, barriers must be removed in existing buildings where it is easy to do so without much difficulty or expense.

Courses and examinations related to professional licensing, certifications, or credentialing must be provided in a place and manner accessible to people with disabilities, or alternative arrangements must be made.

Commercial facilities, such as factories and warehouses, must comply with the ADA's architectural standards for new construction and alterations.

These regulations require

- changing eligibility criteria that screen out persons with disabilities
- making reasonable changes to policies and practices
- providing auxiliary aids and services
- removing architectural and communications barriers if it can be done with little difficulty or expense, or providing alternatives for persons with disabilities when it cannot

Priority should be given, in the following order, to providing access to areas where goods or services are offered; public restrooms; and entrances and exits.

Real estate companies must make their facilities accessible to persons with disabilities wherever cost or difficulty does not make that access prohibitory. This includes wheelchair ramps or doors that can be easily be opened by elderly persons. Bathroom facilities should be altered to include accessible toilets and sinks. When accessibility is not accomplished, other arrangements must be made to provide services.

The real estate professional should also be prepared to offer guidance to clients with regard to compliance with these regulations. The entrepreneur planning to open a restaurant needs guidance when selecting a property to house his or her new business. A savvy agent can offer advice so that additional expenses for providing accessibility can be avoided. Where the professional is involved in the development of residential multiunit properties, his or her expertise can ensure that ground floor units are built with residents with disabilities in mind so that alterations need not be made after completion. Private clubs and religious organizations are exempt from accommodation requirements.

---

[1] www.ada.gov/cguide.htm

Real estate firms that operate real estate schools must keep in mind that their facilities and curricula are required to accommodate persons with disabilities.

When contemplating any modifications that need to be made to facilities, one must remember not to think of any changes required to facilities or policies as onerous regulations, but as an investment in an opportunity to reach a neglected and growing market segment.

Equal Employment

There are a number of federal laws prohibiting discrimination in the workplace:

- The Civil Rights Act of 1964 (Title VII) prohibits employment discrimination based on race, color, sex, or national origin.
- The Equal Pay Act of 1963 (EPA) requires that men and women who perform the same work receive the same pay.
- The Age Discrimination in Employment Act of 1967 protects individuals 40 years of age and older from discrimination.
- The Americans with Disabilities Act was discussed earlier in this chapter.
- The Civil Rights Act of 1991 provides monetary damages for intentional employment discrimination.

The broker/owner is responsible for his or her firm's compliance with these regulations.

Federal Taxes

The tax liabilities of a firm depend on its ownership structure. This topic is too large for a full discussion in this book. For more complex forms of ownership, an accountant or lawyer, or both, should be consulted.

The broker/owner is responsible for withholding and reporting federal taxes and Social Security for the firm's employees. Where other licensees are independent contractors, as is usually the case, they are responsible for their own taxes.

The Real Estate Settlement and Procedures Act (RESPA) was discussed in Chapter 4. The supervising broker and the broker/owner are responsible for monitoring adherence to its regulations, particularly those prohibiting kickbacks and channeling.

State Laws and Regulations

The type of business organization of a real estate company can affect liability and taxes. How the business is registered with the state depends on the particular state. There are several different organization types.

- A **sole proprietorship** has one owner, who assumes all responsibilities. The business may use a trade name, but for most purposes it does not have a legal existence apart from the owner. There are fewer legal restrictions, and taxes are filed on the owner's individual return. However, the owner has all fiscal and legal liability.
- A **limited liability company (LLC)** has the limited liability advantage of a corporation with the tax status of a sole proprietor or partnership. The LLC is governed by an operating agreement.

- A **limited partnership (LP)** includes a general partner and one or more limited partners. The limited partners invest capital, but do not participate in day-to-day operations. A partnership agreement governs how the company operates. The general partners have unlimited liability.

- A **general partnership (GP)** allows two or more persons to share profits and liabilities. As in a sole proprietorship, the partners have unlimited liability.

- **Corporations** are very structured and are governed by a corporate charter. Owner liability is limited to their investment. Corporations require extensive record keeping.

- A **C-corporation** is double taxed: Both the company and the shareholders pay taxes on the earnings.

- In an **S-corporation**, the shareholders pay taxes on their personal returns. There are restrictions in the number of shareholders and other requirements.

State Real Estate Regulations

Most real estate regulation takes place at the state level. The broker/owner and, to an extent, the supervising broker are responsible for adherence to the regulations. This can become especially complex, especially if a company has offices in more than one state. Areas where the state regulates real estate companies and personnel include the following.

Licensing

The broker/owner needs to know who within the organization needs to be licensed. States have different rules governing licensing for tasks such as showing properties. An unlicensed employee performing a task that requires a license can result in legal consequences.

In addition to staff licensing, the organization may need a license. The broker/owner must know the various requirements for operation in his or her state.

Commissions

The broker/owner sets policy regarding commission amounts. As indicated in Chapter 4, there can be no arrangements made between real estate firms and commission rates or territories. Any such agreement would be an antitrust violation.

In most states, commissions must pass through the broker. The sales associate cannot receive the money directly at closing.

Trust (Escrow) Monies

Most states have regulations about money held in trust by real estate firms. For example, down payments may need to be deposited in a separate, non–interest bearing bank account. There may be a limitation on the banks that can be used. Money received may need to be deposited or returned within a specified time.

Miscellaneous

There may be other state regulations governing

- office location
- business name and sign, business cards, and lawn signs
- branch office licensing
- maintaining documents: disclosure forms, listings, offers, or closing statements
- delivery of documents
- licensing for nonresidents
- personal participation by licensees in real estate transactions

Local Business Regulations

It is rare that local regulations are specific to real estate firms. However, the broker/owner will need to confirm general business regulations.

Zoning

Real estate offices are retail businesses and must be located in an area that is zoned for such businesses. The offices must adhere to local regulations regarding hours and days of operation.

Signs

In addition to real estate-specific regulations regarding signage, there may be local ordinances restricting size and location.

Taxes

A real estate firm may be required to pay local taxes. For example, if the company owns the building housing its office, it will be responsible for the real estate taxes.

Staffing

The broker/owner recruits employees and independent contractors. He or she also negotiates contracts with the independent contractors that specify the conditions of their employment, the percentage of commissions they will receive, and policies regarding expenses. It's a good idea to tie the contract to the firm's policies and procedures manual. Signing the contract then acknowledges that the contractor has read and will abide by the policies and procedures.

Policies and Procedures

A company in an industry as highly regulated as real estate should have a written record of its policies and procedures. Topics in the manual can include

- agency
- commissions
- cooperation with other brokers
- arbitration of disputes
- expenses
- use of office equipment and supplies
- computer usage
- e-mail
- dress code
- keys
- listing policies
- advertising
- referrals

Staff should be required to acknowledge that they have received and read a copy of the policies and procedures manual. It is important to keep the manual up to date, so it conforms to new regulations and covers new industry practices.

Record Keeping

An essential task in any business is accurate record keeping. Proper documentation can protect the firm and its staff from litigation. Improper documentation can lead to lost lawsuits and fines. The firm should have definitive policies regarding the maintenance of records for all transactions.

The Internal Revenue Service (IRS) requires that income tax records be maintained for seven years. Housing and Urban Development (HUD) regulations require that lead-based paint disclosures be kept for three years. In general, HUD requires that records related to transactions be maintained for a minimum of three years.

Each state will have its own regulations regarding disclosure forms, listings, offers, and closing statements. Some states have regulations regarding the retention of e-mail correspondence. Always remember that proper risk reduction activities include maintenance of all pertinent paperwork in a transaction.

Special FREE Offer from LearningExpress

LearningExpress will help you ace the broker exam

Go to the LearningExpress Practice Center at www.LearningExpressFreeOffer.com, an interactive online resource exclusively for LearningExpress customers.

Now that you've purchased LearningExpress's *Real Estate Broker Exam*, you have **FREE** access to:

- **Full-length practice tests** that mirror the national format and content of the AMP, PSI, Promissor, and Thomson Prometric exams
- **Immediate scoring** and **detailed answer explanations**
- Benchmark your skills and focus your study with our **customized diagnostic reports**

Follow the simple instructions on the scratch card in your copy of *Real Estate Broker Exam*. Use your individualized access code found on the scratch card and go to www.LearningExpressFreeOffer.com to sign in. Start practicing online for the broker exam right away!

Once you've logged on, use the spaces below to write in your access code and newly created password for easy reference:

Access Code: _____   Password: _____